Self-Determined Kids

Self-Determined Kids

Raising Satisfied and Successful Children

by

Dennis E. Mithaug

Lexington Books

D.C. Heath and Company · *Lexington, Massachusetts* · *Toronto*

Library of Congress Cataloging-in-Publication Data

Mithaug, Dennis E.
Self-determined kids: raising satisfied and successful children /
by Dennis E. Mithaug.
p.   cm.
Includes bibliographical references and index.
ISBN 0-669-27140-3
1. Autonomy in children.   2. Autonomy in youth.   3. Success—
Psychological aspects.   I. Title.
BF723.A87M57   1991
155.4′1383—dc20   90-20111
                                                                  CIP

Published simultaneously in Canada
Printed in the United States of America
International Standard Book Number: 0–669–27140–3
Library of Congress Catalog Card Number: 90–20111

The paper used in this publication meets the minimum requirements of
American National Standard for Information Sciences—Permanence
of Paper for Printed Library Materials, ANSI Z39.48-1984.

Year and number of this printing:

91 92 93 94 95 8 7 6 5 4 3 2 1

To my self-determined kids:
Derek
Dana
Deirdre
Dustin

Contents

Introduction

In every school in this country a few children succeed regardless of the instruction they receive. Teachers identify these students early because they have purpose in their lives. They know what they like, what they can do, what they want, and how to get it. These young people *self-direct* and *self-correct* in order to succeed. They are *self-determined.*

But each succeeding year teachers find fewer self-determined students. Something is happening to the way families raise children and to how our culture encourages their independence. Increasingly, our young people are exceptional in a different way. They're out of touch.

Today, American youth grow up in a fantasy world that encourages them to believe that their adolescent life-style will follow them into adulthood. Nothing they learn at home or in school counters this view. Thus, when they leave home and school to face the world on their own, they're shocked by reality. For the first time in their lives they must use their minds to decide and their initiative to survive. Living with mom and dad was easy and secure. Life away from their parents is threatening and uncertain. What a surprise to discover that getting ahead requires hustle and resourcefulness. Too bad there are no multiple-choice answers to one of life's most significant questions: "How do I succeed?"

The real world forces many young adults to withdraw. Growing up "entitled" has weakened their need to succeed. Youth don't know how to self-direct, and even less about how to self-correct. So they give up. Rather than using life's setbacks to move forward, they fall back in retreat. Failure challenges their self-esteem, saps their confidence, and encourages negative views of the world and themselves. Their future seems bleak. Our country is at risk. And parents tell themselves "We did everything we could," "We gave them all they wanted," and wonder why their children's lives are going so wrong.

Youth problems are regular features on the evening news. Education expenditures are up, but Scholastic Aptitude Test scores are down. Suicide rates and cocaine use have increased, but living independently of parents has decreased. And teen pregnancies and sexually transmitted diseases are on the rise, while knowledge of science, economics, and geography is on the decline.

The problem-solving capacities of our young people are shrinking just as our country's need for creative thinking is expanding. And their underdeveloped minds seem to be undermining their own development. Why? Who's responsible? And what's to be done? Are parents and teachers less effective? Or are our youth problems today reflections of dangers forecast a quarter of a century ago by John Holt in his *How Children Fail?*[1]

We have been struggling to reverse youth declines for decades. And nothing has worked. More money for education hasn't helped. Higher salaries for teachers won't help. And neither will more and longer schooldays or stiffer math and science requirements for graduation. Nothing proposed so far will solve our ballooning youth crisis. Why? Because these remedies miss the target by treating symptoms, not problems.

The real problem facing youth today is their *lack of desire and ability to succeed.* This lack is compounded by the inability of their parents and teachers to inspire and teach youth to think and act successfully. As educators and business leaders worry about helping students to catch up with their foreign counterparts, they forget what's ultimately important for all children to learn: how to think and act independently in order to get what they want from life. Consequently, youth never learn the self-determination skills needed to succeed. No one teaches them the universal principles we all must obey in order to get what we want. So youth never discover their own route to happiness and personal fulfillment.

Problems and Solutions

For three decades an avalanche of reports has chronicled the crises youth face and the unfortunate decisions they make. Today Americans agree that the significant problems facing the country *are not* budget deficits, trade deficits, terrorism, inflation, recession, communism, pollution, abortion, school prayer, or economic domination by Japan. Most (74 percent) believe that youth problems are worse than when we were young, and they are right. Recently a reader wrote Ann Landers complaining about those who think the Depression generation had it tough compared to today's kids:

DEAR ANN LANDERS:
The reader signed "Georgia," who lived through the Depression and described how hard it was to be a teenager in the '30s, said kids today have an easy time of it compared to teens in his day. You said you couldn't argue with him. Well, I can.

Let me ask your generation a few questions:

Are your parents divorced? Almost every one of my friends comes from a broken home.

Were you thinking about suicide when you were 12?

Did you have an ulcer when you were 16?

Did your best friend lose her virginity to a guy she went out with twice?

You may have had to worry about VD, but did you have to worry about AIDS?

Did your classmates carry guns and knives?

How many kids in your class came to school regularly drunk, stoned or high on drugs?

Did any of your friends have their brains fried from using PCP?

What percentage of your graduating class also graduated from a drug and alcohol rehabilitation center?

Did your school have armed security guards in the halls?

Did you ever live in a neighborhood where the sound of gunfire at night was "normal"?

You talk a lot about being dirt poor and having no money. *Since when does money mean happiness? The kids at school who have the expensive cars and designer clothes are the most miserable.*

When I am your age, Georgia, I won't do much looking back, I'll just thank God that I survived.—**Other Side of the Story in Indianapolis** [italics added][2]

What a contrast to 30 years ago when American youth supposedly had the world by the tail! Parents, teachers, and media sang the same refrain. The baby boom generation would be more talented, better educated, healthier, happier, and more productive than any previous generation. Expectations soared. What youth wanted, they got. Nothing was too good for this new breed.

Expectations peaked in the 1970s. The entitlement generation received a dose of reality, as disillusionment replaced unbridled ambition. Boomers competed with each other for jobs, housing, and favorable positions on the corporate ladder. The value of college degrees plummeted while the cost of owning a home skyrocketed.

Some boomers took change, hardship, and challenge in stride, demonstrating persistence, resilience, and adaptability. They channeled frustration and impatience into entrepreneurial activities to create what corporate America couldn't: positions at the head of the boardroom table. Others suffered, taking longer than usual to find their way.

Now baby boomers are parent boomers, producing record numbers of babies each year. In 1988 births hit 3.8 million, the most since 1964, the last year of boom births. Census analyst Amara Bachu says that boom mothers "[have] been postponing motherhood. Many probably finished college and are established in jobs. Once in their 30s, they decide, 'Now we should have our babies.'" Today 54 percent of all childless wives in their early 30s want babies. This figure is up from 34 percent in 1975.[3] The result will be the "babyboom echo"—*the generation that will lead us into the 21st century.*

How will boom parents raise their children? And what will they expect from schools? Will they allow their children to follow the educational and social declines characterizing youth today? Or have we learned something from the past 30 years to help them reverse these trends?

Chapter 1, *Decline,* documents youth problems at home, at school, and at work. The message is always the same. Youth lack direction and purpose in their lives. They don't know where they're going or where they've been. Their day-to-day drift maps an unhappy journey searching for "highs" and trying to avoid "lows."

Can today's parents prepare their children to lead our country into the next century? *Self-Determined Kids* says "yes!" It lays out the problem, its causes, and the solutions. In the next 11 chapters, I describe how youth fail (chapter 1), why they fail (chapter 2), and what we have learned from their experiences (chapter 3). I show how changes in our values (chapter 4) affect what makes us happy today (chapter 5), and how success (chapter 6) and achievement (chapter 7) help us meet our own expectations for fulfillment. I describe how parents and teachers can help young people achieve self-determination by *developing their talents* (chapter 8), *maximizing their intelligence* (chapter 9), and *persisting at their goals* (chapter 10). Finally, in chapter 11, I describe *three success principles* and *ten parenting steps* to change youth incompetence to competence, unintelligence to intelligence, and surrender to persistence. As a result of these changes, youth will develop the "true grit" that characterized previous generations. They'll become internally motivated rather than externally stimulated, self-directed rather than peer-dominated, and self-reliant rather than other-dependent.

What the next generation of Americans needs for its own well-being and for the well-being of the country is *self-determination.*

Underdeveloped Minds Undermine Development

Chapter 1, *Decline,* describes how youth fail. The twenty-five indicators that follow illustrate the range of problems they face.

1. Today most youth are more interested in having fun than in becoming successful.
2. 68 percent of all 4th graders, 64 percent of all 8th graders, and 43 percent of all 11th graders spend *three or more hours watching television each day.*[4]
3. 80 percent of all 4th graders, 61 percent of all 8th graders, and 59 percent of all 11th graders spend *less than one hour on homework each day.*[5]
4. 80 percent of high school seniors do not use their own money to plan for their future.[6]
5. Cocaine use among American youth, already the highest in the industrialized world, has nearly doubled in the past decade.[7]
6. From 1950 to 1985, sexually transmitted diseases have increased 218 percent for youth aged 15 to 24.[8]
7. Births to unmarried women between the ages of 15 and 19 have increased 251 percent from 1950 to 1985.[9]
8. For youth 18 and younger, arrests for drunk driving and

drug abuse have increased over 1200 percent from 1965 to 1985.[10]

9. Voting by eligible 18- to 24-year-olds has decreased from 52 to 42 percent from 1972 to 1984.[11]

10. From 1960 to 1985, suicides among youth between ages 15 and 19 increased 194 percent for males and 47 percent for females.[12]

11. From 1960 to 1980, homicides involving youth between ages 15 and 19 have increased 165 percent.[13]

12. Public school expenditures per student have *increased* 168 percent from 1955 to 1987.[14]

13. Pupil/teacher ratios in public schools have *decreased* 34 percent from 1955 to 1987.[15]

14. According to the U.S. Department of Education, the U.S. ranked second among 15 industrialized nations in instructional expenditures per pupil in 1985.[16]

15. In international mathematics tests, U.S. 8th graders ranked 13th among students from 18 countries in 1982.[17]

16. In science, U.S. elementary and high school students knew less in 1983 than their counterparts did in 1970.[18]

17. In a 1986 survey of economic knowledge, only 34 percent of American high school students correctly defined profits, and only 39 percent could define the Gross National Product.[19]

18. In 1983, high school achievement scores were lower than when the Soviet Union launched Sputniks I and II in 1957.[20]

19. Scholastic Aptitude Test scores for college-bound high school seniors have decreased dramatically since the 1950s.[21]

20. Remedial math courses in public four-year colleges have increased 72 percent from 1975 to 1980.[22]

21. Business and military leaders have spent millions of dollars on remedial programs to teach young workers and recruits math and reading skills.[23]

22. Over 30 percent of American companies with 10,000 or more employees provided remedial education for large numbers of their workers in 1987.[24]

23. Social scientists and journalists report that millions of college graduates have difficulty finding themselves and making vocational decisions after leaving school.[25]
24. The U.S. Census Bureau reports more young people between ages 18 and 24 were living at home with their parents in 1985.[26]
25. Parents of 20- to 30-year-old adults say their children take longer than expected to grow up and become financially and emotionally independent.[27]

Childhood Entitlement, Adulthood Disillusionment

How do we explain these declines? Are youth themselves solely responsible or have we contributed to their troubles? Chapter 2, *Entitlement,* explains how our own values and behaviors reinforce youth belief in a "play now, pay never" philosophy. The prosperity that began in the 1950s gave us 40 years of good living and entitled expectations.

Today, most youth are products of "wishful" parenting that inadvertently increases expectations but decreases initiative. Rather than giving children a reason to achieve, we give them every reason not to. And when they leave home, we discover they don't have the interest *or* the ability to make it on their own. *Then* we understand why they postpone adulthood and prolong childhood.

We should have learned something from the baby boom generation's postschool experience. They were the first to leave home with "entitlement values." They expected to find a world waiting for their advice, direction, and leadership, but instead found Vietnam, assassinations, Watergate, and stagflation. In addition, they had to compete with each other for jobs, promotions, and housing.

Chapter 3, *Disillusionment,* describes the consequences of these experiences. The value of family declined as fast as the American dollar. Childhood went "out" and adulthood came "in" as the boom generation led us from the "Me" decade of the 1970s to the "Mine" decade of the 1980s. Now politicians worry that we'll be unable "to replace ourselves with enough stable children born to families with the ability to raise successful children."[28] They may be right.

Over a decade ago, sociologist James Coleman noted that the boom generation would not be able to raise their children effectively: "Child rearing is one of the biggest casualties of the modern age that is being ushered in by this generation. We are becoming the first species in the history of the world which is unable to care for its young."[29]

The Fulfillment Request, the Happiness Quest

In spite of dire predictions from the past and ominous warnings about the future, there *is* a silver lining. Decades of near-addictive consumption and self-aggrandizement have at least left us parents more introspective. The material rewards that drove us in the beginning turned out to be incidental satisfactions in the end. Decades of "me" and "mine" yielded an understanding of the ultimate rewards in the "good" life. No longer were wealth, status, and power sufficient motivators for superachievement. *Fulfillment* became the principal goal.

In the 1950s family and career were kept separate. Dad worked 9:00 to 5:00 at a job he disliked or only tolerated. Then he returned to enjoy his family. Personal and work paths rarely crossed. Boomers rejected this schizophrenic split between heart and mind, insisting on success *in all areas of their lives*. They expected to do *what they liked to get what they wanted*.

Chapter 4, *Fulfillment*, describes the baby boomers' discovery of self-improvement power. Baby boomers believed in their ability to make things happen. When activism failed to change the world in the 1960s and 1970s, boomers decided to change themselves in the 1980s. They fomented a new kind of antiestablishment revolution, introducing self-help in marriage counseling, parent training, and health awareness. Boomers took charge of their careers too, demanding a match between their interests, talents, and careers. For the first time in history, a generation of well-educated workers refused jobs that were inconsistent with their personal goals. The integration of personal and professional life became an ultimate end. Boomers were not satisfied with occasional, off-the-job happiness and satisfaction. They wanted these feelings on the job too. They sought fulfillment!

Chapter 5, *Happiness,* unveils the *secret* to the search for happiness. Superachievers who *have found happiness* contradict popular views that parents are responsible. Satisfaction and enjoyment are not negotiable commodities to be given and withheld by others. Happiness comes from within. It's a consequence of actions consistent with one's interests, needs, and abilities, and which *consistently* approximate important goals. Happiness is the positive feeling that results from *doing what we like to get what we want.*

If it's that simple, why aren't more people happy? And why don't parents teach their children how to make themselves happy?

Success and the Self-Determined Achiever

When raising children, we spend so much time looking at immediate peer averages that we neglect future challenges. By comparing Dick and Jane with others their own age, we assure ourselves that they walk, talk, read, and write on schedule. We know what they need for where they've been, but not what they'll need for where they're going. When they don't measure up, we take steps to help them catch up. But what's the "what" they're supposed to catch? Developmental milestones? Peer averages?

When it's too late we learn that they *are* just like their peers after all. And their peers are failing too. Check those 25 indicators again. Do you really want your children to turn out like most of their peers?

If children are to succeed in life, they must learn the self-determination skills that make a difference in the real world. What works in daily living is not the same as what works in the classroom. Good grades and high I.Q. scores are poor predictors of success in life. Every year we graduate our "brightest" and "most capable" students from high school to college and back home again where they sit and wait for some external force to move them in the "right" direction.

"Making it" in life requires more than scoring well during exams. Our young people are not learning the behaviors and skills that will make a difference in their lives. If they're to have a shot at getting what they want, making their mark, or possibly even contributing to future generations, then they must learn to think, feel, and act *like people who succeed.*

They need to be less like their peers and more like their heroes. They need to conform less and aspire more. They must understand that all people who succeed follow the same laws. There are no shortcuts. Contrary to the lessons of television, success is a way of living, not a reward for sitting.

So what are those self-determination skills people use to succeed? And how can we teach them to our children so that they can find their own happiness and personal fulfillment?

Chapter 6, *Success,* lays out the most recent and most enduring findings on success. Over 50 years of research on the most successful and influential people in our nation's history has generated a common core of essentials that explain success. People who succeed get the right start early in life. They develop their talents and competencies. They maximize their intelligence through effective mental self-management. And then they persist at solving problems that get in the way of their goals. We must teach these same critical thought and action strategies to our children.

Chapter 7, *Achievement,* describes how young people develop their talents, maximize their intelligence, and persist at their goals. As a consequence of learning these critical patterns, they:

1. Become *aware* of their own needs, interests, and abilities
2. Learn *self-direction* by setting their own goals and developing their own plans
3. Gain *self-confidence* by increasing their skills and abilities to perform important tasks well
4. Become more *self-reliant* by learning to initiate "risky actions" on their own
5. Increase their *self-esteem* by achieving intermediate successes in their talent areas
6. Take *responsibility* for positive *and* negative results by evaluating themselves objectively and then deciding what to adjust to improve next time

To parents and teachers, these young achievers seem internally motivated, independent, and intelligent. They are. Every day, they demonstrate their competence, intelligence, and persistence. They are *self-determined achievers.*

Success Principle #1: *Competence*

**"ALL PEOPLE WHO SUCCEED ARE COMPETENT;
NOT ALL COMPETENT PEOPLE ARE SUCCESSFUL."**

Competence is the first of *three principles* to account for why some succeed and others don't. It's the sine qua non of achievement. No one succeeds without it. And everyone works to get it. There are no exceptions. We're born with potential but strive for achievement. Innate ability may be free, but competence costs a bundle—anywhere from ten years to life. That's what superachievers pay to excel in their talent areas.

In his review of research on world-class achievers, Eugene Griessman concludes that "natural gifts are not sufficient in and of themselves in explaining these extra ordinary accomplishments. Unless there is a long and intensive process of encouragement, nurturance, education, and training, the individuals will not attain world class in their respective fields."[30]

Chapter 8, *Competence*, lays out the requirements for children and youth preparing themselves in their own talent areas. The experiences of such superachievers as W. Clement Stone, Jack Nicklaus, Lee Trevino, Mary Kay Ash, Charles Schulz, James Michener, Nadja Salerno-Sonnenberg, and Yo-Yo Ma testify to the costs of competency development.

The price tag for developing talent is usually out of reach for most children. Unless they get help from parents and teachers who know how to *lead, mentor,* and *befriend,* they won't realize their potential. This is why youth are in trouble today. No one has footed the bill. No one started them early, built their skills systematically, or encouraged their achievements broadly.

Success Principle #2: *Intelligence*

**"ALL PEOPLE WHO SUCCEED ARE INTELLIGENT;
NOT ALL INTELLIGENT PEOPLE ARE SUCCESSFUL."**

Intelligence is the second of the success principles. But it's not the same as I.Q., which fails to give valid assessments of true intellectual ability. Robert Sternberg, author of *The Triarchic Mind,* notes that intelligence involves the ability *to adapt* to one's environment.[31] Howard Gardner, author of *Frames of Mind*, defines it as "the ability *to solve problems or to create products* that are valued within one or more cultural settings [italics]."[32] And Napoleon Hill states that "Success in life, no matter what one may call success, is very largely a matter of *adaptation to environment* in such a manner that there is harmony between the individual and his environment [italics added]."[33]

Chapter 9, *Intelligence*, demonstrates how intelligent people harmonize with their environments *in order to* achieve their goals. First, they set goals commensurate with their needs, interests, and abilities. Second, they find environments that value what they have to offer. Third, they give the environment what it wants *in return* for opportunities to get what they want: goal attainment. They are intelligent mental managers.

Youth adapt intelligently to their environments by acquiring the five determinants of intelligent competency management: *passion, direction, organization, actions,* and *reactions.* Parents and teachers help them develop these behaviors by: (1) demonstrating, expecting, and providing opportunities for self-determination, (2) teaching the self-determination strategy, and (3) encouraging its use to solve problems at home and at school.

Success Principle #3: Persistence

**"ALL PEOPLE WHO SUCCEED ARE PERSISTENT;
NOT ALL PERSISTENT PEOPLE ARE SUCCESSFUL."**

Persistence is the third and last principle of success. Like Rodney Dangerfield, it too gets little respect, even though it does what neither competence nor intelligence alone can do. *Persistence goes the extra mile.* "When the going gets tough, the tough get going" by means of persistent, continuous problem solving. All accomplishments, great and small, require ample doses of this potent potion.

Twentieth-century titans Henry Ford and Thomas Edison found their place in American history through their unswerving, single-minded, persistent actions while trying to achieve important goals. Napoleon Hill notes: "I had the happy privilege of analyzing both Mr. Edison and Mr. Ford, year by year, over a long period of years, and therefore, the opportunity to study them at close range, so I speak with actual knowledge when I say that *I found no quality save persistence,* in either of them that even remotely suggested the major source of their stupendous achievements" [italics added].[34]

Chapter 10, *Persistence,* describes the cumulative effects of competence, intelligence, and persistence. Self-determined people get what they want in life because: (1) they've *developed their talents;* (2) they use their abilities to *adapt intelligently* to environments they like; and (3) they *persist* at removing obstacles in the way of their goals.

Superachievers Steve Jobs, who founded Apple Computers, Robert Swanson, who founded premier biotechnology firm Genentec, and Ted Turner, who built CNN and TBS, are contemporary models for lifelong striving and accomplishment. They demonstrate repeatedly that it's as important to doggedly *pursue* opportunity as it is to adapt competently and intelligently once it appears.

Parents and teachers can encourage persistence the same way they promote competence and intelligence—by leading, mentoring, and befriending. They *lead* by demonstrating persistence themselves, expecting youth to stick with difficult tasks, and by providing challenges that stretch endurance. They *mentor* by teaching concentration, follow-through, and persistent, daily problem solving in the quest of distant goals. And they *befriend* by supporting youth as they learn the attempts-to-accomplishment ratio that governs real-life outcomes.

No one achieves worthwhile goals with unblemished records. Jobs, Swanson, and Turner logged as many failures as successes, maybe even more. But they persisted, trying harder and more often than their peers. This gave themselves *more chances* to succeed.

Ten Steps to Parenting the Self-Determined Child

The *Law of Success* states that "All people who succeed are competent, intelligent, and persistent," and that "All people who are competent, intelligent, and persistent will succeed." Therefore, if you want your children to be successful in their adult lives, you must help them develop their potential, maximize their intelligence, and commit themselves to challenging and fulfilling goals.

Unfortunately, coming from an educated family with middle-class expectations is no longer the great advantage it once was. The entitlements of the past 40 years are too persuasive and too pervasive.

Guaranteed affluent living and unrestricted freedoms during childhood are detriments to self-determined success in adulthood. Chapter 11, *Finale,* describes how the three principles that comprise the *Law of Success* can guide your approach to parenting. The chapter presents ten steps to implement those principles. If you follow them, you'll develop the leadership, mentorship, and friendship skills necessary to start your children down that path toward *self-determination* and *personal achievement.*

Self-Determined Kids

1

Decline

The values gap between generations has narrowed. Youth finally share many values with their parents. They too want happiness, fulfillment, and success. That's the good news. The bad news is that they lack the skills and the will to achieve. Look at the record. Achievement declines are so precipitous that even politicians are alarmed. Former Colorado governor Richard Lamm writes: "Future historians will see best the multiple factors that led to the decline of America. But I suggest one of those major factors will be the failure to replace ourselves with enough stable children born to families with the ability to raise successful children."[1] According to *Newsweek* reporter Kenneth Woodward, "By 1972 sociologist James Coleman had discerned the regressive character of the burgeoning new youth culture: locked in a world of their own creation, with their own music and money and licence to do as they wished, the young saw no reason to abandon this 'pleasing surrogate for maturity'."[2] Woodward's analysis of youth problems led him to conclude that "young Americans entering the twenty-first century are far less mature than their ancestors were at the beginning of the twentieth. The difference is evident in all areas of youthful development: sex, love, marriage, education and work."[3]

Indicators of Decline

Many youth take wrong turns early, a truth documented by accelerating trends in teen pregnancies, homicides, suicides, and drug use. They also distract easily from what's ultimately important.

Lack of concentration lowers their motivation and decreases their performance. Employers complain that high school graduates can't compete. Parents complain that they can't adjust. The symptoms are pervasive.

Students' Values

Unlike students of the rebellious 1960s, young people today agree with their parents about the importance of education, what to do with their lives, roles of women, the value of religion, how to dress, and racial issues. This apparent rapprochement closes the "generation gap" that widened to a chasm 20 years ago. In 1986 87 percent of high school seniors reported that having a happy family life was "very important," this figure compares to 82 percent in 1974. More youth expressed interest in living closer to mom and dad and remaining in their home town area. But today's youth are also more materialistic and less humanistic. In 1975 18 percent of youth placed a high value on having money, and by 1986 this figure increased to 22 percent. Meanwhile, youth's concern about correcting inequalities decreased from 26 to 11 percent. They were also less interested in community leadership. Since 1972 the importance of being successful at work has decreased from 85 to 81 percent.[4]

Student Behaviors

The materialism-leisure value shows up in spending habits, daily routines, drug use, sexual behavior, citizenship, mental health, and academic performance. Youth are so caught up in conspicuous consumption and immediate gratification that they have little time for anything else. They've become the advertiser's ideal target group.

SPENDING HABITS. Today's young people are the beneficiaries of America's unprecedented wealth, convenience, and abundance. Their base necessities include televisions, VCRs, Nintendo systems, compact disk players, designer clothes, cars, and "walking around" money. In 1986 56 percent of youth 16 and older worked part-time, a rate comparable to 1950. The big difference between today and yesterday was how they spent their money. Over two-thirds of all contemporary seniors *did not* use the money they earned for education, car expenses, long-term savings, or to help their families. One-quarter didn't even use their earnings for clothes, records, or personal care. Instead, they used their money for entertainment.[5] No wonder youth don't plan, prepare, and build for that good life. They already have it!

According to Jill Lawrence from the Associated Press, "American teenagers are working in droves, much of their cash going for cars, clothes, beer and sometimes drugs. They are perhaps learning the work ethic. But they also are learning conspicuous consumption, and some critics say they are compromising their education as well."[6] When asked about the priorities of working students, 1989 National Teacher of the Year Mary Bicouvaris said: "They are very busy people. What I find deplorable many times is they work school into the business schedule rather than fit business into the school schedule."[7] English teacher Patrick Welsh agrees: "They will tell you, 'I just don't have time to do that assignment. I have to work,' and they expect you to buy that. I don't buy it. But what happens is a gradual and subtle erosion of standards and the amount of work you're going to hit kids with. It's happening all over the country."[8] Sociologist James Coleman warned us in the 1970s that youth were becoming consumers before learning how to produce. Temple University psychology professor Lawrence Steinberg says that the United States has the highest rate of working students in the world (Canada is a distant second): "Working while one goes to high school is unheard of in Japan. The Japanese society is organized such that school is the only thing that kids are to be concerned about while they're teen-agers."[9] Newsweek reporter Woodward connects teens' work habits with a need for instant gratification: "In short, teenage employment has only intensified the adolescent drive for immediate gratification. Instead of learning how to delay desires, students are indulging what University of Michigan researcher Jerald Bachman calls 'premature affluence.'"[10]

ACTIVITIES. In 1985 72 percent of all high school seniors spent most of their time watching television; the rate was the same in 1976.[11] Viewing patterns develop early and change little as youth grow older. In 1984 68 percent of all 4th graders, 64 percent of all 8th graders, and 43 percent of all 11th graders spent *three or more hours* watching television each day. In the same year 80 percent of all 4th graders, 61 percent of all 8th graders, and 59 percent of all 11th graders spent *less than one hour* on homework each day.[12] From 1976 to 1985 the percentage of high school seniors who read books, magazines, or newspapers each day decreased from 59 to 51 percent. And less than 30 percent develop their talents and interests by pursuing such activities as playing musical instruments, working on special projects, or writing.[13] Television is always the number-one vote getter, absorbing their time and pacifying their attention. Television itself partly explains delayed maturity, reinforcing youth for passively watching the tube and listening to music for hours and hours. Ultimately, they are incapable of making that transition to active responsibility taking, which is a "major passage from childhood to adulthood."[14]

DRUGS. From 1975 to 1981, the percentage of high school seniors who admitted to using illicit drugs increased from 55 to 66 percent. The percentage of students using cocaine increased from 9 to 17 percent. Easy money and easy access contributed to these increases. In one survey, 86 percent of high school students said that marijuana was easy to get; 66 percent reported the same for amphetamines, 55 percent for tranquilizers, 51 percent for barbiturates, 49 percent for cocaine, and 21 percent for heroin.[15]

The incidence of drug dealing and drug use is so high that many children even incorporate it into their games. Reports from Lebanon, Pennsylvania, indicate that "A group of children used a playground as headquarters for a make-believe drug ring, selling neatly packaged bags of sugar and grass clippings that looked like cocaine and marijuana."[16] Pervasive drug use infects all youth regardless of sex or ethnic origin. Atlanta-based PRIDE surveyed 296,180 white students and 59,989 black students in grades 6–12 from 958 schools in 38 states during the 1988–89 school year. The poll revealed that cocaine is twice as available to black students but *they use it less often* than white students. Only 4 percent of black, 12th-grade students reported cocaine use at least once in the previous year compared to 7 percent of their white peers. Drug use was highest among white males, followed by black males, white females, and black females.[17]

SEX. Sexually transmitted disease among young people is also on the rise. According to a 1986 Harris survey, 57 percent of youth have sex before they reach 18.[18] This correlates with a 318 percent jump in gonorrhea from 1950 to 1985 for youth between 15 and 19. For this same age group and time period, births to unmarried women increased 251 percent, while births to unmarried, 20- to 24-year-old women increased 220 percent.[19] Glen Gabbard of the Menninger Clinic thinks this is a symptom of deeper problems: "In this age group you see many young women who have had multiple abortions. The ease with which they choose to abort reflects a *disturbing sense of self-absorption and an alarming indifference to the moral gravity of their actions and an inability to make commitments*" [italics added].[20]

CITIZENSHIP. In 1950 youth under the age of 18 accounted for only 15 percent of all arrests for persons 34 and younger. By 1985 they accounted for 47 percent. From 1965 to 1985 arrests for drunk driving and drug abuse for youth under 18 increased over 1200 percent! At the same time, more youth are becoming victims of crimes, with 82 percent of youth 19 years or younger becoming victims of robbery, assault, or rape.[21]

They're less interested in the democratic process too. From 1964 to 1984 the percentage of eligible 18- to 24-year-olds who voted decreased from 52 to 42 percent. This pattern is consistent across ethnic groups.[22] Youth are less involved in their communities, less concerned about others, more materialistic, and more inclined to get into trouble with the law.

HEALTH. On a brighter note, the *physical* health of young people has improved in the past 35 years. Deaths are down 55 percent for 5- to 14-year-olds and down 26 percent for 15- to 24-year-olds. Fewer lethal accidents and better treatment for such major illnesses as cancer, heart disease, pneumonia/influenza are responsible. Unfortunately, *mental* health is following the opposite trajectory. Suicides for males and females between 15 and 19 have increased 197 and 47 percent respectively. During the same period homicides increased 178 percent for youth aged 15 to 19 and 120 percent for youth aged 20 to 24.[23]

ACADEMIC ACHIEVEMENT. Academic trends are grim too. Public educational institutions can barely hold their own, in spite of decreasing pupil/teacher ratios and increasing dollar per student expenditures.

In 1984 test scores showed that poor writing skills correlated with excessive television viewing. Literacy tests in 1985 indicated that nearly half of our youth were unable to perform moderately complex tasks such as balancing a checkbook or using a map.[24] In 1982, international mathematics tests of 8th graders placed U.S. students 13th among the students from 18 countries. Students from Japan, the Netherlands, Hungary, (Flemish) Belgium, France, Canada, (French) Belgium, (Ontario) Canada, Scotland, England, Finland, and New Zealand all scored higher in arithmetic, algebra, geometry, measurement, and statistics.[25] In science, U.S. elementary and high school students knew less in 1983 than their counterparts did in 1970. English and Japanese pupils outscored them in physics, chemistry, and biology.[26]

In economics, American high school students are equally ignorant. A 1986 survey of 8,205 11th and 12th graders in public and private high schools in 42 states found that only 34 percent could correctly define profits as "revenues minus costs" and only 39 percent could select the correct definition of Gross National Product: "the market value of the nation's output of final goods and services."[27] A 1989 Gallup poll of 696 seniors from 67 colleges and universities found that only two in five knew that the "shot heard round the world" that started the American Revolution was fired at Concord, Massachusetts, and 42 percent did not know in which half-century the Civil War occurred. Americans finished 6th among 10 nations in a survey conducted by the National Geographic Society. Persons between 18 and 24 scored lower than anyone, averaging 6.9 correct answers compared to 8.4 for Americans aged 55 or older.[28]

Today's students are less prepared to enter college after graduating from high school than American students of previous generations. The average Scholastic Aptitude Test (SAT) score for college-bound high school seniors decreased dramatically from 1960 to 1981. In 1983 the secretary of education's blue-ribbon panel published *A Nation at Risk*, pointing out that three out of four U.S. students leave school unprepared to meet the basic problem-solving demands of college or work. Today's average high school and college graduate is not as well educated as graduates 25 years ago. "If an unfriendly foreign power had attempted to impose on America the mediocre educational performance that exists today, we might well have viewed it as an act of war."[29]

Al Shanker, professor of Education at Harvard, told fellow educators that eight years of educational reform have failed to make a significant difference in student outcomes: "In any other country, these students . . . could not get into a college or a university. . . . That means that the overwhelming majority of parents who think their kids are doing well because they are in college are wrong because we have no standards in higher education."[30] The National Assessment of Educational Progress indicates that only 3 to 6 percent of 17-year-old students can solve two-step math problems, write simple essays, or read complex sentences.[31]

Shanker charges that schools treat students as nonthinking automatons which decreases their incentive to learn and solve problems on their own: "[They're] like inanimate things on an assembly line, moving from one place to another" to be assembled without having to react or interact with the assembler. Shanker concludes: "*No one can educate you or force you to learn. It is something you have to do for yourself.*"[32] *Chicago Tribune* columnist Mike Royko complains that "the majority of youth are materialistic, indifferent to the country and world around them, politically ignorant and primarily interested in finding lucrative jobs and having a good time."[33]

Adjustments after High School

Students leave high school carrying entitlement symptoms with them. They require colleges and universities to "gear up" instruction and "water down" content. Business and industry must do the same with remedial programs to teach young workers reading and math.

In 1988 Motorola's newly established quality control system at a plant in Arcade, New York, discovered that its employees lacked the mathematical skills needed to run the system. So the company had to provide six hours of remedial training in grade-school mathematics for all workers.[34] Similarly, the Polaroid Corporation had to set up a tutorial program to teach 300 of its 10,000 employees material typically taught in the 1st through 12th grades. "We view this as absolutely necessary to be effective today in the work place and necessary to move into the future,"[35] said Charles E. LaPier, manager of human resource development. This is an increasing problem. In many companies the introduction of new technologies meets stiff opposition from uneducated and poorly prepared workers. A 1980 report by the U.S. Departments of Education and Labor stated that "The concerns of the business community for a skilled work force have never been greater. In survey after survey, employers have identified the need for workers with stronger basic skills to accomplish tasks in the work place of today and to adapt to the work place of tomorrow."[36]

A 1987 survey conducted by *Training* magazine found that 30 percent of American companies with 10,000 or more employees provided remedial education for workers, a 2 percent increase from the previous year.[37] And Curtis Plot, of the American Society of Training and Development, estimates that twice as many companies today offer such programs as did ten years ago.[38] In 1988 Joseph Kellman, the Chicago businessman who spearheaded the $3 million Corporate/Community School in Chicago, stated that "Each year, corporate America spends $30 billion to $40 billion teaching people things they should have learned in school."[39] But this isn't the only problem. Many young adults simply don't want to work. Jay M. Wilson of Steeltin Can Corporation in Baltimore says that there are plenty of candidates for $6.50 per hour starting jobs, but keeping workers at those jobs is tough: "Some fail drug tests, some are surprised at how hard the work is, and others simply have little notion of what is involved in holding any job."[40]

Even college students don't measure up. A Carnegie Foundation survey of 5,450 campus faculty reported that "College teachers are generally satisfied with their jobs but disdain . . . *lazy, grade-grubbing students who lack basic skills.* . . . Three-quarters consider their students 'seriously unprepared in basic skills,' and 68 percent feel colleges spend too much time and money teaching students what they should have learned in high school. 'Public education, despite six years of reform, is still producing inadequately prepared students.'. . . Fifty-five percent agreed that most undergraduates at their schools 'only do enough to get by.' "[41] Woodward found similar patterns in an annual survey conducted by UCLA's Higher Education Research Institute which reported that:

> Forty-three percent of all students who had entered a four-year college or university in 1984 had flunked at least one course, and over 30 percent had taken special courses to strengthen basic reading, study, or other scholastic skills. Even professors at elite schools see a

difference. "A third of my students are illiterate," says Robert Bellah, a distinguished professor of sociology at the University of California, Berkeley. "By that I mean they are unable to understand a complex sentence, or write one that makes much sense."[42]

In a monthly report to faculty and staff, former University of Colorado president Gordon G. Gee wrote:

Educational studies and statistics confirm casual observation: even with improved test scores in recent years, today's high school seniors are pathetically ill-equipped for informed citizenship. Their knowledge of history, literature, social processes, mathematics, and science is often utterly inadequate. Their attention spans and retentive powers have been reduced by mindless television and various popular magazines and newspapers. And they often do not know how to go about solving a problem, much less to obtain a correct solution.[43]

Adjustments after College

Parents see similar problems. Their adult children cannot survive on their own. Between 1960 and 1985 the percentage of 18- to 24-year-old adults living at home with parents increased from 43 to 54 percent. Parents reported that their adult children had difficulties establishing themselves in the mainstream. They were more dependent than any generation before them. In *Adult Children Who Won't Grow Up*, Dr. Larry Stockman and Cynthia Graves wrote:

it would not be unreasonable to estimate that at least 40 percent of the current group of young adults (eighteen to forty years of age) are excessively dependent. This would mean that approximately 36 million young adults are taking an unhealthy length of time to severe the ties of adolescence.
. . . The scope of the problem is enormous, and the need to cope with it is urgent. For *if we have a generation of unhealthy and overly dependent young adults beginning to raise their own children, they are unlikely to be able to teach their children how to be independent. And the problem will snowball.* [italics added][44]

Susan Littwin's *The Postponed Generation* describes the same pattern. Young people growing up in the 1980s are incapable of facing the "real world" on their own. They never learned the skills or developed the determination required for independence:

> It seems almost impossible to untangle the real and practical problems from the emotional ones. Perhaps it is best to look at it as a social problem that arises from their history. *These were the special children of perfect parents, and they've had very little practice in dealing with failure or rejection. But fate has taken these bright, charming middle-class aristocrats and dumped them into a rude, tightfisted world. They tried independence; it didn't work, and that sapped their confidence and sent them home crying.* [italics added][45]

Adrienne Miller and Andrew Goldblatt identify yet another group of youth who refuse to grow up, Hamlets, "Overthinkers Who Underachieve":

> Almost every Hamlet has at least one personality trait that predisposes him to the syndrome. *He may never have developed the taste for risk required for success in a free market economy. He may have been humiliated by defeat once too often to engage in competition. He may have little patience for details or knotty problems. He may lack self-confidence. He may hate work. He may be a procrastinator, figuring that he'll get around to a career sometime in the future. Or he may be passive by nature, counting himself a victim of forces beyond his control.* [italics added][46]

In *Young beyond Their Years*, Kenneth L. Woodward reports that "Something happened on the way to the 21st century: American youth, in a sharp reversal of historical trends, are taking longer to grow up. As the 20th century winds down, more young Americans are enrolled in college, but fewer are graduating—and they are taking longer to get their degrees. They take longer to establish careers, too, and longer yet to marry. Many, unable or unwilling to pay for housing, return to the nest—or are slow to leave it. They postpone choices and spurn long-term commitments. Life's on hold; adulthood can wait."[47] Here is a sample of their problems:

> Sandy and Marvin Miller have three children, ages 19 to 25, and are wondering when they'll grow up. Though the younger two come and go, all three consider their parents' lavish house in Encino, Calif., home. Each child's bedroom is equipped with a stereo and a color TV set. "Our kids were spoiled rotten," Sandy admits.
> . . . But the real problem is Todd, the oldest child. With a loan from

his parents, Todd started a limousine business from the family home. His parents have given him till the year's end to move out and have even offered him money to buy a house. But Todd refuses to budge. He pays no rent and gets his clothes laundered free by the family maid. "I grew up here," he argues. "You're throwing me out of my own house." "I don't want to throw them out in the street," Sandy Miller says of her children. *"But they've got to take responsibility and stand on their own two feet. They've got to grow up."*[48]

Novelist-film writer Hal Dresner worries that his daughter won't measure up when she has to face "Mr. Reality."

"My daughter and her friends wanted, no doubt about it, an easy, air-conditioned elevator ride right to the top; in fact, they expected it. . . . In her early teens, my daughter revealed that her professional goal was to 'be famous.' 'As what?' I asked, more amused than concerned. 'Model-actress-whatever.' In Hollywood, believe it or not, that is an accepted job definition. When I learned that all of her friends also wanted big-money 'fun jobs'—animal photographer, tennis-clothes designer, party consultant—I became less amused, more concerned. Was this the inevitable by-product of the Me generation—a spoiled subculture of wanna-be celebrities?"[49]

Some parents, like 52-year-old freelance writer Joan France, are fed up with being the "Caretaker Generation." France finally stopped assuming responsibility for her son's drug-addiction treatment program. "I want to call a halt to this exploitation of parents. Specifically, I want to sound a warning to my own generation. We are rapidly becoming a caretaker generation."[50] Woodward summarizes: "[Adulthood] implies the development of character, competence, and commitment, qualities essential for self-discipline, cooperation, and taking care of others. *By these standards, young Americans entering the 21st century are far less mature than their ancestors were at the beginning of the 20th. The difference is evident in all areas of youthful development: sex, love, marriage, education, and work"* [italics added].[51]

The Meaning of Decline

Youth decline bodes ill for the nation's future. Former governor of Colorado Richard Lamm, author of *Megatraumas: America in the Year 2000*, writes:

America is not replacing itself with a skilled enough workforce to keep it economically healthy and socially stable. *By no standards are American students and young adults coming close to having the skills, motivation and talents of our economic competitors. Our children are in the bottom third of industrial nations on all education comparisons. Our major economic competitors have children who are ahead of ours from the moment they enter the first grade and these nations graduate far more of their 18-year-olds from high school than we do. Additionally, those they graduate are better educated, more knowledgeable and more motivated.* [italics added][52]

The Washington, D.C., Council on Competitiveness found that growth in Americans' standard of living lagged behind other major industrialized nations in 1988, despite a surge in U.S. export sales. For the past 16 years the U.S. hasn't kept pace with its major trading partners. The council's "competitiveness index" measures U.S. standing in the world economy in terms that have meaning to the average American.[53]

A 1989 Joint Economic Committee report from Congress states that "Our country has been driven for most of this decade not by investment but rather by a *binge of consumption* that threatens our long-run standard of living and our standing as the world's leading economic power."[54] To compete internationally, the U.S. must boost savings, increase investment, and increase productivity. In the last decade the government led consumption with its huge federal deficit. Business followed with a 20 percent drop in new investment. And then consumers did their part by doubling credit card use and racking up a total debt of more than $700 billion.[55]

The average per capita income in Japan far outpaced the rest of the world in 1989, rising from $15,840 to $21,040. Japanese life expectancy is 78, the highest in the world. The U.S. ranks fifth in per capita income behind Switzerland, Japan, Iceland, and Norway. Japan, Switzerland, France, and Sweden all have higher life expectancies. Ours is 69 years.[56] A recent poll indicated that 59 percent of Americans believe that Japanese economic competition is a greater threat to national security than the cold war.[57]

Every year, evidence for the Asian ascendency mounts. Once American services dominated world markets. In construction, companies like Bechtel, Brown, and Root and Westinghouse took the lion's share of engineering contracts. Today, they compete head-to-head with world-class firms like Japan's Chiyoda Engineering and Kumagai Gumi and Korea's Hyundai and Lucky Goldstar.[58] The same has happened in financial markets. Japan owns 25 of the top 50 international banks in total assets. The top 12 are all Japanese. *The United States only has 2 in the top 50,* Citibank at number 27 and Bank of America in San Francisco at number 44. We're behind Germany's seven, France and Great Britain's four each, and Switzerland's three. Seven of California's largest banks are Japanese-owned.[59]

We approach the 21st century in a twenty-year nosedive. And the young people who'll ultimately be responsible for pulling us out can't even fly. They don't know how to compete and don't believe they need to. Their entitlement culture has led them to believe that wealth and prosperity come with membership in the middle class.

How did this happen?

2

Entitlement

"**G**reed . . . is good. Greed is right. Greed clarifies, cuts through and captures the essence of the evolutionary spirit. . . . Greed—mark my words—will save . . . the U.S.A."[1] So said *Wall Street's* Gordon Gekko, reflecting the spirit of the 1980s. Greed's first cousin, "play now, pay later," also found its way into the national ethos, creating the greatest consumptive binge in history. The "Me Generation" of the 1970s became the "Mine Generation" of the 1980s as government, industry, and consumers spent, spent, and spent some more. Avarice and consumption yoked themselves for mutual benefit. The result?

The national product doubled, the national debt tripled, and corporate and personal debt soared. Americans and their institutions *spent $1 trillion more than they produced.* The U.S. went from being the world's largest creditor in 1980 to the world's largest debtor. The Tokyo Stock Exchange surpassed the New York Stock Exchange in total value, Japanese per capita income surpassed ours, and the Japanese gained financial control of Rockefeller Center, Columbia Pictures, and much of Waikiki Beach.[2]

In *Time's* "Freed from Greed," Otto Friedrich writes: "The atmosphere of the 1980s, along with actual crimes, spread a general sense that anything goes. Get rich, borrow, spend, enjoy. Not only Gordon Gekko said greed is good; so did Ivan Boesky, the dapper king of arbitrage, before he ended up going to prison."[3] Billionaire H. Ross Perot says: "The '80s is the decade that we gave away our industrial lead and acted totally irresponsibly in wrecking some of our big corporations through leveraged buyouts. We felt affluent because we were living off borrowed money. We've got to clean up education, clean up the deficit, clean up the drugs, clean up the justice system, clean up industry. But right now it's like Lawrence Welk music: it's just wonderful, wonderful, wonderful."[4]

Era of Self-Sufficiency[5]

Clearly, there's more to American aspirations than consumption, leveraged buyouts, and junk bond get-rich schemes. Today's technological conveniences didn't just "happen." Someone, somewhere in our past contributed to the "good life" we enjoy today. Industrial giants like Henry Ford blazed trails and prodigious inventors like Thomas Edison lit pathways. "Never give up" was their clarion call. The light bulb epitomized that try-try-try-again philosophy. Edison even quantified it: "I have not failed 10,000 times. I have successfully found 10,000 ways that will not work."

Where is that personal persistence today? Has the Ford-Edison kind of "true grit" that sustained our parents and grandparents through two world wars, a depression, the Korean conflict, and the cold war seeped from the American spirit? Young people today believe that "modern" history begins with Woodstock, Watergate, Watts, and the Vietnam War. True, the 1960s were eventful times. But they contributed little to our position as the greatest economic and technological power of the 20th century. Pre-1950s achievements are responsible for the country's meteoric rise that climaxed act 2 of *The American Dream* when America the beautiful became America the bountiful. The 1950s was America's "coming out" party which we've been celebrating ever since. Who delivered this bounty to us and what price did they pay? These are questions we rarely hear anyone ask.

The Accomplishments

Three generations of "True-Gritters" are responsible for where we are today. The first generation revolutionized how we communicate and how we travel. Cellular phones and satellite communication systems began with Fessenden's radio transmission of human speech via radio waves in 1900 and Marconi's telegraphic radio messages in 1901. Mechanized land and air travel started when J. P. Morgan organized the U.S. Steel Corporation in 1901, Henry Ford founded the Ford Motor Company in 1902, and Wilbur Wright piloted a 40-minute air flight in 1907. And the nuclear age introduced itself in 1915 when Albert Einstein developed his "General Theory of Relativity."

By 1925, a second generation of Americans accelerated the pace of innovation and development. Alexander Graham Bell made telegraphic contact with Dr. Thomas Watson from New York to San Francisco; the United States became the world leader in coal and steel production; the Ford Motor Company produced its 10 millionth car; and Americans listened to 2.5 million radios throughout the country. A few years later, Charles Lindbergh completed his nonstop flight from New York to Paris in 1927; and television made its debut in Schenectady, New York, in 1928. In 1929, the year of the Great Crash, "talking pictures" replaced silent films, Bell Laboratories developed color television, and Kodak introduced 16 mm color films. Even the Depression years had sparkle. Walt Disney introduced *Snow White and the Seven Dwarfs* in 1937, and by the end of the decade 20,000 New Yorkers were watching TV while 30 million American families listened to radio.

The third generation of True-Gritters projected our technological prowess onto the world scene. Within two decades we became an undisputed world force. Military applications of science dominated the 1940s with the splitting of the atom by Enrico Fermi, the development of the first computer in 1942, and the first successful atomic bomb test in 1945. Domestic innovations kept pace with Chester Carlson's introduction of the Xerographic process in 1946 and Bell Laboratories development of transistors in 1947. The decade ended with air-space conquests as a 1949 U.S. Air Force jet flew across the U.S. in 3 hours and 46 minutes, and the U.S. launched a guided missile 250 miles in the air—the highest altitude ever reached by man.

The cumulative effect of these first 50 years was no less than profound. By the time color television made its debut in 1951, 1.5 million homes had already converted dining rooms into monochromed TV rooms. Three years later black and white viewing reached 29 million homes, and overnight the U.S. was sporting a standard of living unmatched anywhere. With only 6 percent of the world's population, Americans drove 60 percent of all cars, communicated on

58 percent of all telephones, listened to 45 percent of all radios, and traveled on 34 percent of all railroads. This *was* America the bountiful, the largest concentration of wealth anywhere in the world right here at home. No wonder the 1950s seemed so good. They were! No other country achieved as much, accumulated as much, or believed in itself as much. But there were costs. Pre-1950s generations remember. That's why they're True-Gritters—surviving, achieving, innovating against all odds.

The Challenges

Baby boomers look back to the 1960s and wonder how the country survived. But decades earlier the pre-1950s generations wondered too. Their worries were life threatening, decade after decade: World War I, the Great Depression, World War II, the Korean War, the cold war. Even so, those generations reached beyond themselves to leave a legacy that would become our grubstake for a better life in the second half of the 20th century.

Our parents, grandparents, and great-grandparents were True-Gritters. So were our post-1950s presidents: Dwight D. Eisenhower (b. 1890), John F. Kennedy (b. 1917), Lyndon B. Johnson (b. 1908), Richard M. Nixon (b. 1913), Gerald R. Ford (b. 1913); Jimmy Carter (b. 1924), Ronald R. Reagan (b. 1911) and George Bush (b. 1924). They grew up when "self-sufficiency" was the bulwark of the American value structure and Thomas Hobbes and Adam Smith were its philosopher-kings.

They witnessed the start of the century with Germany united and Russia not yet the USSR. Eisenhower was 24 years old when Archduke Francis Ferdinand, heir to the Austrian throne, was assassinated in Sarajevo, causing Germany to declare war on Russia and France and Britain to declare war on Germany. In 1916 German saboteurs blew up a munitions arsenal in New Jersey, provoking the United States to declare war on Germany, Hungary, and Austria. And by 1918 the war was over. Germany and Austria agreed to President Wilson's demands and retreated to their own territory. The same year, the Bolsheviks executed Czar Nicholas II and his family.

Four years later, when Ronald Reagan was 11 and Lyndon B. Johnson was 14, the seeds of war were germinating once again.

Mussolini marched on Rome to form the Fascist government in Italy while the communists absorbed the Baltic states into the USSR. In 1927 the German economic system collapsed on "Black Friday." Two years later, October 28th decimated the New York Stock Exchange to set off a world economic crisis. U.S. securities lost $26 billion in value. When Dwight Eisenhower was 38, John F. Kennedy 12, Ronald Reagan 18, and George Bush 15, the industrialized world teetered on financial ruin, the Nazis established their first concentration camps in Germany, and the boycott of Jews began.

There were ominous signs elsewhere too. In 1933 the Japanese premier was assassinated, and three years later Japan withdrew from the League of Nations. During the same period Britain abandoned the gold standard. Famine spread across the USSR. By 1935 revolution in Austria overturned the Social Democrats, and the world news reported five political assassinations: Austria's chancellor, Yugoslavia's king and foreign minister, Stalin's associate Serge Kirov, and Louisiana's Huey Long. The European political and social order continued to decline. A general strike erupted in France; Hitler became "Fuhrer"; Germany passed the Nuremberg Laws against the Jews; and Mussolini invaded Abyssinia.

Across the Atlantic, Americans were doing their best to stay out of trouble. But in 1938, one year before World War II broke out, German troops invaded the Rhineland, Mussolini and Hitler proclaimed the Rome-Berlin Axis, Japan seized five cities in China, Mao Tse-tung started a revolution in China, and Japanese planes sank a U.S. gunboat in Chinese waters.

World War II was about to begin and our post-1950s presidents were now adults. Richard Nixon was 25, Ronald Reagan 27, and Jimmy Carter and George Bush 15. In 1939 Roosevelt asked Congress for $552 million for defense and then demanded assurances that Hitler and Mussolini would not attack 31 European countries. It was too late. Germany invaded Poland from the west and the USSR invaded Poland from the east. Britain and France declared war on Germany and the USSR invaded Finland. In 1940 Germany invaded and occupied Norway, Denmark, Holland, Belgium, Luxembourg, and France. Italy declared war on France and Britain. The next year Germany invaded Russia and advanced to the outskirts of Leningrad. Then, on December 7th, the Japanese bombed Pearl Harbor; the United States and Britain declared war on Japan the next day. Four years later, 35 million were dead, 10 million were in German concentration camps, and Europe and Japan were devastated, their economies in shambles and their people demoralized. Italy capitulated in 1943. Germany surrendered in 1945. The United States dropped atomic bombs on Hiroshima and Nagasaki on August 6th and 9th. Japan surrendered on August 14.

The United States was the only winner. The war ravaged allies and foes, but left us an atomic power. For the second time in 20 years, the U.S. entry into world conflict made the difference. Confidence soared. We sent General MacArthur to rebuild Japan's shattered economy, passed the Marshall Plan to reconstruct Europe, and welcomed home over a million veterans with the G.I. Bill of Rights. By 1950, we had a baby boom and a new era.

The Era of Entitlement[6]

Freedom and democracy triumphed. The work ethic was paying generous dividends and plenty of babies were being born to enjoy them. World wars and a depression were enough. It was time for a better life and a new ethic. War Mobilization and Reconversion director Fred Vison remarked that "the American people are in the pleasant predicament of having to learn to live fifty percent better than they ever have before."[7]

Young Americans responded to this new prosperity by leaving home earlier, marrying younger, and having more children. "The fertility boom coincided with the greatest economic expansion this country has ever seen. In June 1946, *Fortune* reported that women were lining up by the hundreds for new nylon stockings and concluded that 'this is the dream era, this is what everyone was waiting through the blackouts for. . . . The Great American Boom is on.'"[8] From 1946 to 1964, 76 million American babies entered the world. Magazines, television soap operas, and commercials extolled the virtues of motherhood. *Look* magazine dubbed mother a wondrous creature "who bears more babies and looks and acts far more feminine than the emancipated girls of the twenties and thirties."[9] Soap operas described the fertility option as a way of attracting mates.

The "Procreation Ethic" developed a moral tone that cast aspersions on those choosing to remain single or to forgo children. Nearly all families had more than three. Childless couples, bachelors, and spinsters nearly disappeared. Better education and higher income no longer correlated with lower birth rates. The opposite occurred. The couples with more education and higher incomes had more children. By 1958 the number of families with two or more children increased 46 percent to 5.2 million. Young people started outnumbering all other age groups. In 1964, the last year of the boom, 40 percent of the U.S. population was under 20.[10]

The New American Family

Security, prosperity, and the baby boom transformed postwar America. Overnight, the extended family which had held together millions of Americans for generations disappeared. In 1790 the average number of persons per household was 5.7. In 1890 it was 4.9, but by 1960 it was 3.6. At the same time, families moved out of the cities and into the suburbs in their search for extra room for children. Between 1950 and 1970 the suburban population doubled from 36 million to 72 million.[11]

Millions of acres of farmland made way for 11 million homes for new families. Home ownership doubled between 1940 and 1960. The 1950s building boom accounted for 25 percent of all homes ever built in the U.S.[12] The new suburbia was "big and lush and uniform—a combination made to order for the comprehending marketer."[13] It was a "servantless society" with such labor-saving conveniences as washing machines, electric clothes dryers, branch stores, and finally, the ultimate symbol of suburban living, the station wagon. From 1945 to 1960 car registrations increased 231 percent. The number of two-car families doubled from 1951 to 1958.[14]

There were other changes as well. In 1946, the first year of the boom, there were barely 6000 television sets. Seven years later the industry was producing 7 million per year; by 1967 98 percent of all homes had televisions. This increase surpassed adoption rates for all other technological innovations in this century. Not even telephones, radios, or automobiles matched television's meteoric rate of acceptance.[15]

The "New American Family" was here: nuclear sized, suburban settled, and TV-room anchored. Movie attendance dropped as parents turned to Lucy Ricardo in *I Love Lucy* and boom children tuned in the *Mickey Mouse Club* and *Howdy Doody*. Families shared their viewing pleasures in *The Adventures of Ozzie and Harriet, Father Knows Best, The Life of Riley,* and *Leave It to Beaver*.[16]

The new family rejected self-sacrifice, preferring consumption to savings and convenience to deferred gratification. Television advertising reinforced the new values every hour every day. How different this was from Christopher Larsch's archetypical embodiment of the American dream: "[a man who] owed his advancement to habits of industry, sobriety, moderation, self-discipline, and avoidance of debt . . . [who] lived for the future, shunning self-indulgence in favor of patient, painstaking accumulation."[17] Baby boomers learned to walk, talk, and watch television to the tune of "the New Ethics." By adulthood, they were consummate consumers, quintessential representatives of entitlement.

The Cult of the Child

Baby boomers secured starring roles in *The American Dream* because their moms and dads arranged risk-free auditions. No reason for failure or frustration. The country had suffered enough. Parents rejected Dr. L. Emmett Holt's scientific method of childrearing that warned against too much coddling, playing, kissing, and rocking. They had no use for Granville Stanley Hall's recommendation for more spanking, or behaviorist John B. Watson's plan for clockwork feeding and toilet training either. Dr. Benjamin Spock's 1946 *Common Sense Book of Baby and Child Care* was the new parents' bible. It encouraged parents to be natural, to love, and to enjoy their children. The Pocket Books edition sold 30 million copies in 29 languages, becoming the best-selling title in the United States.[18]

The new authority placed children where they belonged, in the center of the family circle. Infant demand feeding replaced scheduled feedings and "permissive" childrearing came of age. By the time boomers entered school, the curriculum was different too. Emphasis on rote learning of facts and figures to get ahead in a tight-fisted world gave way to social development. Now children were to be "well-adjusted" and "well-rounded." They needed to cooperate, express themselves creatively, and increase their self-esteem and self-confidence. So they were enrolled in Cub Scouts, Girl Scouts, and

Brownies in record numbers. They converged on America's favorite sport, baseball, swelling the ranks of Little Leagues by 735 percent.[19]

Parents produced and directed every scene. They organized and planned meaningful social experiences and accounted for every precious minute. This was a golden age of boundless optimism. Entry into school was especially significant. Parents banded together to form PTAs to improve education. From 1950 to 1960 spending on elementary and secondary schools increased 281 percent; in 1958 alone, 62,000 new classrooms came on line at an average cost of $40,000 each. The rallying cry heard across the land was "Our children deserve the very best!"[20]

Parents moved to the suburbs to find more room to raise their children. They organized activities to promote healthier experiences. They built new schools and bought new textbooks to improve their children's education. And they enhanced their children's self-esteem and self-confidence with continuous streams of reminders that they were special and that they would inherit the best of all possible worlds. Parents *wanted* their children to feel special. And they did.

By 1956 many boomer children were almost boomer teens, ready for "Blue Suede Shoes," the King, and *American Bandstand*. On August 8, 1957, Dick Clark's ABC debut found boomers in 67 cities watching and listening to Jerry Lee Lewis perform "Whole Lotta Shakin' Goin' On." Soon *American Bandstand* was attracting 20 million daily viewers who wrote 50,000 fan letters a week. This was an important event, especially for advertisers. A new market was born. During the 1950s the number of teenagers increased from 10 million to 15 million; by 1970 there were 20 million of these young adults with significant financial backing. What Jack and Jill wanted today, parents bought for them tomorrow.[21]

Teenagers were unexpected sources of consumer spending too, accounting for 55 percent of all soft drinks purchased, 53 percent of all movie tickets, and 43 percent of all records sold in the U.S. Meanwhile, parents reinforced the consumptive binge by adding second and third cars, second TVs, and, of course, the children's phone. Teenage girls, representing only 11 percent of the total population, spent 20 percent of all money exchanged for cosmetics and toiletries, while teenage boys spent over $120 million a year for comparable "needs." Teenagers were convinced the biggest problem they faced was acne.[22]

The nation was enthralled with it all. As Jones notes, "The editors of *Time* honored the 'Under-25 Generation' as its Man of the Year in 1967. In its lifetime, *Time* wrote, this promising generation could land on the moon, cure cancer and the common cold, lay out blight-proof, smog-free cities, help end racial prejudice, enrich the underdeveloped world and, no doubt, write an end to poverty and war."[23]

By the time boomers reached adulthood their values and expectations mirrored what their parents, teachers, and the media had told them for years. They were special—a new breed, set apart historically and economically from past generations of suffering and sacrifice. "What other generations have thought *privileges*, the baby boomers thought were rights."[24]

Baby boomers were the entitlement generation.

Disillusionment

Baby boomers were the first heirs to post–World War II prosperity, first children of nuclear families, first citizens of suburban sprawl, first "swooners" of rock and roll, first youth consumers of Madison Avenue, and first full-time television viewers. Isolated and insulated by their size as a group, they developed a culture of their own. Parents and grandparents had less influence on them than they had on each other. Television reinforced entitlements and advertisers encouraged consumption. For the first time in American history, external forces overpowered family forces. Dad's stories of the Great Depression and grandmother's advice on the work ethic never registered. Relatives lived in other cities, dad was usually at the office, and mom was out shopping. Meanwhile, boomers were watching television.

TV ownership jumped from a few thousand in 1948 to 15 million in 1952. Patterns of family living changed. A Cornell study reported that the 40-year decline in time children spent with parents was due to television.[1] Boom children watching TV from age two accumulated up to 5000 hours by age six. By the sixth grade they watched an average of four and one-half hours each weekday and up to thirteen hours on weekends. At 18 the average boomer watched four hours per day or about 24,000 hours—one quarter of their waking life. The only activity that took more time was sleep.[2]

As viewing increased, reading, movie going, socializing, daydreaming, and traveling decreased. Children with televisions were physically present but mentally absent. Parents lost touch with them for long periods each day. Family problems on television were resolved in 30 minutes and long-term struggle, hardship, and despair never surfaced. Solutions were neat, painless. "Beaver Cleaver never had to worry if his parents would announce a trial separation. And if Ozzie Nelson had a drinking problem or was otherwise unemployable—why else was he always hanging around the house?"[3]

Gradually, but inexorably, boomers drifted from the cultural moorings that anchored them to the past. The nuclear family disconnected them physically and television separated them mentally. New value structures emerged as the entitlement ethic replaced the work ethic. Expectations increased along with a youthful sense of power. Media exposures imprinted "made for TV" beliefs and attitudes. Parents had no control, teachers had no control, and boomers had no control. They were on an evolutionary roll guided only by their boundless expectations. The gap between generations widened. No one could help them more than they could help themselves. American history shrunk to 30-minute TV scenarios depicting truth, justice, and the American way.

But when boomers set out on their own they discovered assassinations, Vietnam, Watergate, and stagflation. They also discovered that membership in a population bulge was no longer empowering, especially when it came to finding jobs, securing promotions, and buying houses. Suddenly, life wasn't fair. They reacted by postponing commitments. Rather than marriage first and career last, they put career first and family last. They postponed marriage and downgraded family. The beneficiaries of the "cult of the child" instituted the "cult for adults." For the first time in American history, children and family were absent from the typical wish list. BMWs, Bloomingdale's clothes, and exotic weekend vacations were there instead.

The social costs of these choices are still with us. Devaluation of the American dollar paralleled devaluation of the American family. Children and childrearing vanished with the quest for "me" and "mine." The new values and expectations widened the "generation gap" as boomers discovered the "reality gap."

The Generation Gap

Boomer children grew up expecting easy living and abundant rewards. Parents, teachers, and media had joined to perpetuate this message. Nowhere was contrary evidence apparent. It's no surprise their worldview was different. How could they comprehend pre-1950s hardships and sacrifices? Occasional reminders from parents and grandparents were no match for thousands of hours of television that portrayed the good life—the way things were, the way things should be, the way things would always be. No one burdened the boomers with a past adults wanted to forget. Spare them. This was a better world. America was strong. America was beautiful. America was bountiful.

By the time they graduated from high school, the boomers were ready to take on the world. But first college. From 1963 to 1973 enrollment in colleges and universities doubled to reach an annual growth rate of 9 percent per year. The number of college graduates present in the general population increased from 10 million in 1965 to 19 million in 1980.[4] The effect was profound. There were so many boomers they became the campus "fourth estate," demanding courses and assignments that met *their* needs and *their* interests. They convinced administrators to expand offerings and to make courses "relevant." More sociology, psychology, and religion, but no history. Why waste time studying the mistakes of the past? "History was the academic equivalent of the voice of their parents, harping on an irrelevant past. Why should they compare their experience to anything else? The whole point was that theirs was the *unique* generation, without parallel, *sui generis*."[5]

By the mid-1960s civil rights and Vietnam caught their attention. So they marched, sat in, demonstrated, and dropped out—en masse. They "had no use for their parents' skills or wisdom. . . . [they] had made their peers their ultimate authority. Further, they were abandoning what they said was the sterile, empty, materialistic world of their parents to shop in a supermarket of new ideas and life-styles."[6] This *was* the generation gap: "The child-oriented parents of the forties and fifties, who had made their children their religion, were devastated. The idea of their children—so fortunate in the affluence and attention lavished on them—rejecting the society that made it possible seemed almost obscene. They had seen enough of human waste during the Depression—but at least they could understand that tragedy. But how had they failed their own children?"[7]

The "Reality Gap"[8]

Unfortunately, boomer life after 18 was never as good as promised. There were signs earlier, but they never penetrated the fantasy shield of suburban living.

The Cold War

In 1948 the USSR stopped road and rail traffic between Berlin and the West. The next year 11 U.S. communists were found guilty of conspiracy to overthrow the government and the USSR successfully tested its first atomic bomb. We were no longer its sole proprietors. The threat of thermonuclear war was here. So was the cold war. In 1950 North Korea invaded South Korea to capture Seoul; within a year General MacArthur was leading U.S. and U.N. forces to regain lost territory. Fear of communism and the threat of nuclear war started runs on bomb shelters as Americans planned for the worst. Schools prepared too with weekly drills. Jeff Greenfield remembers that "we would drop from our chairs, pull ourselves into a fetal position, and crouch under our desks, and wait until the A-bomb had fallen."[9]

In 1955 the Soviets challenged our technological superiority by announcing plans to launch an earth satellite. Two years later they delivered Sputniks I and II. We answered with 31-pound Explorer the next year. They countered with 3,000-pound Sputnik III. Our confidence was shaken. What had happened?

While the chosen generation was learning to get along in school, express itself, and be creative, Soviet students were learning math and science. Our educational system had failed and the country had lost a technological edge that had taken 50 years to establish. In 1958 we launched a moon rocket that failed to reach its destination, and the following year the USSR's Lunick II reached the moon and photographed its surface. In 1960 they shot down a U-2 airplane and captured pilot Francis Gary Powers who confessed to aerial reconnaissance over the USSR.

The First Assassination

The country was ready for change. John F. Kennedy, the country's youngest president, encouraged exiled rebels to invade Cuba at the Bay of Pigs. A year later, Khrushchev installed a missile base in Cuba and Kennedy blockaded Cuba to force its removal. The nation and world watched as the superpowers teetered at the brink. Meanwhile, James Meredith was denied admission to the University of Mississippi and U.S. marshalls backed by 3,000 soldiers suppressed riots so he could begin classes. Racial unrest spread to Birmingham, Alabama, as whites and police beat blacks during riots leading to the arrest of Martin Luther King. Kennedy ordered 3,000 troops to quell the unrest as 200,000 black and white "Freedom Marchers" moved on Washington, D.C. Then, on November 22, 1963, John F. Kennedy was assassinated by Lee Harvey Oswald, ending the country's Camelot presidency. Two days later Lee Harvey Oswald was shot and killed by Jack Ruby while America watched on TV. The boomers saw it all.

Civil Rights and the War

"Good life" prospects suddenly went from bad to worse. While the Warren Commission investigated the Kennedy assassination, U.S. aircraft attacked North Vietnamese bases, North Vietnamese MIG aircraft shot down U.S. jets, and the USSR admitted supplying arms to Hanoi. At home, race riots erupted in Harlem and New York City, Black Muslim leader Malcolm X was assassinated, violence and Ku Klux Klan shootings rocked Selma, Alabama, and severe race riots in Watts killed 35 and sent 4,000 to jail.

Meanwhile, Vietnam festered on. Heavyweight boxing champion Muhammad Ali refused induction into the armed services while 5,000 persons rioted against the war in Hong Kong, 700,000 in New York marched down Fifth Avenue in support of the war, 50,000 demonstrated against the war at Lincoln Memorial in Washington, D.C., and Martin Luther King led an antiwar march in New York. In 1968 Reverend Martin Luther King, Jr., winner of the 1964 Nobel Peace Prize, was assassinated in Memphis, and Senator Robert F. Kennedy was assassinated in Los Angeles.

War protests at college campuses resulted in four students killed and nine wounded. Higher education was under siege. By the end of the war, 58,000 Americans were dead and another 153,000 had been wounded. The majority were baby boomers.

Boomers no longer saw the world as their private playground. Landon Jones captured the reactions of one baby boomer from California who became a New York magazine editor: "We went through a hell of a lot. If you went through it and emerged from it, you emerged so much stronger. I think there is a way of seeing the worst. You know you're not going to see it that bad anymore. Therefore, you have a lot more strength and drive to go on and get about your life and do well. I weathered my father's death, a suicide, and the sixties. Nothing scares me."[10] The "sheltered generation" received a stiff dose of reality:

> The optimism and hope that the boom generation took into the Vietnam years only made its eventual disenchantment more devastating. They had been young and idealistic and Vietnam made them old and cynical. Their parents had come out of World War II with renewed confidence, but the boom generation came out of Vietnam with little to believe in of its own. . . . It is trite now to say that Vietnam marked America's end of innocence. But the boom generation did receive then its first personal taste of life as tragedy.[11]

Watergate and Stagflation

In 1972 Richard Nixon won a reelection landslide victory over George McGovern and then surprised the world with a daring visit to China. From these heights he fell precipitously as a thread connected to his reelection bid began to unravel. The District of Columbia police arrested five men for breaking and entering the Democratic National Headquarters and the Watergate cover-up began. The following year Nixon aides Haldeman and Ehrlichman resigned; John Dean III implicated Nixon in a cover-up; John Mitchell and Maurice Stans were indicted by a grand jury; Attorney General Elliot Richardson resigned; Congress began impeachment considerations, and Vice President Spiro Agnew resigned after pleading nolo contendere to one count of income tax evasion.

Prosperity had ended too. In 1970 the Dow Jones stock exchange index fell to 631, the lowest level in eight years, and by 1973 OPEC's oil embargo impacted on heating and transportation services and eliminated 100,000 jobs. Worldwide inflation increased the cost of fuel, food, and materials and slowed economic growth to near zero in most industrialized nations.[12] Baby boomers coming out of college discovered that their higher education meant little in an economy headed nowhere. Too many degrees chased too few opportunities.

The 1970s unfolded slowly, painfully, with one wrenching event leading to another. In 1974 Nixon agreed to pay $432,787 in back taxes, while a grand jury secretly named him as an unindicted co-

conspirator in the Watergate cover-up. The U.S. Supreme Court followed with a unanimous decision to turn over additional White House tapes to the special prosecutor. And the House Judiciary Committee recommended three articles of impeachment. On August 9, 1974, Richard Nixon resigned and Vice President Gerald R. Ford became the 39th president.

The next year OPEC raised its oil prices another 10 percent. Britain's inflation rate jumped to 25 percent, unemployment in the U.S. reached 9.2 percent—the highest level since 1941, and New York City appealed to the federal government for cash to avert financial collapse. Meanwhile, former White House aides and cabinet members received sentences. Maurice H. Stans was the third Nixon cabinet member convicted. John N. Mitchell, John D. Ehrlichman, and H. R. Haldeman received sentences of up to eight years in prison. Nixon aides Robert C. Mardian, John W. Dean III, Herbert W. Kalmbach, Jeb Stuart Magruder, Charles Colson, James W. McCord, E. Howard Hunt, and G. Gordon Liddy also served time.

Politically and economically, the nation was on the ropes. Only the judiciary branch of government seemed to work. Politicians were liars and economists were stupid. The American dream was a fraud and the giant of free enterprise was adrift, with no captain and no engine. The decade ended with decreased initiative and diminished opportunity. Production was down and inflation was up—an economic anomaly economists finally called "stagflation."

Boomer Reactions

For a generation raised on 30-minute bites of plastic living and shallow thinking, the 1960s and 1970s were shockers—assassinations, riots, demonstrations, resignations, convictions, inflation, unemployment. Where *were* truth, justice, and the American way? Boomers no longer believed what they were told. In school they had learned about textbook America and at home they had watched "good guy-bad guy" TV. They never suspected a charade. Increasing disillusionment did not end with the Vietnam War. Baby boomers fresh out of college faced yet another obstacle: themselves. They swamped the degree markets, the job markets, and the housing markets, depressing the value of their education and inflating the value of everything else. They entered adulthood during the worst recession since the 1930s and experienced the highest inflation since World War II. Getting started was tough.

"Me Now, Children Never"

Marriage and family were the first to go. In 1967 44 percent of first-year college women identified home and family as their personal goals. A decade later only 20 percent valued these goals.[13] Surviving the economic challenge came first. This meant career women, pooled incomes, and down payments on the "good life." Boomers set new standards for living well. Although single incomes fell short of 1950s purchasing power, combined incomes leveraged a decent life-style by any standard.

The values of aspiring young adults also changed. Personal and material needs replaced family and children. The quest for happiness and immediate gratification postponed personal commitments. Many boomers rejected staying married "for the sake of the children." Others avoided commitment altogether. Divorce rates skyrocketed. From 1958 to 1978 divorces per 1,000 persons increased 148 percent while marriages increased only 25 percent. During that same period, birth rates per thousand persons decreased 38 percent. By 1980 the median age for first marriages for males was 25.9 years—the highest since 1900; and the median age for females was 23.6 for 1970 and 1980—the highest for the century.[14]

Boomers also committed themselves less to jobs. They were impatient with setbacks and refused to wait for promotions. According to a 1970s Yankelovich survey, "the number of workers who look on their jobs as their primary source of fulfillment has been halved since the late sixties. The number who think 'hard work always pays off has dropped from 58 percent to 43 percent.'"[15] Increasingly, values shifted from sacrificing self to gratifying self. Jobs, spouses, and family no longer came first. This was the "Me" decade. Unlimited options for self-gratification turned out to be as unfulfilling as the more restricted menus of the past. Boomers continued their search for meaning in life. "'Uncertainty was the legacy of our generation,' a 32-year-old told the *Boston Globe* in a revealing use of the past tense. 'Our parents' generation was sure of certain values. We weren't. We had freedom, but the flip side of freedom is instability.' Born into an affluent society, the young baby boomers never had a chance to test their character. Then, in the seventies, they were overwhelmed by a world that seemed to offer limitless choice."[16]

Effects on Parenting

The "cult of the child" was an immediate casualty of the new values. Never again would the country worship its children as it did in the 1950s and 1960s. A University of Michigan survey found that between the 1960s and 1970s, the percentage of female college graduates who felt positive about having children decreased from 50 percent to 28 percent.[17] In the late 1970s, Daniel Yankelovich polled baby-boomer parents (whom he called the "New Breed") and found them to be less child-oriented and more self-oriented than previous generations of parents.[18]

Twenty-five percent of "New Breed" fathers believed that children should learn proper health and nutritional habits at school.[19] The parental overprotectionism of the 1950s and 1960s was gone. Father and mother were no longer breadwinners and homemakers. Mothers worked and marriages dissolved. In fact, New Breed parents really didn't know what they wanted for their children. Transferring the cultural heritage to the country's future citizens was up for grabs. What values should children learn? What parenting methods should they use? Certainly *not* the ones their parents had used.

Entitlements gave youth everything externally stimulating and nothing internally motivating. As a consequence, youth conditions deteriorated faster than ever. "Sizable numbers of people currently believe that many things have become worse since they were young. For example, 33 percent feel that the quality of education is now worse, 43 percent say unemployment has grown worse, and *52 percent believe family life is worse today*" [italics added].[20] Even wealth didn't make things right. While only 40 percent of all adults felt that children got a good education, a substantial proportion believed that children were unhappy (52 percent) and did not have loving parents (47 percent).[21] It's not surprising that prospective baby boom parents were confused. "Isolated from their parents, besieged by experts, and unsure of their own roles, these baby-boom parents had lost the inner maps that were supposed to guide them through parenthood. 'Child rearing is one of the biggest casualties of the modern age that is being ushered in by this generation,' says sociologist James Coleman. 'We are becoming the first species in the history of the world which is unable to care for its young.'"[22]

The parenting practices of the past failed to instill the self-righting gyroscopes essential for sustained, purposeful accomplishment. Consequently, young people don't know how to maximize their potential, become independent of their parents, and find their own measure of happiness, success, and fulfillment as adults. They live day to day, seeking one source of immediate reinforcement after another. They have no notion of how the world works or what accomplishment takes.

Would-be parents who want to do a better job don't know how. Just as the authoritarian approaches of the 1930s were out of step with the 1950s, the permissive parenting of recent decades is out of touch with the 1990s. The cult of the child is over. So what, if *anything*, will take its place? Are there alternative roles for modern parents who want to help their children direct themselves and the country into the next century? And what about the children of immature parents and broken homes? How will they survive in the next century?

Parenthood had been devalued. America was no longer a society dominated by children or even by families. As families continued to break down, more and more children were caught up in divorce and grew up with a different idea—if any idea at all—of how the traditional family operated. Many of these children are emotionally and psychologically wounded. A decade earlier, the psychiatric field of childhood depression did not exist. Now it is a growth industry. Children as young as six and seven are trying to kill themselves in numbers previously unthinkable. Yet these are the same people who will carry us through the twenty-first century. Three out of every four children born in 1980 can expect to live to the year 2045; one-half will reach 2055, and one out of every four will reach 2056. They will be the legacy of the boom generation.[23]

From 1983 to 1987 violent crimes committed by persons under 18 increased 31 percent and property crimes committed by youth increased 41 percent.[24] Some lawmakers want to make parents responsible. California and Florida passed controversial laws to punish parents, sometimes with jail time, for their children's actions.

According to Los Angeles County District Attorney Ira Reiner, "Traditionally, the law about contributing to the delinquency of a minor meant contributing to the delinquency of someone else's child, not your own. This law [California's] has been slightly modified, so that by the omission of certain acts, your failure to exercise necessary control, you can then be charged with the crime of contributing to the delinquency of your own child."[25] Reiner argues that legislation like this encourages parents to control their children. Families at all income levels experience the consequences of raising children who don't adjust outside their home. In *Why Good Parents Have Bad Kids*, Kent Hayes writes:

> Children raised in middle- and upper-income homes are no longer immune to the indignities of the prison environment. The belief that all prisoners are poverty stricken and ignorant is a twentieth-century wives' tale. Other well-meaning mothers and fathers who own homes on treelined streets in communities all over the United States are suffering as their children struggle to maintain sanity in mental hospitals, or praying to understand why their loved one chose suicide rather than continue the struggle.[26]

Now, more children grow up in single-parent homes or have two working parents. They're home alone, unsupervised for long periods of time, with no idea of how to manage their time appropriately and productively. Current parenting methods fail to recognize this significant problem, much less how to solve it. According to Lawrence Kutner, "A recent study found that eighth graders left at home alone more than 11 hours a week were twice as likely to use alcohol, tobacco and marijuana as children the same age who spent all their time after school supervised by adults."[27] Dr. Jean L. Richardson, the University of Southern California associate professor who directed the study, concluded that "This increased risk appeared no matter what the sex, race or socioeconomic status of children."[28]

There's also a deep-seated misconception that children need affluent life-styles to grow up "normally." What happened to those old-fashioned ideals about children learning to earn their way? Today parents guarantee such "necessities" as spending money, designer clothes, and cars, even though this method violates a fundamental motivational principle: "People who don't need don't succeed."

When youth don't need to be responsible, they don't learn responsibility; when they don't need to succeed, they don't learn to succeed; and when they don't need to adjust, they don't learn independence. Instead they learn how to search for quick fixes—like those portrayed on television and at the movies. Some even get themselves into trouble with their dependent, childlike behaviors. And a few become so desperate that they end their lives. Although many parents like to believe that solutions to these problems rest with the schools, the psychiatric hospitals, and the courts, they don't. They rest with us. We are responsible for teaching our children how to succeed at whatever they choose to do.

The next four chapters describe the goals and strategies all people use to get what they want in life. They're simple, logical, time-tested universals we all know, but may not know we know. It's time to recall them from our cultural consciousness and show our children how they work, when they work, and why they work. It's taken generations of reflective superachievers to isolate what works and what doesn't on that road to success. So why not help our children minimize that trial-and-error search for fulfillment and happiness? Chapters 4 and 5 describe the conditional properties of fulfillment and happiness and how they relate to *personal needs and abilities.* And Chapters 6 and 7 describe success strategies and achievement tactics that produce those end states.

4

Fulfillment

We had thought life was free and would never run out. There were good people and bad people and we could tell them apart by a look or by words spoken in code. We were certain we belonged to a generation that was special. We did not need or care about history because we had sprung from nowhere.[1]

Sara Davidson's *Loose Change* captured post-1960s disappointments: the decade was over and the world was the same. "For four years I felt I had blown it, my generation had blown it, the Sixties had blown it, and we would never again see the heights."[2] After years of sit-ins and marches, the great pendulum of social change reversed directions—from a cold war to a hot one, from prosperity to stagflation. And for what? Instead of a new age of brotherhood and enlightenment with boomers leading the march hand-in-hand to the promised land, it was the same "me first" rat race, this time with boom sisters and boom brothers competing with each other for the same jobs, promotions, and houses.

The flower children of the 1960s were disillusioned adults by the 1970s. While "worry" among most adults remained constant between 1957 and 1976, it increased as a concern from 30 to 50 percent for baby boomers entering the 21- to 39-year-old-group.[3] A 1979 New York Times/CBS poll found that pessimism about the future was highest with young people.[4] By the end of the decade, boomers turned inward. If they couldn't change the world, improve society, and get a fast promotion, they could still find happiness. So they jogged, climbed mountains, and played racquetball.

The entitlement ethic was still alive. Some demands remained nonnegotiable. Achieving the good life was one. Boomers were humanitarians on the outside, but hard-core Skinnarians inside. They weren't going to live with a "tie" ball game. They still wanted that big win. Unlike the generations of youth that have since followed them, boomers believed they could still score, if not for the world then at least for themselves. So they led the charge into self-help and career fulfillment, taking the rest of the nation with them. Why spend a lifetime in dead-end, uninspiring work just to pay rent and feed families? "Endure the job to enjoy the home" was out. "Enjoy the job *and* the home" was in. Separation between personal and professional rewards was artificial, wasteful, and illogical. If something isn't fun, challenging, and fulfilling, don't do it. Work, money, status, and pleasure became members of the same team. In the titular words of author Marsha Sinetar: *Do What You Love, the Money Will Follow.*[5]

Self-Help

As boomers sought happiness inside, their attitudes soured outside. A decade of political assassinations, presidential deceptions, and congressional incompetence ended any residual faith they had in the institutional solution. In 1966 Harris and Associates reported public confidence in the military at 61 percent, in higher education at 61 percent, and in medicine at 73 percent. Twenty years later only 36 percent of those polled expressed confidence in the military, only 34 percent believed in higher education, and only 33 percent trusted the medical profession. Other tarnished images included the U.S. Supreme Court—down 22 points, TV news—with an 18 point loss, leaders of organized religion—down 20 points, and the presidency—minus 12 points. Confidence in business leaders dropped from 55 to 16 percent, and trust in the press decreased from 30 to 19 percent. Even the White House lost ground, from 41 percent in 1966 to 18 percent in 1986. Members of Congress went from a high of 42 percent in 1966 to 21 percent in 1986.[6] John Naisbitt, author of *Megatrends,* noted:

> During the 1970s, Americans began to disengage from the institutions that had disillusioned them and *to relearn the ability to take action on their own.*
>
> In a sense, we have come full circle. We are reclaiming America's traditional sense of self-reliance after four decades of trusting in institutional help.

It is important to recall that the Great Depression was the most traumatic event that America experienced in this century. During the 1930s our traditional faith in ourselves was badly shaken. We began to think that only with the strength of large institutions behind us could we effectively counter life's blows.

More and more, we relied on government to provide the basic needs. Government's traditional function is to safeguard citizens. We also asked that it provide food, shelter, and jobs. But by the 1960s government's role had grown to testing toys and regulating the environment and much of the economy. [italics added][7]

By the early 1980s 15 million of these New Age, rugged individualists formed over 500,000 self-help groups to take on such diverse problems as retirement, weight control, alcohol and drug abuse, widowhood, mental illness, child abuse, divorce, single parenthood, sickness, joblessness, and childrearing.[8] Alan Gartner and Frank Riessman, codirectors of the City University of New York's Self-Help Clearinghouse, attribute the movement to "people [who] feel unable to control 'big government' and the distant bureaucracies and so are drawn to mutual-aid groups that enable them to deal directly with some immediate problems of everyday life."[9] Social critic Peter Drucker told *U.S. News & World Report* that "Nobody really believes anymore that government delivers."[10]

Baby boomers grew up with group problem solving. By the 1970s when distrust of older generations peaked, they turned to each other for support. Self-help was the quintessential "groupy" solution. And *this time,* the rest of the country was with them. As housing costs increased 127 percent and rents doubled, self-helpers came to the rescue, making houses livable *and* affordable. In cities like South Bend, Washington, D.C., Denver, St. Louis, Savannah, Astoria, New York, and Miami, self-help renovation and redevelopment projects converted deteriorated structures into livable homes that people could afford.[11] Other self-helpers tackled such intractable problems as failed parenting, broken marriages, declining health, and unfulfilled careers.

Health Self-Help

From 1960 to 1980 the number of exercising Americans increased 100 percent to 100 million. At the same time fat intake decreased

20 to 30 percent. Smoking decreased 28 percent for men and 13 percent for women. Consumption of hard liquor decreased as Americans turned away from distilled spirits and to wine. In 1968 there were only 1,200 health food stores in the United States: by 1981 the number had increased to 8,300—a 692 percent increase! Business and industry responded to the new health kick by providing in-house fitness centers. Xerox, Johnson and Johnson, PepsiCo, Chase Manhattan, Mobil Oil, and Exxon were first. Republic Steel Corporation began testing its workers for high blood pressure, and other companies started similar programs. The Mendocino County Office of Education of California even offered $500 incentives for employees who stayed healthy, which reduced medical claims by 60 percent.[12]

For 30 years the boom generation *was* the youth movement— new ideals, new ideas, energy, and vitality—signs of the up and coming. But by age 30, even the most robust saw morbidity in deepened wrinkles and drooping jowels. "Over the hill" signs today, hypertension, heart disease, and cancer tomorrow. Prevention was better than cure. By the way, where *was* that cancer wonder drug promised a decade ago?

Boomers also challenged the medical establishment's monopoly on health wisdom. Instead of obediently following doctors' orders for annual physical exams, drugs, and surgery, boomers experimented with New Age treatments like acupuncture, vitamin therapy, preventative health care through diet and exercise, and even charismatic faith healing. *Boomers reclaimed responsibility for their own health.* According to Dr. Tom Ferguson, author of *Medical Self-Care,* "I think we are on the edge of a very major change in our health care system. People are learning to make decisions about their own symptoms and to take care of themselves."[13] The patient-oriented responsibility trend coincided with alternative health perspectives. Mechanistic treatments that dissected patients into healthy and unhealthy parts gave way to wholistic approaches:

The new wholistic health approach has opened up a new area in the search for health and wellness: the human mind. At the radical end of the spectrum is the belief that there is no disease that cannot be cured through the powers of the mind and a positive attitude.

But even traditional medicine has acknowledged that the mind has a role in the prevention and healing of disease. This was dramatized when Norman Cousins shared with millions of readers the story of how with his doctor's help he healed himself of what was thought to be an incurable disease with vitamin C and laughter.[14]

In *Mind Over Back Pain*, Dr. John Sarno, professor of Clinical Rehabilitation Medicine at the New York University School of Medicine, says that 80 to 90 percent of Americans experience medically untreatable pains in the neck, shoulder, or back during their lifetime. Mind-producing tension is the cause. "I have learned in working with TMS [tension myositis syndrome] *that human beings have great capacities for self-healing*; but those powers must be recognized and unleashed. In my view this is the best medicine: releasing the potential within individuals to heal themselves"[15] [italics added].

Dr. Bernie Siegel, professor of medicine at Yale University Medical School, agrees:

Despite the insights of these eminent doctors [Osler, Hippocrates, Pasteur, and Bernard], medicine still focuses on disease, giving it a failure orientation. Its practitioners still act as though disease catches people, rather than understanding that people catch disease by becoming susceptible to the seeds of illness to which we are all constantly exposed. Although the best physicians have always known better, medicine as a whole has rarely studied the people who *don't* get sick. Most doctors seldom consider how a patient's attitude towards life shapes that life's quantity and quality.[16]

Dr. Siegel's patients beat cancer's challenge by "manifest[ing] the will to live in its most potent form. *They take charge of their lives even if they were never able to before, and they work hard to achieve health and peace of mind.* They do not rely on doctors to take the initiative but rather use them as members of a team, demanding the utmost in technique, resourcefulness, concern, and open mindedness. If they're not satisfied, they change doctors" [italics added].[17]

Robert Kowalski, author of *The Eight-Week Cholesterol Cure*, also reclaimed responsibility for his health. A heart attack and two coronary bypass surgeries convinced him to be a dutiful patient and follow the American Heart Association's recommended diet. But it only reduced his cholesterol by 13 points, hardly enough to stave off future attacks. So Kowalski took charge. He researched the medical literature, analyzed the effects of different treatments, and constructed the best cholesterol reduction diet he could find. Within eight weeks his dangerously high 284 reading dropped to 169, reducing his risk of heart attack by more than half.[18]

Suddenly, personal responsibility became more than just exercising regularly and eating prudently. It also includes feeling positively and thinking strategically. Behavioral research finally confirms what positive thinking gurus have been saying for years. Our thoughts affect our health and our health affects our thoughts. According to Dr. Redford Williams, director of Duke University's Behavioral Medicine Research Center, "We now have clear evidence that hostility and anger are the 'toxic elements' that put Type H's at risk of coronary disease."[19] Apparently, simmering anger stresses blood vessels which, in turn, elevates "bad" cholesterol. People who control their anger and manage their thoughts calmly decrease their risks of disease. They can even improve their chances of surviving life-threatening diseases.

Boomers made the connection between responsibility and prevention. If you want the "good life," be responsible for preventing the "bad life." No other generation saw it so clearly or acted upon it so quickly. Overnight a new industry swept the country as 15.5 million Americans raced to join health clubs, 1.7 million more than in 1988. There's a fitness routine for every need too—from aerobics, computerized bicycling, and weight lifting to swimming, programable Stairmasters, saunas, and steam rooms.[20]

Career Self-Help

Even traditional career paths changed direction. Baby boomer Dale Dauten wanted to be corporate president but didn't like waiting. He also wanted the personal freedom, spontaneity, and self-actualization that his company couldn't provide. So he changed companies. This wasn't the answer either: "I kept picturing myself as president. And guess what I saw? One dull job. Twenty years of sacrifice, luck, and achievement, and maybe, just maybe, I would move to the head of the conference table . . . same tedious meetings, same blurry printouts of nums and figs (that's 'numbers and figures' to those of you who don't speak corporatese), same weary, wary lifestyle."[21] So he quit again, took a vacation, and then set out on this own. Dauten is one of hundreds of thousands of boomers who wanted to achieve but refused to wait. So he started his own business.

> The baby boomers were not just another generation of idealists, though. Their numbers made them a megageneration, an army that was not easily absorbed in society. And the 1970s, when their ranks hit the job front, were not exactly booming times. Consequently, some baby boomers were forced into self-employment, even entrepreneurship, by a weak job market. Others who had cherished independence in the 1960s and given it up for high-paying corporate jobs in the 1970s were, all the while, saving, learning, and plotting their escape into entrepreneurship.
>
> In the late 1970s it all exploded into an entrepreneurial boom.[22]

In the 1950s there were only 93,000 new businesses each year. By the end of 1980 the rate increased to 600,000 per year, and today the average is 700,000. In 1986 the total number of new businesses surpassed the 1 million mark, with nearly half started by women.[23] According to MIT researcher David Birch, small businesses have fueled the nation's economy since the mid-1970s. In *Growing A Business*, Paul Hawken explains why:

> This movement toward new enterprises must reflect a certain amount of alienation of the work force from the conditions of their jobs. . . . Conformity within a large bureaucracy was the meal ticket for most people in the fifties, but I believe that the ability to strike out on one's own will be the most dynamic means of developing a "career" in the late 1980s and the 1990s. *This path will lead to the greatest job satisfaction and personal development.* Knowing how to grow one's own business will be critical. The person who chooses to hide within some bureaucracy may be left behind. [italics added][24]

Boom generation folk heroes like Steve Jobs, Bill Gates, and Donald Trump epitomize a new breed of rugged individualists who challenge conventional wisdom and corporate muscle by doing their own thing, loving it, and setting new standards for achievement. The entrepreneurs of the 1970s and 1980s accomplished what their boom brothers and sisters always wanted to accomplish.

Those of us adults born after World War II, the baby boomers, are children of Positive Thinkers, raised in the Era of Unlimited Possibilities. We intellectually suckled on "Whatever the mind of man can conceive and believe, it can achieve." None of this "low self-esteem" stuff for us. . . . Never has a generation had such high expectations. We were the first generation expected to graduate from college. And we did—nearly twenty million of us since 1960, the largest glut of educated labor in the history of the paycheck. Hard work. Ambition. Money.

But along the way we also absorbed the message of the hippies, giving us another set of expectations: the brotherhood of man, spontaneity, individuality.

So where does that leave us? We are the Expectations Generation— twenty million of us crowded into line for success.

Never have so many asked so much: freedom and individuality, as well as status and wealth. And be quick about it. [italics added][25]

Career Fulfillment

Self-help returned control to the group and power to the individual. When bodies aged, exercise and nutritional eating increased. When children rebelled, parental love toughened. And when careers stalled, new businesses flourished. Self-reliance, individuality, and personal responsibility returned—values resurrected from decades past. Boomers also decided that job security and family life were not enough. The good life was more. Landon Jones concluded that what boomers wanted was *fulfillment.*

> As the largest, most widely studied, and most publicized generation ever, the baby boomers gained from the start an acutely felt self-awareness and sense of their own destiny. This generation wanted everything: to be the best educated, to reform society, to integrate motherhood and career, to integrate a husband's job with a wife's job, and to have healthy, fulfilled lives on top of it all. Even when they saw the naivete of their aspirations, they could not turn them off. "I live with a desire to excel or be productive," said one baby-boom woman to the *Los Angeles Times.* "But," she apologized, "I realize through it all that it is bourgeois."[26]

In the 1940s and 1950s dad worked and mother raised children. Job and home were separate. Who knows what Jim Anderson of

Father Knows Best did for a living? And in the 1950s, who cared? Occupations were irrelevant in Boomerville happiness. "The boom generation will have nothing of this. They do not see a dichotomy between private and social values and have no intention of denying their 'real selves' on the job. In their minds, self-fulfillment and successful careers should not be incompatible. The purpose of a job, they argue, is not to satisfy their material needs but to satisfy their emotional needs."[27] This has become a national sentiment. Young workers no longer settle for money and security. They want job satisfaction too. Pollster Louis Harris asked workers to rank the importance of five major work attractions: accomplishment, advancement, pay, security, and hours. He found:

> at the head of the list, singled out by 48%, was that "*the work be important and give you a real feeling of accomplishment.*" This sense of a job having a larger meaning is obviously critically important in today's job market. Next is "the chance to advance," with 20%. Getting ahead is important. Close behind is the former number-one motivator, high pay, now singled out by only 19% as most important. Far down the list, at only 7%, is "no danger of being fired," a former sacred cow. Finally, cited by only 3%, is "to be able to work shorter hours in order to have lots of free time." [italics added][28]

Daniel Yankelovich also discovered that baby boomers

> did not believe that women should stay home. The men were not willing to put up with drawbacks in their jobs. They were not selflessly loyal to organizations. They did not blindly acquiesce to authority. They did not define their identities through their work. They thought there was more to life than slavishly earning money. They did not think conventional success was necessarily related to their self-fulfillment.[29]

Yankelovich concluded that the new values were "advance signs of life in the 21st century of the third millennium"[30] and already spreading to the rest of the working population: "By the late seventies, my firm's studies showed more than seven out of ten Americans (72 percent) spending a great deal of time thinking about themselves and their inner lives—this is a nation once notorious for its impatience with inwardness. The rage for self-fulfillment, our surveys indicated, had now spread to virtually the entire U.S. population."[31] But, of course, not everyone finds fulfillment, as Dr. Jan Halper documents in *Quiet Desperation: The Truth about Successful Men:* "Jim Gabbert, who owned a broadcasting empire, radio and TV stations up and down the West Coast and in Hawaii, told me, 'I went through a midlife crisis. I woke up one morning and asked myself if it was worth it. I wanted to learn how to fly. I wanted to travel. I wanted some time with the people in my life who mattered. I had amassed an empire. I knew if I continued I would make millions, but it wasn't worth it to me anymore.'"[32]

Ignoring personal needs is common in other cultures too. Associated Press writer Elaine Kurtenbach reports that "Japanese businessmen aren't concerned just about market shares and interest rates anymore. Now they're wondering whether their jobs will kill them. It's called 'Karoshi'—death from overwork, or 'pokkuri byo'—sudden death. The number of such deaths among harried Japanese businessmen is growing at an alarming rate, researchers say." Dr. Kiyoyasu Arikawa found that sudden deaths among top executives increased from 10 in 1969 to 150 in 1985. Persons in their 40s and 50s were common victims, including such prominent figures as publishing executive Koremichi Noma, trading company president Hirotoshi Inui, Fanuc Company president Nobuo Hanaoka, and chairman of the mass media group Fuji Sankei, Haruo Shikanai. Researchers claim "the underlying cause of sudden death is the excessive competition inherent in Japanese society and working life. . . . Competition and stress permeate the lives of overwork victims, coupled with poor health habits attributable mostly to their busy work schedules."[33]

Fulfillment in one's work and personal life may yield more than just happiness. It saves lives. Boomers on the entrepreneurial track enjoy their work and the increased control it provides. They've eliminated corporate waits for promotion and don't worry about office politics and interdepartmental one-upsmanship. They control their destiny. Dr. Halper asked top executives three questions: "Do you feel your life has meaning and direction?", "Have you made personal sacrifices to achieve your success?", and "Would you make them again?" Results were not surprising: 91 percent of the entrepreneurs had no regrets, whereas only 68 percent of the senior-level executives were happy professionally. Nearly half the executives "admitted they regretted spending so many hours at the job and if they were to do it over would spend more time with their wife and children from the onset. *At the middle-management level, 58 percent admitted they had wasted years "striving for and achieving their goals, only to find their life empty and meaningless"* [italics added].[34]

When career goals change, success symbols do too. Arnold Mitchell of SRI International noted that past symbols included fame, being in *Who's Who*, a five-figure salary, college degree, splendid house, executive position, new car every year, and membership in the club. Today, the symbols are unlisted phone numbers, Swiss bank accounts, connections with celebrities, deskless offices, ownership of second and third rare foreign cars, being a vice president, being published, and engaging in frequent and unpredictable world travel. His list for tomorrow includes free time anytime, recognition as a creative person, oneness of work and play, rewarded less by money than by honor and affection, major societal commitments, easy laughter, unembarrassed tears, wide-ranging interests and activities, philosophical independence, loving, in touch with self.[35]

People who discover fulfillment are confident in their capacity for independent thought and action. They know what they like, what they can do. They use this information to define what they want and how they can get it. They make proactive, responsible choices and then back them with personal commitment. They give unconditionally to the work they love in return for the meaning and satisfaction it generates. This is fulfillment.

5

Happiness

Individuals who find fulfillment harmonize person with profession. They know what they like and what they can do. And they know how to use what they have to get what they want. They change themselves to fit environments while changing environments to fit themselves. They negotiate and adjust their way into happiness, uniting mind, body, and spirit to do best what they like most. Unlike their fathers who escaped work at the office to seek fulfillment at home, "fulfillers" connect livelihood with personhood by matching interests with abilities. They strive for Maslow's self-actualization.[1] Ambitious? Yes. Unrealistic? Maybe not. Today, more Americans seek fulfillment than ever. A supersalesman and author of *Nice Guys Finish Rich,* Jim Hasberger says: "I truly believe you can have it all—a deep spiritual faith, extremely close relationships with your friends and family, physical fitness, and a positive attitude—and make a million dollars a year."[2]

Unfortunately, the "how" is not immediately apparent. Many parents want their children to be successful, happy, and fulfilled but have no idea how to help them to achieve these goals. They think happiness is a condition to "bestow." Ron Howard's movie *Parenthood* portrays three boom parents trying to give their children the best. Steve Martin tries to give his son "confidence." Martin's younger sister Harley Kozak and her husband Rick Moranis try to give their three-year-old daughter "intelligence." And Martin's older sister Dianne Wiest tries to give her 16-year-old daughter and 13-year-old son "happiness." The movie ends with Wiest explaining that all she ever wanted was to make her children happy—even if it meant telling her daughter to stay with her adolescent husband, "that Todd." The drama was humorous and revealing, showing confused and semicompetent attempts to give what children must ultimately achieve *on their own*.

Unhappiness

As parents, we want everything for our children: talent, intelligence, education, success, and, if possible, wealth. During the 1950s many parents believed positive experiences and unbridled expectations were sufficient to meet those goals. Now we know better. The achievement path of recent generations discredits those wishful thoughts. Today, some baby boomers have achieved wealth and found success and happiness in spite of unexpected difficulties. Others, especially those born since the 1960s, continue their struggle to free themselves of their indulgent past. Susan Littwin found that adults in their 20s and 30s have trouble finding themselves, much less fulfillment. Littwin describes some of their problems:

> It is hard enough to establish an adult identity, even in the best of times. But to do it with such a jarring conflict between expectations and reality is a stunning task. What many of today's twenty- to thirty-year-olds have elected to do is continue the identity search while avoiding reality, and that makes it exceedingly slow work. Unless they are fortunate enough to be born with the talent or inclination to go into a field where their expectations are met—such as high technology—they find themselves in their late twenties or early thirties before they have any sense of who they are or where they are going in life.[3]

In *The Hamlet Syndrome*, Miller and Goldblatt identify "millions of real Americans" who overthink and underachieve—persons in their twenties and thirties long on education, talent, and skills, but short on initiative, decisiveness, and commitment. Their "reluctance to take risks . . . loathing for competition, . . . low threshold of frustration, lack of self-confidence, . . . distaste for work, procrastination, [and] passivity . . . [generates] . . . an aversion to responsibility, and good old-fashioned fear."[4] In *Adult Children Who Won't Grow Up* Stockman and Graves describe young adults who take "an unhealthy length of time to sever the ties of adolescence. They live at home with their parents and display a pattern of extended dependency." And in *Boomerang Kids,* Okimoto and Stegall describe young adults who are too dependent to make it alone:

> There is usually a kind of war going on inside most young adults, a conflict played out between two parts of themselves. One part of them really wants to be totally independent from parents: free, strong, confident, self-assured, and secure in the knowledge that they can completely take care of themselves, not needing their parents for anything. But the other part of them wants very much to be taken care of; it yearns for the blissful state of turning everything over to some benevolent presence who will think of everything, take care of everything, nurture, support, protect—meet their every need.[5]

The psychological profile of young people from entitlement cultures is not encouraging. Studies by the University of Michigan's Institute for Social Research and by Yankelovich, Skelly, and White indicate that young Americans are increasingly goal-less and anxious.[6] Too many 20- to 30-year-olds are afraid to take risks and compete in a world that demands commitments. They dislike working, avoid reality, and reject authority. They experience depression and anger in a world in which they are passive participants. Parents report that their adult children make excuses, provoke crises, and run home when things don't go right. At the same time, they are ungrateful for help they receive, displaying a sense that their parents and the world owe them something. They compound feelings of frustration with financial dependence, chronic unemployment, and job hopping. At a deeper level, observers report that these young people lack self-direction, self-confidence, self-esteem, self-validation, and self-discipline. An albatross of self-pity hangs round their necks bowing their spirits and their initiative. They match Dennis Wholey's description of unhappiness: "people [who] are consumed by anger and resentment. They are critical of others; they live in fear; they worry and they procrastinate; they wallow in self-pity and depression; they try to change other people instead of themselves."[7]

Causes

How can well-intentioned, loving, devoted parents raise so many misguided and confused adults? Since the 1950s, moms and dads replaced strict, disciplinarian childrearing practices with tolerant ones. Dr. Benjamin Spock's 1945 best-seller, *The Common Sense Book of Baby and Child Care,* started them thinking about free expression, creativity, and flexible expectations. According to Beth Brophy of *U.S. News & World Report,* the book "was seized upon by war-weary Americans who were looking for ways to free themselves of old conventions and who interpreted his emphasis on nurturing, gentleness and following common-sense instincts as a sanction for permissiveness."[8] Permissive childrearing also received a boost from Scottish educator A. S. Neill's report on the Summerhill School in Suffolk, England. Neill's philosophy, expressed in *Summerhill: A Radical Approach to Child Rearing,* influenced teaching and parenting practices through the 1960s, providing the basis for open classrooms, alternative schools, and communes. His premise—that students do better when they choose what and when they will learn—suggested that teachers facilitate rather than direct.

This approach never worked. When given unrestricted choice between reading and television, youth viewed more and read less; and when given the choice between play now and work later, they enjoyed now and deferred forever. Immediate rewards and postponed consequences disconnected expectations from reality. As Glenn and Nelson note, "And by providing so much for our children without teaching them the means of achieving these things and respect for those means, we might be literally threatening their chances to survive through adolescence. Young people are led to believe that shoes, food, and cars will come to them automatically, and that badgering, manipulating, and wishing guarantee that they will be able to go first class."[9]

Permissive, indulgent parenting produced unhappy, maladjusted children who never learned how to succeed and, as a consequence, how to make themselves happy. In *Kids Who Succeed,* Dr. Beverly Feldman reports:

> In all my years of experience in working with parents, I have never known so many to be so worried about their children's economic futures. Nor have I encountered so many young adults who share their apprehension. One concerned father came to me recently and said, "I have three teenage sons and only one of them has a clear idea of what work he wants to pursue in life. The other two don't seem to think about tomorrow at all. They say they want to be rich, to have nice things, to travel, to have a better life than my wife and I

have. That's fine with us—but *how are they going to achieve a life even as good as ours? They don't seem to be concerned about the how.*"[10]

Parents believe it's important to help keep their children up with the Jones's children. Abundant, noncontingent financial support during the early years will provide a secure base for success during the later years. Right? Wrong! The seeds of long-term happiness fail to germinate from wealth alone. A different kind of nurturing is necessary, the kind that understands the deepest and most enduring source for happiness.

Happiness[11]

Can we help our children find happiness? Or is it a crapshoot from the start, just the luck of the draw? Certainly when they're young we can help. A little physical and emotional support will dry a tear and bring a smile. But that disappears fast. Soon they want what we cannot afford, have unpleasant experiences we cannot erase, and contract diseases we are powerless to cure. Still, we do what we can to minimize hurt and maximize joy. But ultimately, they must manage for themselves. *Happiness is their responsibility.*

Some kids do grow up with sufficient self-knowledge, self-direction, and self-reliance to find happiness. They know how to persevere, benefit from mistakes, and adjust to results. They enjoy the process as well as the product of their endeavors. They're as positive about their ability to fit into the scheme of things as they are about scheming for a new fit of things. They act and react to change while progressing toward personal and professional goals. Dennis Wholey describes these people in his book, *Are You Happy?* They are:

optimistic . . . know[ing] that feeling good is the way you are supposed to feel. They seem to operate on a philosophy of positive thoughts, positive expectations, positive action, positive results. They always look at a half-full, not half-empty glass. Happy people accept life and see it as an adventure.

Unhappy people always seem to want something different, while happy people like what they have. If happy people don't like what they have they put in the extra effort to change it.[12]

Norman Cousins, author of *Anatomy of an Illness,* describes some ways people find happiness:

> To some it is nothing more complicated than the absence of pain; to others enough money in the bank to cover outstanding checks; or babies who have stopped crying in the middle of the night; or having your bag come off first on the airport carousel; or sinking a thirty-foot putt on the first hole; or finding an Italian restaurant that really knows how to make a meat-free tomato sauce. . . . Whatever it is or isn't, just be glad you're around to think about it.[13]

Whatever it is, it *comes from within.* It's not something we can secure from others or from external sources. Actress and comedienne Pat Carroll says: "Our responsibility is to be happy. It's not your parents' responsibility. It's not your teachers' responsibility. It's not your neighbor's responsibility. It's your responsibility to be happy."[14] Academy Award winner Burt Bacharach, who wrote the music for *Butch Cassidy and the Sundance Kid,* says: "You've got to get inner peace to be happy."[15] New York psychiatrist Dr. Theodore Isaac Rubin says: "If happiness is to come it will not come from anything additional, from the outside; it must come from a rearrangement of how one perceives oneself vis-a-vis the world one lives in."[16]

Happiness also comes from *doing what we enjoy.* Anthropologist Ashley Montagu says: "It is within your power to make yourself happy or unhappy by setting yourself such goals as are within your range, and that you will enjoy achieving." He recalls: "Once a man I knew, a very unhappy man, had almost a billion dollars at his disposal. He gave each of his children $28 million on his or her twenty-first birthday. *It ruined their lives. The worst thing you can do to young people is to take away from them the necessity of making something of themselves*" [italics added].[17] For Dr. Rubin happiness is "Going through the struggle of becoming an expert, becoming well educated, learning a craft well, understanding it thoroughly, making a contribution—training, work, energy, time with other people—are really what life ought to be about."[18] Dr. Benjamin Spock says that "Happiness is mostly a by-product of doing what makes us feel fulfilled. Certainly that definition applies to me. Happiness is not something that we get by deliberately grabbing for it."[19] And for Malcolm Forbes, former editor of *Forbes* magazine, success does not produce happiness, *happiness produces success*:

> People often ask me, "How do I become successful?" I say, "Whatever you like to do, just find a way to do it."
>
> The biggest mistake people make in life is not trying to make a living at doing what they most enjoy. There's no job that's all joy. But to work at a job you hate is probably the biggest waste in life. If you don't care about it or you can get by with it and if you're not really consumed to do anything else, fine. But that's a waste. We're all responsive to something and we do our best when we're doing something that has a turn-on to it. There is no other way to go.[20]

Obviously there are *two types* of happiness, one that comes from the *activity* itself, what I call "activity happiness," and the other that comes from the *results* of that activity, what I call "outcome happiness." Burt Bacharach describes his "high" from "outcome happiness": "Winning the Academy Award gives you a happy moment, the highest kind of feeling, totally on top of the world. Euphoric. You wanted it, you've missed it before, you were nominated, you finally get it. You finally win two Academy Awards—not one, but two. You walk out of the Chandler Pavilion, you're the happiest person in the world. You stay happy through the night."[21] Actress Ruby Dee echoes this sentiment: "Happiness is a feeling of fulfillment. It's *achieving a specific goal* that you set out to achieve. It's a fleeting state, not a permanent one" [italics added].[22]

She's right, it is only temporary. Bacharach was "happy through the night." He recalls that "The next day you put those two Oscars up there on the mantelpiece above the fireplace. Three days after you win the Academy Awards, you go through the whole day without thinking about them or even noticing them in the living room. *The externals don't work, they just are temporary things* [italics added]."[23] Ruby Dee says that "One of the attributes of [outcome] happiness is that *you forget what it was that made you happy the last time you were happy.* . . . Happy results from so many things. It's nebulous, will-o'-the-wisp. *It's the pure enjoyment of a moment*" [italics added].[24]

Now consider less euphoric, more enduring *activity happiness.* Dr. Rubin describes it: "If you are totally goal-oriented in a success-oriented culture, and if the product is the goal, you have destroyed much of the possibility for happiness in your life, *since almost all of your life has to be the process and not the product. . . . I'd say we're in the process 98 percent of the time. If you're living just for that final 2 percent, you're in trouble. The truth is that most of the population is in trouble*" [italics added].[25] Tom Peters, coauthor of *In Search of Excellence* and *A Passion for Excellence,* sees *activity* happiness at all levels in the workplace:

> Happiness, at all levels of the work place, *has to do with being engaged.* Whether it's making a Chrysler, going to see your route if you're a bus driver, or battling in the internal politics of the company where you work, you want to get up in the morning and do it. It's almost action for action's sake. Probably the closest operating definition to loneliness or unhappiness I can invent is not being engaged in whatever it is that you're doing. . . . *Being engaged literally means being excited in any sense of the word about any task.* [italics added][26]

Helen Thomas, United Press International bureau chief at the White House, says: "When you get up in the morning you should really want to go to work. If it's exciting and you have some sense that you're going to learn something and be a part of something, I think that's one of the most fulfilling rewards in life. My job does make me happy."[27] Burt Bacharach feels that way when composing music: "The music is hard, but I like going back to the room and writing. I'm happy because I push myself into a discipline. I get into a groove where I'm playing the piano and melodies start to flow and I'm happy."[28] Novelist and poet May Sarton says: "My definition of happiness is writing a poem. I'm absolutely alone then and I'm in a state of great intensity of feeling and intellect. I'm perfectly balanced and nothing else exists. Time doesn't exist. Happiness has a lot to do with timelessness—those times when you are not pressured by the feeling 'I've got to get somewhere.'"[29]

Activity happiness also comes from stretching to the limit, as *Megatrends* author John Naisbitt describes:

> A sense of personal worth has to do with realizing your full potential and not just being satisfied with some of your potential. People who work for a sense of personal worth keep working at it. They want to push and stretch. They want to experience their potential. They want

to get right out there to the edge, and that's what they keep pushing for. How can you know what your full potential is unless you put it at risk? You have to put it at risk. The only universal either/or is either you grow or you die. That's true of you and me and a tree or a city or a country. It is either growing or it's dying. . . . *That has a lot to do with happiness and unhappiness. I think happiness is a journey. I don't think it's a goal.* [italics added][30]

President Kennedy frequently quoted a saying from the ancient Greeks: "Happiness is the fullest use of one's powers along the lines of excellence."[31]

Happy people are responsible people. They control their destinies by finding what works and changing what doesn't. They're action-oriented optimists, confident in their ability to get what they want by doing what they like. They optimize inner states by: (1) taking responsibility for achieving happiness; (2) setting goals that require pleasurable activities; and (3) achieving goals that have pleasurable outcomes. Happy people know where they want to go and how to get there. They carry their capacity for well-being with them, infecting others with enthusiasm and optimism as they go. Their perpetual "highs" contrast with the emotional "lows" of their polar opposites who chronically worry, lament, and complain. Unhappy people search outside themselves for answers, always hoping their luck will change, people will change, or the world will change. Their feelings of helplessness drive them to distraction through television, alcohol, and drugs.

For years, we've heard that people who succeed are not really happy, and people who are happy don't really succeed. This is nonsense. A few people know themselves well enough to put it together, to set goals and pursue activities that give pleasure. They have the best of both worlds. Happiness from their work and happiness from their accomplishments. *They do what they like best to get what they want most.* How do they do it? They followed the same *success principles* that were effective for Andrew Carnegie, Thomas Edison, Mary Kay Ash, Steve Jobs, and Sandra Day O'Connor.

Success

people everywhere are searching for that secret formula to make it big. Is it going to a prestigious college, looking stylish, speaking with authority, knowing the right people, mastering the computer? Rivaling diet books in popularity are those with such titles as Getting Yours, Winning With Deception and Bluff *and* How to Get Ahead by "Psyching Out" Your Boss and Co-workers.[1]

After two decades of neglect, success finally returned to America, once again promising the American dream to all who believed, worked, and persevered. Across the country seminars and workshops preached the basic think-and-grow-rich formula while adding such aggressive touches as "Getting Yours" and "Winning with Deception and Bluff." The rags-to-riches allure was as powerful as ever. "Anyone can do it, maybe even you!"

Horatio Alger (1834–99) introduced the American dream in *Ragged Dick, Luck and Pluck,* and *Tattered Tom,* books that described how underprivileged youth won fame and fortune by practicing honesty, diligence, and perseverance. He wrote more than 100 such works to demonstrate the power of the work ethic. Andrew Carnegie, American philanthropist, industrialist, and founder of the Carnegie Steel Company, was contemporary proof of the Alger myth. Born in Dunfermline, Scotland, in 1835, Carnegie came to the United States at age 13 and began work as a bobbin boy in a cotton mill in Allegheny, Pennsylvania, where he earned only $1.20 a week. From there he worked his way up to messenger boy in a Pittsburgh telegraph office, private secretary and telegrapher to a railroad official, and superintendent of the Pittsburgh division of the railroad. After the Civil War, he formed his own company and constructed iron railroad bridges. By 1899 Carnegie controlled 25 percent of all American iron and steel production, and in 1901 he retired after selling his company to the United States Steel Corporation for $250 million. He never received a formal education.

In the 1920s Carnegie helped translate the Alger myth into a workable philosophy by challenging Napoleon Hill to study successful people and identify factors that explained their success: "What is there in the climate of this great nation that I, a foreigner, can build a business and acquire wealth? How is it that anyone here can achieve success? I challenge you to devote twenty years of your life to the study of American achievement and come up with an answer. Will you accept?"[2] He did. For the next 20 years Hill studied over 500 of the most famous and successful men in American industry, including Henry Ford, Theodore Roosevelt, James J. Hill, Wilbur Wright, William Jennings Bryan, George Eastman, Woodrow Wilson, William Howard Taft, Luther Burbank, Clarence Darrow, Dr. Alexander Graham Bell, John D. Rockefeller, Thomas A. Edison, and F. W. Woolworth. In 1928 Hill reported his findings in *Law of Success.* A decade later he published *Think and Grow Rich,* the most influential self-help book ever written, and two decades after that he collaborated with W. Clement Stone in *Success through a Positive Mental Attitude.* These works became the philosophical godparents of such standards as Og Mandino's *The Greatest Salesman in the World,* Dr. Norman Vincent Peale's *Power of Positive Thinking,* Denis Waitley's *Seeds of Greatness,* and the Reverend Robert H. Schuller's *Discover Your Possibilities.*

So what is the secret? There are actually three not one: mental self-management, competence, and persistence. Hill used them in his five-step plan, which included:

1. Choice of a definite goal to be obtained
2. Development of sufficient power to attain one's goal
3. Perfection of a practical plan for attaining one's goal
4. Accumulation of specialized knowledge necessary for the attainment of one's goal
5. Persistence in carrying out the plan[3]

Steps 1 through 3 describe *mental self-management,* step 4 is *competence,* and step 5 is *persistent problem solving.* Thirty years after *Think and Grow Rich,* Gallup and Gallup published their study of successful people, *The Great American Success Story: Factors that Affect Achievement.* They interviewed a random sample of 1500 people listed in the 83rd annual edition of Marquis's *Who's Who in America.* The top three characteristics for success that they discovered were common sense, special knowledge of one's field, and self-reliance. *Common sense* is mental self-management—the ability to make decisions consistent with one's purpose and with environmental conditions. *Special knowledge* is a component of competence. And *self-reliance* is also persistent problem solving. "Self-reliant people will typically be able to rely on themselves to set well-defined goals and to apply willpower to *persevere* and realize those goals" [italics added].[4]

In *The Achievement Factors* Dr. Eugene Griessman describes "what made famous people famous—from the famous people themselves." In a series of public affairs television programs he hosted during the mid-1970s Griessman interviewed leading musicians, politicians, scientists, religious leaders, businessmen, celebrities, and sports stars. The interviews helped Griessman identify 30 achievement factors. The three most important were: *doing what you enjoy, competence,* and *persistence*—the same factors that Hill identified in 1937 and that Gallup and Gallup described in 1986.

"Doing what you enjoy," a component of effective mental self-management, received 9.9 on the 10-point importance scale. Persons who understand their needs, interests, and abilities direct themselves with the conviction and passion needed to succeed.

The competence factor received a 9.8 score. "High achievers *may* attain breadth of knowledge, but they *always* attain depth of knowledge in some one area."[5] Hill had said the same thing 50 years earlier: Specialized knowledge is his "fourth step toward riches."[6]

The persistence factor received a 9.3 score. "Clearly, high achievers possess the ability to keep at the tasks and careers they choose. They finish the jobs that they consider important and they stick by their guns when attacked. . . . They think about the future, but not too much. Mainly they are intent on doing well what comes to them each day."[7] Hill said that you need "persistence in carrying out the plan," and Gallup and Gallup talked about the importance of "will power to *persevere* and realize those goals."[8]

Factor 1: Intelligent Mental Management

A distinguished friend of the family once asked me, "If you're so intelligent, why aren't you rich?" I said I was seeking knowledge, not money (which was only partly true). That question and my lame answer has always bothered me. There *should be* a correlation between intelligence and results, but usually there isn't. That's because we equate intelligence with I.Q. but we should know how poorly that score relates to real-life problem solving. People who score well on paper-and-pencil tests aren't necessarily better at their jobs, as Yale psychology professor Robert Sternberg points out:

> That "academic" intelligence is insufficient for successful performance in real-world settings is suggested by the low typical correlation (about .2 on a scale from 0 to 1) between occupational performance and performance on either IQ or employment tests reported by several researchers. Correlations of this magnitude indicate that hardly any variance (*only about 4 percent*) in occupational performance is accounted for by IQ level. [italics added][9]

Although this is common knowledge among testing professionals, it's news to others. IQ is an *incomplete* measure of intelligence, as research over the past several decades has demonstrated. Contemporary views of intelligence such as Sternberg's *The Triarchic Mind: A New Theory of Human Intelligence* and Howard Gardner's *Frames of Mind: The Theory of Multiple Intelligences* account for some of these discrepancies. According to Sternberg, "intelligence can be defined as a kind of *mental self-management*—the mental management of one's life in a constructive, purposeful way. . . . Mental self-management, too, can be said to have three basic elements: adapting to environments, selecting new environments, and shaping environments."[10] Sternberg explains:

> Intelligence involves the shaping of, adaptation to, and selection of your environment. . . . there may be no single set of behaviors that is intelligent for everyone. . . . *What does appear to be common among successful people is the ability to capitalize on their strengths and compensate for their weaknesses. Successful people are not only able to adapt well to their environment but also to modify this environment in order to increase the fit between the environment and their adaptive skills.* [italics added][11]

Mental self-management is the CEO of thought and action. It maximizes strengths and compensates for weaknesses to achieve targeted outcomes. Mental self-managers self-direct and self-correct. They plan what to do, follow through, evaluate results, and then adjust and adapt. Sternberg describes seven executive processes in intelligent self-management.

[M]y own research and that of others suggests that they are among the most important, because they must be used in the solution of almost every real-world problem. The processes are: recognizing the existence of the problem, defining the nature of the problem, generating the set of steps needed to solve the problem, combining these steps into a workable strategy for problem solution, deciding how to represent information about the problem, allocating mental and physical resources to solving the problem and monitoring the solution to the problem.[12]

The Garfield Studies

Charles Garfield interviewed over 1500 high achievers in business, science, sports, and the arts to determine what distinguished them from their peers. He found five factors. Peak performers achieved remarkable results because they:

1. Defined and pursued missions that motivated
2. Developed plans and engaged in purposeful activities directed toward achieving goals that contributed to the mission
3. Engaged in self-observation and effective thinking that assured maximum performance
4. Corrected and adjusted activities to remain on the critical path to the goal
5. Anticipated and adapted to major change while maintaining momentum within an overall game plan.

Peak performers are powerful mental self-managers. They engage in thoughtful planning, follow through with effective action, and then adjust to results for improvements next time.

MISSIONS AND PLANS. When formulating their mission, peak performers see patterns in the things and thoughts that get people moving.

They assess their resources, and then translate their feelings into words. This is Hill's definition of purpose: "the knowledge of what one wants, and a burning desire to possess it."[13] Peak performers set goals, plan resource development, and establish timelines. They acquire new skills and competencies as they go, usually through self-education rather than formal schooling. Peak performers renew their specialized knowledge and skills continually in order to succeed over a lifetime.

Gallup and Gallup's specialized knowledge ranked second behind common sense; Napoleon Hill included it in his step 4, the accumulation of specialized knowledge necessary for the attainment of one's goal, and W. Clement Stone, author of *The Success System that Never Fails* ranked it third in his success formula:

1. Inspiration to action: that which motivates you to act because you want to.
2. Know-how: the particular techniques and skills that consistently get results for you when applied. It is the proper application of knowledge. Know-how becomes habit through actual repetitive experience.
3. *Activity knowledge: knowledge of the activity, service, product, methods, techniques, and skills with which you are particularly concerned.* [italics added][14]

Sternberg calls it "tacit Knowledge"—which is "practical rather than academic, informal rather than formal, and usually not directly taught. Knowing how best to get along with your colleagues or your boss is an example of tacit knowledge."[15]

PERFORMANCE. Peak performers also succeed because they manage their performances effectively. They see themselves "as the originator of actions in [their] life . . . [viewing] events in life as opportunities for taking action and [seeing] themselves as the agents who must precipitate action."[16] Other characteristics setting them apart include self-understanding, self-confidence, effectiveness, and self-evaluation. Self-evaluation is the ability to seek out feedback and use it positively to adjust subsequent performance:

A key to self-management is the capacity for self-observation. "A strong self-watchfulness, self-surveillance . . . that constantly searches for improvement, excellence, and respect," is what C. Jackson Grayson, chairman of the American Productivity Center, calls it. This is not overcriticism, judgmentalism, or the well-known paralysis by analysis. It is familiarity with your own standards of excellence, of what you consider to be quality, and maintaining enough of a detached perspective to evaluate your performance.[17]

Peak performers also improve their performance in key situations by rehearsing mental images of what they plan to do and say:

> In business, peak performers report using mental rehearsal for specific micro situations: presentations at board meetings, a sales encounter with a difficult customer, a speech to a large group. They may be unaware of using a formally defined skill. Few in our study were acquainted with the term mental rehearsal. I frequently hear responses like "Yes, I imagine things in advance, sometimes over and over. But I never knew that had a name."[18]

Napoleon Hill called it "autosuggestion," recommending its use to increase self-reliance, willpower, and persistence. Gallup and Gallup noted that successful performers have "courage to take definitive action to get things moving in their life." They have "will power" and "the ability to get things done."[19]

ADAPTABILITY. Actions don't always produce expected outcomes—a disturbing discovery for persons who misinterpret feedback and believe they've failed. But peak performers know the score. They examine all feedback, positive and negative, objectively. They use it to decide what to change and how to improve. They adapt to, select, and shape their environments to maximize results. Garfield calls this *course corrections* and *change management*. Peak performers manage change by *learning continuously,* expecting to succeed, mapping alternative futures, and updating their missions.

Course Corrections. Peak performers excel because they know how to adjust their plans and behaviors in order to achieve objectives on time. They fine-tune their perceptions and then act with mental agility, concentration, and self-corrections. *Mental agility* is the ability to examine a problem from different perspectives:

> A key to the strength that mental agility generates is flexibility. This is not the same as bending before every breeze. It is, rather, the kind

of brainstorming one sees in original thinkers. These people do not keep running dumbly down empty tunnels. They look at what is in there, look from a dozen different angles, argue for things and against them just to see what happens. . . . Nobody who is firmly glued to conventional categories of thinking and his or her own past attitudes, can be flexible enough for major course corrections. A reasonable detachment, a more objective view, is essential.[20]

Concentration includes (1) endurance under stress for long hours, (2) resilience under stress, and (3) adaptability. Peak performers also *learn from mistakes,* the third essential for effective course correction. Finely tuned sensitivities to environmental cues tell them what works and what doesn't long before others notice. "It may be obvious to other people that you are on the path or off it; but for an individual in the middle of a job, the cues can be subtle and easy to ignore."[21]

Change Management. When conditions change drastically no amount of fine tuning will help. Recall what happened to the auto industry. After years of manufacturing large, inefficient, mediocre cars, Detroit discovered that Japan owned the small car market. Change managers anticipate new conditions and adapt by discarding what no longer works, keeping what does, and developing what's missing.

Lifelong Learning. Unfortunately, there are no road maps to success. No one knows *exactly* what's necessary to reach a goal. Peak performers understand this reality. They recognize that they'll never have all the information, skills, and resources they need to start. But they proceed anyway, expecting to figure out what they need to know along the way. They have confidence in their ability to solve problems. All successful people learn as they go. This is the only route to unknown destinations.

Expecting to Succeed. Peak performers are confident too. Past accomplishment reinforces belief in self and builds courage to act again and again. Achievers reduce risk by mastering details and by practicing before acting. They leave little to chance. They "develop powerful mental images of the behaviors that lead to desired results. They see in their mind's eye the result they want and the actions leading to it. They rehearse. They give new meaning, a positive excitement, to the statement 'I can't take my mind off my work.' They visualize—not [as] a substitute for thorough preparation and hard work—but as an indispensable adjunct."[22]

Mapping Alternative Futures. Superachievers anticipate the future through contingency planning. "What will happen if. . . . ?" They understand that nothing is forever and that change is certain. So they seek out information on probable trends and then prepare themselves to act and adapt. "The key is not to predict the future with unnatural precision, but to look about for clues to the general directions of change that are going to affect one's mission—and to follow the critical path for achieving it."[23]

Updating the Mission. Periodically, achievers go back to ground zero to reassess their mission. Have business conditions changed? Do they require fundamentally different products and services? Good answers to good questions mean the difference between staying on top or going under. How many eight-mile-per-gallon cars are on the road today? Peak performers update what they're about so they can manage rather than react to change.

The Intelligence of Successful People

Successful people like Garfield's peak performers are highly intelligent. Although they may not score well on standardized IQ tests, they *do* score well on reality tests—the tests that count. They engage in effective and efficient mental self-management. They think first, act decisively, and then think about what they have accomplished. Their thoughts and actions are always productive, never counterproductive. They don't engage in purposeless, self-defeating behaviors. They act in their own best interests by first asking: (1) "What do I need and what do I want?," (2) "What do I like and what can I do to get it?," and (3) "What else must I do to get what I need and want?" These questions define their mission and set their goals. They place them in the big picture context by showing specific people, places, events, times, and their relationships to the mission. It gives substance to dreams by suggesting directions, routes, and steps that get from here to there.

At the same time, successful people attend to details, the day-to-day tasks that get them started and keep them going. They take macro and micro snapshots of where they're going and what they're doing. They fulfill Alvin Toffler's recommendation that "You've got to think about 'big things' while you're doing small things so all the small things go in the right direction."[24]

Successful people master daily self-management by asking themselves: (1) what do I need to do, (2) what am I going to do, (3) what am I doing, (4) what have I done, and (5) what do I need to do tomorrow? This practice keeps them focused. After identifying the most important tasks (what do I need to do?) and planning how to complete these tasks (what am I going to do?), they monitor their performance ("what am I doing?"), and then evaluate "what have I done?" Last, they identify changes necessary to improve their performance next time (what do I need to do tomorrow?).

Factor 2: Competence

Effective mental self-management is necessary *but not sufficient* for success. All successful people are effective mental self-managers. But not all effective self-managers are successful. Some know what they want, set goals, plan actions, follow through, evaluate, and adjust— *but still never get what they want.* They fail because they lack the skills, talents, and specialized knowledge necessary for success in the area they've chosen. No matter how effectively I manage my thoughts and actions, I'll never be a world-class pianist. I don't have the competence needed for that career. The necessary and sufficient rule applies to the converse situation as well. People who are competent don't always become successful. Experience is replete with talented, brilliant, and competent people who never get what they want because they don't manage their mental resources effectively. To be successful, you must be intelligent *and* be competent.

Developing Competence

Competence is a *pattern* of thought, feeling, and action that completes tasks effectively and efficiently. This definition applies to everything we do to get results—from playing the piano, dancing a ballet, replacing a transmission, making a speech, solving a math problem, and painting a portrait to washing dishes, mowing grass, and making beds. All tasks require coordination of thought, feeling (attitude), and action. Nobel laureate Herbert A. Simon and his colleagues say that "There's no magic going on in the human head. . . . The expert has stored in memory a large number of patterns, which he recognizes when they occur in the situation around him. The grand master chess player, for example, has stored a large number of patterns, which he recognizes when they occur on a chess board before him."[25]

Experts recognize more patterns than others do. Call it what they may—brilliance, intuition, or blind instinct—it's really just the patterns of thinking, feeling, and responding stored in memory from thousands of learning episodes. Researchers estimate that experts have tens of thousands of these patterns that they call upon to solve problems in their specialty area. Simon likens this to the vocabulary acquired by an educated adult.

> Using simple probability models, as well as computer simulation of the chess perception process, quantitative estimates were made of the "vocabulary" of familiar chunks in a master's memory. The estimates obtained by several different procedures all fall in the range of twenty-five thousand to one hundred thousand chunks—that is, a vocabulary of roughly the same size as the vocabulary of an educated adult in his native language.[26]

Expert or not, all of us learn the survival competencies for day-to-day living. We dress ourselves, clean the house, and make dinner. We learn these competencies early and perform them routinely, almost without thinking. We're less likely to learn other competencies like winning a chess match, quarterbacking a football team, or walking a high wire. They take years to master, and require more effort and longer periods of commitment. Consequently, only a few become masters of such skills. Simon estimates it takes a minimum of ten years to master a professional discipline sufficiently well to qualify as an expert.[27] "Research done by my colleague John R. Hayes and I indicates that nobody reaches world class in less than ten years of diligent application. Bobby Fischer became a chess grand master in slightly less than ten years. It took a bit more than ten years for Mozart. Mozart was a slow learner."[28] Griessman noted that for superachievement "researchers concluded that natural gifts are not sufficient in and of themselves in explaining these extraordinary accomplishments. Unless there is a long and intensive process of encouragement, nurturance, education, and training, the individuals will not attain world class in their respective fields."[29]

Unfortunately, prodigious competence doesn't just descend "naturally," although its guardian angels, interest and talent, certainly help. Parents can look for typical signs in their children if they're interested in early starts. Children who discover early what they like and can do get a "head start" on the ten-year competency trek. They can focus their energies, develop their talents, and build skills in areas that are most "natural," even enjoyable. *They learn to do well what they like most to do.*

Although it makes sense to fit competency development with natural ability, few parents do it. That's why so many young people enter school without the slightest notion of their likes and potentials. And by then, their choices narrow considerably. Linguistic and mathematical competencies are all that count. Suddenly, students who felt pretty good about themselves before school must reappraise themselves. If they don't read and compute as well as their peers, they feel *incompetent*. Some end up in classes for "slow" and "special" learners.

Yes, some students *are* slower than others. That's no surprise. What is surprising and, indeed, unfortunate, is our reaction to differences. Slow reading and slow calculating do not mean slow everything else. But that's the message most children and their parents receive and accept as true. All children and adults have strengths *and* weaknesses. The trick is to find which is which, and to maximize the one while minimizing the effects of the other. That's intelligent self-management. Remember: Andrew Carnegie amassed one of the country's greatest fortunes without the benefits of a formal education. What, then, are the multiple talents that people can develop to get what they want in life?

Multiple Talents

In *Frames of Mind: The Theory of Multiple Intelligences*, Harvard psychologist Howard Gardner describes the *multiple* intelligences and talents we use "to solve problems, or to create products, that are valued within one or more cultural settings."[30] These talents are independent of each other. Persons with one talent typically lack comparable ability in another. Across-the-board talent in all areas is uncommon—even for people scoring highest on I.Q. tests. Each of us has *relative* strengths and weaknesses in different areas: "each intelligence is relatively independent of the others, and . . . an individual's intellectual gifts in, say, music, cannot be inferred from his or her skills in mathematics, language, or interpersonal understanding."[31] Many children go through school with abilities and talents unnoticed by their parents and teachers. Consider the range of talent areas *outside the core curriculum* in which children may have ability: spatial reasoning, visual expression, musical expression, fine and gross motor coordination, and social and personal sensitivity. In Gardner's view, "it should be possible to identify an individual's intellectual profile (or proclivities) at an early age and then draw upon this knowledge to enhance that person's educational opportunities and options. One could channel individuals with unusual talents into special programs, even as one could devise prosthetics and special enrichment programs for individuals presenting an atypical or a dysfunctional profile of intellectual competencies."[32] Gardner identified six talent areas from which all our competencies emerge: linguistic, logical-mathematical, spatial, bodily-kinesthetic, musical, and personal.

LANGUAGE COMPETENCE. People with exceptional linguistic talents use them to: (1) convince others of a course of action, (2) remember information, and (3) explain and teach through "oral instructions, employing verse, collections of adages, or simple explanations; and now, increasingly, through the word in its written form."[33] Usually children display linguistic skill when they learn to talk. The range of capacities here is vast. While some youngsters don't talk until rather late, others form understandable phrases at year one. "Young Jean-Paul Sartre was extremely precocious in these regards. The future author was so skilled at mimicking adults, including their style and register of talk, that by age five he could enchant audiences with his linguistic fluency. Shortly thereafter, he began to write, soon completing whole books."[34] And by age nine, he was passionate about language:

> By writing I was existing. . . . My pen raced away so fast that often my wrist ached. I would throw the filled notebooks on the floor, I

would eventually forget about them, they would disappear. . . . I wrote in order to write. I don't regret it; had I been read, I would have tried to please [as he did in his earlier oral performances]. I would have become a wonder again. Being clandestine I was true.[35]

LOGICAL-MATHEMATICAL COMPETENCE. Logical-mathematical competence is the ability to observe events, think them through abstractly, and then draw valid conclusions about their relationships. These skills enable engineers to build bridges, scientists to calculate pollution indexes, and physicists to determine our position in the galaxy. Abstract deductive thought is unique to this talent area. It's different from linguistics or music.

> According to [mathematician Alfred] Adler, the powers of mathematicians rarely extend beyond the boundary of the discipline. Mathematicians are seldom talented in finance or the law. What characterizes the individual is a love of dealing with abstraction, "the exploration, under the pressure of powerful implosive forces, of difficult problems for whose validity and importance the explorer is eventually held accountable by reality."[36]

Scientists share this talent. They explain rather than examine abstract relationships. Albert Einstein, who was unexceptional linguistically, received a magnetic compass at age four and "was awed by the needle, isolated and unreachable, yet seemingly caught in the grip of an invisible urge that attracted it toward the north. The needle came as a revelation, for it challenged the child's tentative beliefs in an orderly physical world: 'I can still remember—or at least I believe I remember—that this experience made a deep and abiding impression on me.'"[37]

Compare Einstein's *scientific* curiosity provoked by a compass needle with *mathematician* Stanislaw Ulam's childhood fascination with the intricate patterns in an Oriental rug. "The resulting visual picture seemed to produce a 'melody' with relations among the various parts resonating with one another. Ulam speculates that such patterns feature a kind of inherent mathematical regularity and power to which certain young individuals are particularly sensitive."[38]

SPATIAL COMPETENCE. Spatial thinkers solve problems differently from linguistic thinkers. Consider the task of locating a new address in an unfamiliar town. I'm okay if I have a map. But usually I don't, so I stop at a service station and ask directions. The attendant tells me: "Go east five miles, take a left to Main, drive two blocks, and then merge into Meridan for three miles, and take a right on Stevens to the highway heading west." I nod and drive off. Five minutes later I'm lost again. I can't remember a thing. I code *verbal* directions *spatially* in my mind because I think better in pictures. Others, like Dr. Robert Sternberg, solve problems like this *linguistically*:

> Occasionally I visit someone's house for the first time. When people give me verbal directions to get there, I usually have no trouble; but if someone draws a map for me, I have considerable difficulty reading it, especially if I try to do it while driving. Using these maps, I used to get lost frequently in trying to find the person's house. Eventually, I learned that if I am given a map, I need to sit down in advance and write out the directions verbally. (I have also learned to be helpful to others—I now have a set of directions to my own house that includes both a map and a set of verbal instructions for getting there!)[39]

People who solve problems one way—linguistically or spatially for example—have difficulty using the other. Some even argue that spatial thinking is the "other" intelligence. "Dualists speak of two systems of representation—a verbal code and an imagistic code: localizers place the linguistic code in the left hemisphere, the spatial code in the right hemisphere."[40] Psychologist Rudolf Arnheim goes one step further, suggesting that our perception of the world is the foundation of all cognitive processes: "the remarkable mechanisms by which the senses understand the environment are all but identical with the operations described by the psychology of thinking . . . truly productive thinking in whatever area of cognition takes place in the realm of imagery."[41] Gardner cites additional support for this notion that if we cannot produce an image of a concept or problem, we will be unable to think clearly about it:

> In the sciences, the contribution of spatial intelligence is readily apparent. Einstein had an especially well-developed set of capacities. Like Russell he became mesmerized in first reading Euclid; and it was to the visual and spatial forms, and their correspondence, that Einstein was most strongly drawn: "His intuitions were deeply rooted in classical geometry. He had a very visual mind. He thought in terms of images—gedanken experiments, or experiments carried out in the

mind." It can even be conjectured that his most fundamental insights were derived from spatial models rather than from a purely mathematical line of reasoning.[42]

Today, Steven Hawking, Lucasian professor of mathematics at Cambridge University in England, probes black holes of the universe to explain and extend Einstein's theory of relativity. Hawking also has amyotrophic lateral sclerosis and must communicate through a computerized voice synthesizer. Nevertheless, he leads the search for the "Holy Grail" of physics, a unified theory to account for large-scale universal force (gravity), atomic-scale forces that hold atomic nuclei together, and the weak nuclear force responsible for radioactive decay. How does he do it? Like Einstein, he thinks in pictures. When asked about his image of the universe he says: "We all have some mental image of the universe. Mine is just rather more structured and mathematical. *I think in pictures.* I don't really have any feel for equations. Equations are the boring part of mathematics."[43]

PHYSICAL COMPETENCIES. Physical competence comes from another of Gardner's six independent intelligences. These bodily-kinesthetic talents include a full range of competent movements—from the speed and grace of an Olympic pole vaulter to the technical precision of a world-class pianist. Unlike the linguistic, mathematical, and spatial competencies that may take years to gain attention, physical prowess is obvious early. Children who move about gracefully and manipulate their environments deftly are obviously precocious. They develop early competencies in tennis, gymnastics, soccer, baseball, swimming, ice skating, dancing, and nearly anything else they try. Their bodies and limbs are quick, malleable, and adaptable.

My sister and I received early-bird instruction in the late 1940s, aspiring to follow the likes of Ginger Rogers and Fred Astaire. We were tap dancing at three and entering local talent shows at four and five. That was uncommon 40 years ago but near normal today, especially in sports like ice skating, gymnastics, swimming, and tennis. Jack Nicklaus began playing golf at age 10. When most youngsters were in school concentrating on recess and noon hour, he was averaging 300 practice shots and 18 holes of play a day. Imagine the time that took. How many 10-year-olds devote themselves to that kind of development? At age 13 he won the Ohio State Junior Championship, by 15 he qualified for the U.S. Amateur, and at 17 he qualified for the U.S. Open. At 20, ten years after he played his first game, Nicklaus came in second to Arnold Palmer in the U.S. Open.

MUSICAL COMPETENCIES. Musical talent expresses itself as early as physical ability, maybe even earlier. According to Gardner, some authorities claim that "infants as young as two months are able to match the pitch, loudness, and melodic contour of their mother's songs, and that infants at four months can match rhythmic structure as well. These authorities claim that infants are especially predisposed to pick up these aspects of music—far more than they are sensitive to the core properties of speech—and that they can also engage in sound play that clearly exhibits creative, or generative properties."[44]

The accounts of musical prodigies support these claims. Five-year-old Diego Alonso is an example. His mother played scales and repetitive melodies on the violin three times a day when she was pregnant. Diego began singing scales at six months and could read music at age two. By three, he played Bach minuets on the piano, and at four he had an audience before Queen Sofia of Spain.[45]

This is reminiscent of Wolfgang Amadeus Mozart who was a prodigy from age three, sonata composer at five, a symphony performer at ten, and opera composer at twelve. Mozart's father was largely responsible for giving Mozart opportunities for musical expression. Consider what might have happened at a different time and place—possibly with parents who failed to recognize his talent or who could do nothing to help. Would a young Mozart survive and thrive in today's schools? John Lennon didn't think so:

> People like me are aware of their so-called genius at ten, eight, nine. . . . I always wondered, "Why has nobody discovered me? In school, didn't they see that I'm more clever than anybody in this school? That the teachers are stupid, too? That all they had was information that I didn't need." It was obvious to me. Why didn't they put me in art school? Why didn't they train me? I was different, I was always different. Why didn't anybody notice me?[46]

PERSONAL-SOCIAL COMPETENCIES. Gardner's sixth intelligence is personal-social. People with this talent become leaders, helpers, and persuaders. They understand their own needs as well as the needs of others. This insight helps them to assess social situations accurately, sense directions of groups predictably, and position themselves strategically to maximize adaptive fits. They're "in tune" with social environments, often demonstrating an inner strength and confidence that attracts and inspires other people. The highest expression of this delicate balance between understanding self and others comes from such figures as Socrates, Jesus Christ, Mahatma Gandhi, and Eleanor Roosevelt:

> an individual has the option of becoming increasingly autonomous, integrated, or self-actualized, provided that he can make the correct "moves" and arrive at a suitable stance of accepting what cannot be altered. The end-goal of these developing processes is a self that is highly developed and fully differentiated from others: desirable models would include Socrates, Jesus Christ, Mahatma Gandhi, Eleanor Roosevelt—*individuals who appear to have understood much about themselves and about their societies* and to have come to terms successfully with the frailties of the human condition, while at the same time inspiring others around them to lead more productive lives. [italics added][47]

Schools teach splinter components of this talent area, usually focusing on behaviors that prevent trouble and maintain order— hence the importance on "getting along." There's more however. The fully developed personal-social competence is a dynamic and delicate balance between knowing self, knowing others, and acting for mutual benefit. Teachers and counselors are effective because of their inner balance. They're like the Ixils's "daykeeper" in Guatemala:

> He must assess (his patients') situations, their behavior, their concerns. He must also himself lead an exemplary life, or at least try to. Doing all this requires self-analysis as well as an empathic viewpoint for understanding others: it requires an updating, a revising, and a repairing of one's self-image: it requires a conceptualization of others which is added to and revised—a conceptualization that includes attributes and relations which one's clients and their families and friends maintain with each other; it requires an understanding of the

goals and values that motivate people and of the way in which the context or situation can modify these goals and intentions.[48]

Summary of Competencies

All of our skills and competencies derive from these talent areas: language, logical-mathematical, spatial, physical, musical, and personal-social. The relative *independence* of one area from another means that *everyone has* relative *strengths and weaknesses*. If you're competent in one area, you probably lack equivalent ability in others. The trick is to identify which is which. This done, you can move forward vigorously and relentlessly to develop that potential and maximize its benefits. Children should do this when they're young. The evidence on early and sustained development is convincing. People who spend the requisite ten years to reach "expert" levels discover deep satisfaction from connecting "natural" ability and preferred activity with developed capacity. This is the *second* factor needed to succeed.

Factor 3: Persistent Problem Solving

Intelligence and competence are necessary *but not sufficient* to succeed. We all have friends and associates who managed themselves intelligently, performed their work competently, yet never made it as "big" as they expected. Why? Because they gave up too soon. They lacked persistence, the third condition needed to succeed.

People who lack experience with *ambitious* goals usually expect too much too soon and waste time and energy looking for faster and easier routes. They never learned there are no shortcuts. The typical path takes thousands, possibly millions of tiny steps. Consider how many times Jack Nicklaus swung his golf club before winning a national championship, how many dives it took Greg Louganis to win his first gold medal, or how many chess games Bobby Fischer played before winning the world championship. Now recall the 10,000 experiments Thomas Edison conducted to light a single incandescent bulb. According to Napoleon Hill, *persistence* is the only factor that explains the incredible achievements of Henry Ford and Thomas Edison.

What mystical power gives to men of persistence the capacity to master difficulties? Does the quality of persistence set up in one's mind some form of spiritual, mental or chemical activity which gives one access to supernatural forces? Does Infinite Intelligence throw itself on the side of the person who still fights on, after the battle has been lost, with the whole world on the opposing side?

These and many other similar questions have arisen in my mind as I have observed men like Henry Ford, who started at scratch, and built an industrial empire of huge proportions, with little else in the way of a beginning but persistence. Or, Thomas A. Edison, who, with less than three months of schooling, became the world's leading inventor and converted persistence into the talking machine, the moving picture machine, and the incandescent light, to say nothing of half a hundred other useful inventions.

I had the happy privilege of analyzing both Mr. Edison and Mr. Ford, year by year, over a long period of years, and therefore, the opportunity to study them at close range, so I speak from actual knowledge when I say that *I found no quality save persistence, in either of them, that even remotely suggested the major source of their stupendous achievements.* [italics added][49]

People who lack persistence abandon goals rather than concentrate on the difficult problems that get in their way. Persevering achievers, by contrast, take problems one at a time, concentrating their energy on finding its solution before tackling the next. And when they meet obstacles they can't overcome, they figure ways around them. Persistence is not stubbornness. It's sustained problem solving. Voltaire reminds us that "No problem can withstand the assault of sustained thinking."

My father is a sustaining type. I came home from college one summer when he was learning golf. He entered an amputee tournament in Spokane (he lost his left arm in a hunting accident at fourteen). So I volunteered to caddie. It turned out to be the longest day I've ever spent on a course. I worked as hard searching the rough as he did getting balls there. After nine holes, I looked to him for relief. It was time to pack it in. He wasn't going to win, much less produce a "respectable" score. But he said nothing. Every hole, he did his best. Then we searched. Eighteen holes later it ended, mercifully. He said he had work to do. Now, 25 years later, he's an excellent golfer. What he lacks in power he makes up with precision. The episode reminded me that when I was six years old I had watched him pitch softball for his company team. He had one of the best win-loss records in the league. He pitched the ball and then quickly slipped a glove on to field it. No one expected him to make the team, much less to pitch. But he did. He spent hundreds of hours by himself pitching balls between two stakes in the backyard. He practiced and practiced until he mastered techniques that worked for him.

Persistence involves hundreds of thousands of problem-solving episodes all directed toward a single goal. People who focus on solving these tightly interconnected challenges receive greater returns than those who solve an equivalent number of unrelated problems. All superachievers understand this principle. Anthony Robbins's "Ultimate Success Formula" describes how successful people "kept adapting, kept adjusting, kept changing their behavior until they found what worked."[50] Napoleon Hill says that "Lack of persistence is one of the major causes of failure. Moreover, experience with thousands of people has proved that lack of persistence is a weakness common to the majority of men."[51] Griessman reported similar testimonials:

> Helen Gurley Brown, who gives herself high marks on persistence, says that one of the most common mistakes people make in their careers is that they "check out too soon." They don't want to do the grubby stuff. They want to get to the top too quickly.[52]

> [Erskine Caldwell, author of *Tobacco Road* and *God's Little Acre* says that] "I was always willing to undergo hardship or whatever it took to be able to stay with my work. I could have quit many times— given up, because it is no great art in life to be poor and hungry, and that's what I was."[53]

> [Charles Schulz says] "I was not an overnight success, even after I sold the strip. *Peanuts* did not take the world by storm immediately. It was a long grind. It took *Peanuts* about four years to attract nationwide attention, but it took ten years to become really entrenched."[54]

> [Jacques Cousteau, explorer, inventor, and environmentalist also attributes his success to persistence.] "I am obstinate—when I have

something in mind . . . I make a list of things I like to play with: the Amazon, Haiti, the windship. I try, and I don't get the money. I try again, and I don't get the money, and after ten years I get it."[55]

[Edith W. Martin, Ph.D., vice president of Technology of Boeing Electronics Company talks about her persistent problem solving] "If a solution exists, I will find it. That's my tenacity. If a perfect solution does not exist, I will give you the best possible alternative."[56]

General Albert C. Wedemeyer summed up his long and distinguished career in the army thus: "I have not given up easily." Wedemeyer, a recipient of the Distinguished Service Medal, served as American commander in China during World War II. In his eighty-ninth year, the old warrior told me: "I've kept on striving to accomplish my objectives. I've met with disillusionments; I met with disappointments. Sometimes I was confronted with deceit, but I kept on anyway along the avenue that I'd selected, and tried to reach the goals."[57]

Successful people are effective mental self-managers, competent performers, and persistent problem solvers. They use the same three success principles to get what they want in life. If we want our children to succeed, they must use these same principles. This begins with personal achievement—the accomplishment of a single goal.

Achievement

People who achieve success, happiness, and fulfillment follow the same strategy. They assess their needs, determine their wants, and plan their actions. Then they act, monitor, and evaluate to decide what to adjust. They act effectively, solve problems persistently, and adjust to change opportunistically. Every day, week after week and month after month, they plan, work, evaluate, adjust, and readjust. They enjoy the process as much as the outcome. Like Steve Jobs, they know that "The journey is the reward." Their *achievement* begins one task and one problem at a time. Their *success* records net gains and losses en route to a goal. Their *happiness* comes from the passion that their pursuit elicits and the enjoyment that goal attainment returns. And their *fulfillment* is a result of their artful integration of personal and professional passions over time. Figure 1 shows these relationships.

Now you can see why today's youth have such a difficult time finding happiness and fulfillment. They're on the wrong side of the achievement curve with little hope of reversing its direction. They need watered-down content to pass courses in college and remedial training to perform tasks at work. They can't manage themselves intelligently or adapt to their changing world successfully. They prefer to stay at home with mom and dad rather than strive to achieve on their own at work. They lack competence, intelligence, and persistence, the essentials for success, happiness, and fulfillment.

At the root of these problems is their inability to think and act effectively. Youth don't understand what's necessary for independence and self-sufficiency. A 1987 Harris opinion poll found that most Americans agree on the importance of children's ability to

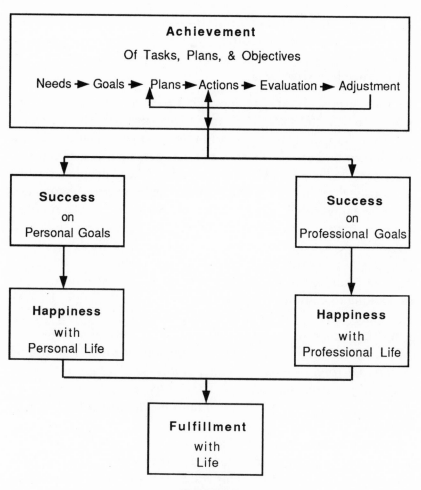

FIGURE 1

From Achievement to Fulfillment

think for themselves.[1] But today's youth can't. The list below summarizes a few of their deficiencies.

1. They have undeveloped talent
2. They are unaware of their own needs, interests, and abilities
3. They lack commitment and purpose in their lives
4. They lack confidence, initiative, and self-esteem
5. They avoid taking responsibility for their behaviors
6. They don't know how to self-adjust

7. They don't persist on difficult tasks
8. They lack internal motivation
9. They depend on others to solve their problems
10. They lack street smarts

It's no surprise they're unhappy. They have no sense of self, competence, or effectiveness. Their most accessible rewards are external. They desperately need opportunities to engage their minds and stretch their bodies—the most common source of satisfaction for all Americans. Pollster Lou Harris reports that when "people are asked to choose what they feel is the greatest single source of happiness, either "great wealth," "good health," or "personal satisfaction from accomplishment," good health wins with 46 percent, followed closely by personal achievement with 44 percent. Wealth trails far behind at 6 percent.[2] While baby boomers rank personal achievement and fulfillment ahead of money, position, and power, youth are looking to cash in with material rewards. According to UCLA's Alexander Astin, who surveyed 250,000 full-time college freshmen, "Students today limit learning to the classroom and the fast-trackers are setting the pace. *They're defining themselves according to external things—money, power, status—and choosing courses that will get them these things. They're terribly preoccupied with their bodies but they've lost touch with mental disciplines*" [italics added].[3]

Youth don't even know the basics of personal achievement. They need to learn how to perform tasks and realize goals that give their lives meaning and direction. This will start them on the path toward success, happiness, and fulfillment. But significant obstacles confront them. Schools offer scant choices for those with different talents and interests. And most parents don't even know about competence, intelligence, and persistence. They believe obedience, good grades, and college are enough. But they're not. *Youth need help learning to think, act, evaluate, and adjust.* They need to learn personal achievement.

Personal Achievement

In *Personal Best,* Dr. George Sheehan, medical editor of *Runner's World* and author of *Running and Being,* describes a life of personal achievement:

We are forever occupied with expressing or discharging what is latent in us. We are maximizers, always trying to make whatever is potential in our personality a living reality. If there is one word for human nature, it is *more*.

... The diligent use of our allotted life span is the secret of the successful life. "There is only one road to greatness," said Sydney Smith, "hard labor." But the right labor done in the right way. Effort is the measure of a man. But it is effort concentrated on the creation and development of the ideal self. [italics added][4]

Happiness comes with accomplishment. It increases confidence and self-esteem. Achievement fosters independence from external forces and increases reliance on personal resources. It connects happiness with responsibility. The Reverend Robert Schuller requested the Gallup Poll to assess the prevalence of self-esteem and its effect on the American public. He found that people with self-esteem were happier, healthier, and more productive than people without it.[5] This is not surprising. German philosopher Arthur Schopenhauer's study of the happy life says that "In general, the wise of all ages have always said the same thing. ... The basic rule for the happy life, according to that consensus is: Develop the self. The rule's application obviously varies from one individual to another—each life becomes a unique manifestation of the principle in action—but the rule stays the same: To be happy, grow."[6]

Comparative Achievement

Young children enjoy learning to walk, talk, and ride their bikes. Each challenge is personal and each accomplishment fulfilling. No need to instruct them on personal achievement. They achieve *personal* goals until age six when they leave home to go to school. Then they become one of many performing the same tasks to achieve peer group goals. Suddenly they compete to achieve. Teachers grade some higher than others. Each year the school gives norm-referenced, standardized tests. A few months later, parents receive readouts, reporting how Jenny and Joey compare with other children their age. They wonder why Jenny is *only average* in reading or why Joey is *only slightly above* the mean in arithmetic. Shouldn't their child be at the top of their class? After all, they *are* special.

Jenny and Joey may be only average, but only on some tasks— like those measured by standardized tests. Jenny and Joey have *in-*

dividual strengths that don't show in stanines. Hopefully they understand this. But do they?

At school, comparisons are common. Children learn that grades depend on how they perform in comparison to how others do. They discover the "curve" that places a few at the top, most in the middle, and a few at the bottom. This system is neither bad nor good, healthy nor unhealthy. It's simply one way to evaluate performance. Some children react positively to comparative evaluations, others don't.

There are three reactions to test results. The first is easiest to understand. Children who score well—because they're good test takers and have above average skills in reading and math—benefit emotionally and psychologically. They view themselves positively and feel confident. A second reaction comes from children who find themselves in the bottom half of the distribution. Results challenge their sense of personal worth. Repeated reports of below average rankings lead them to think they're inadequate. Their confidence suffers, along with their self-esteem. The third reaction comes from children who also score below the norm. But instead of suffering a crisis in confidence they remind themselves that there's more to their net worth than reading and math. They maintain confidence and self-esteem.

Of the three reactions, the first and second are easiest to understand. Group one receives good marks and feels good and group two receives negative results and feels bad. But what about the third group? How do these children maintain poise? Do they know something we don't?

Personal Achievement

Group three children have other ways of evaluating themselves. Positive results they receive from personal, nonschool achievements tell them they're okay. They expect better results *next time*. I was one. Entering first grade a year early, I had trouble with reading, a problem that continued to plague me throughout school. During oral reading I remember counting the number of turns before mine, skipping ahead, and rehearsing the passage silently to avoid embarrassing stops when my turn came. In the ninth grade, my social studies teacher assigned so much reading I had to lock myself in my bedroom for hours at a time to complete the work. I did the same in high school, always allocating enough time to complete the work. My Scholastic Aptitude Test scores for college showed deficits in the verbal section so I studied exam questions and took it again. The results were good enough to squeak by the Dartmouth admissions committee. Still, the problem continued. Freshman year I failed introductory English twice and my academic standing teetered on probation. The next year I improved because I discovered my interests and pursued them vigorously. Today 90 percent of my work requires reading and writing. I'm still not fast, but I get the job done.

Stories like mine are common. That I wasn't as good as my peers on some tasks was not devastating. I didn't like it much but I learned to live with it. I compensated in other areas. My sister and I were successful in music and dance and I knew how to teach myself new skills. Children who achieve excellence in one area have the inner strength and resilience to come back. Even a single competency experience can strengthen resolve, although it doesn't soften the blow. I'll never forget those English courses. Going to an Ivy League school and failing the same course twice was tough but not devastating. I knew I could do better. The confidence was there.

Children develop inner strength and mental toughness through personal achievement. They learn to set ambitious goals, work at them persistently, and overcome obstacles that get in their way. This experience places their less spectacular performances in perspective. Listen to John Holt, author of *How Children Fail*:

> We all agree that all children need to succeed; but do we mean the same thing? My own feeling is that success should not be quick or easy, and should not come all the time. Success implies overcoming an obstacle, including, perhaps, the thought in our minds that we might not succeed. It is turning "I can't" into "I can, and I did."
>
> . . . It is tempting to think that we can arrange the work of unsuccessful students so that they think they are succeeding most of the time. But how can we keep secret from a child what other children of his own age, in his own or other schools, are doing? *What some of these kids need is the experience of doing something really well— so well that they know themselves, without having to be told, that they have done it well.* [italics added][7]

What Children Need to Succeed

Children can avoid the affluent cultural achievement trap by learning that if they want something, they must use their personal resources to get it. They must discover their "competency niche" as early as possible even though conventional wisdom says all they need is a degree from a good school. But grades, test scores, and college education don't guarantee success. Each year hundreds of graduates return home to live with their parents because they are as confused as ever about what they want and what they can do. General education is but a single step toward an opportunity to do what they like and can do best to get what they want most. Karen Thomas reports that "the American emphasis on standardized testing has left students obsessed with *getting the right answer but unable to think toward it. . . .* Numerous recent studies have shown that many students lack thinking skills—to analyze, deduce, understand consequences and make long-range decisions."[8] The lack of these skills, the educators say, leaves them unable to make sound decisions about school, career, marriage, or even what products to buy. Dr. Lauren Resnick of the University of Pittsburgh reports in the *Educational Researcher* that there is a significant difference between the problem solving taught in school and the thinking required to solve problems outside of school, particularly at work.[9]

Educating for Achievement

Young children learn personal achievement by gaining control over their own thoughts, feelings, and behaviors and then organizing those resources to get what they want. At first, this task is difficult. The top half of Figure 2 illustrates the interdependent dynamic of thoughts, feelings, and actions during the early years. Feelings provoke thoughts and behaviors, thoughts affect behaviors and feelings, and behaviors influence thoughts and feelings. Gradually, through contact with others and the environment, order emerges. Children establish inner control and develop sufficient intellectual self-mastery to think, feel, and act intelligently. Now they can address such important self-direction questions as "What do I need and what do I want?" and "What am I willing and able to do to get what I need and want?" They can even generate their own blueprint

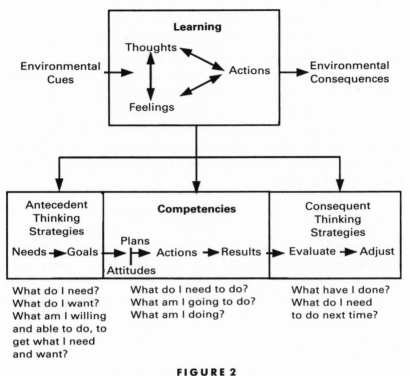

FIGURE 2
Developing Independence

for future achievement: objectives, plans, actions, evaluations, and adjustments. Then they manage themselves to achieve each day by asking themselves (1) "What do I need to do?" (my objective), (2) "What am I going to do?" (my plans), (3) "What am I doing?" (self-monitoring actions), (4) "What have I done?" (self-evaluation), and (5) "What do I need to do next time?" (self-adjustment). These are the basic questions for personal achievement. Antecedent thinking self-directs, competence self-initiates, and consequent thinking self-corrects.

Control

The drive toward mastery of self and the environment is natural. At birth it attempts to control and establish predictability in the service of basic needs. Remember those first months of night-time "calls" for milk and comfort? Crying, emotional outbursts, and even tantrums were powerful attention-getters. But at first they are worrisome. Parents flock to bookstores, pediatricians, and child development experts for answers on discipline—how to teach the rules without discouraging independence. Always, the answer's the same. Never do anything for your child he can do for himself. Let him test, evaluate, and adjust different behaviors to determine what will get him what he wants. He'll learn independence along the way. This is an essential ingredient in the formula for "How to Raise a Responsible Child":

> No matter what age your child is as you read this, there is likely to be some area of his or her life in which you can foster greater independence. Generally this means that you or the other adult who is in closest contact with the child has to allow the child to do something himself or herself that someone else has been doing. *Don't do anything for your child at almost any time that the child can do.* [italics added][10]

Expectations

Pollster Louis Harris reported that the top three characteristics Americans want in their children are honesty, thoughtfulness, and obedience. He concluded: "Of course, a good case could be made for the sound judgment of a people who would bequeath to a new generation a sense of honesty to build character, and an ability to think for themselves as the key to getting ahead in later life. Together, these qualities suggest a model child who combines integrity and mental alertness, a rather formidable formula."[11] On the one hand we want children to obey and to fit in socially—after all, who enjoys calls from school reporting their child in trouble for disobedience. On the other hand, we want our children to think for themselves to solve problems independently. How can they learn both? Are obedience and independence compatible?

Independence

Figure 3 illustrates youth transitions from obedience to independence. At Level 1, parents and teachers make the *antecedent* decisions. They determine what needs and goals are appropriate. They

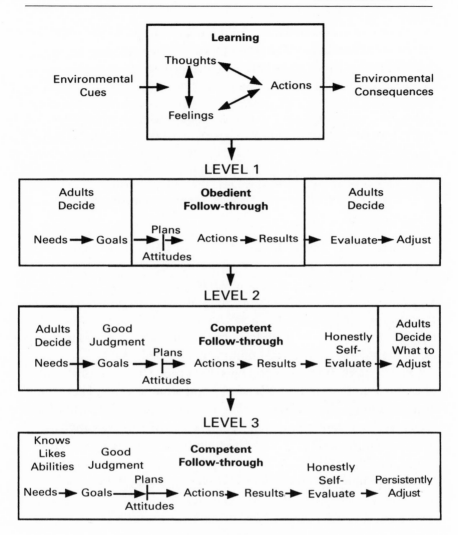

FIGURE 3
Levels of Independence

also make the *consequent* decisions about what children will correct and how they should adjust. Adults are "directors"; children are "directed." This stage should be temporary because it encourages *dependence*. Children should move quickly to Level 2 where parents and teachers mentor rather than direct, when they help children to set goals, to follow through, and to evaluate results.

This role-shift is difficult for adults who enjoy making decisions. What if children choose the wrong goals? After all, they've never made those decisions before. But how can they learn if they never try? John Holt described this dilemma 25 years ago:[12]

> Teachers and schools tend to mistake good behavior for good character. What they prize above all else is docility, suggestibility; the child who will do what he is told; or even better, the child who will do what is wanted without even having to be told. They value most in children what children least value in themselves. Small wonder that their effort to build character is such a failure; they don't know it when they see it.[13]

Unfortunately, few children ever get to Level 3. Consequently, they never display the maturity of thought and action that comes from knowing what they like and what they can do. And their self-awareness never connects important goals with deeply seated needs to impassion achievement. Their lack of good judgment and strategic planning prevents them from channeling their energies to maximize their competencies and minimize their deficits.

Level 3 youth are honest and persistent too. They examine results objectively to determine what works and what doesn't. They don't bother kidding themselves or others about accomplishments that aren't likely or don't occur. They analyze positive and negative feedback with equanimity as they fine-tune their approach to goal setting, planning, and problem solving. They persevere as long as it takes to complete difficult tasks and reach challenging goals.

Independence and Peak Performance

Peak performers use these same patterns of thought and action. The only difference is the intensity and consistency with which they execute. Peak performers work harder than average at matching what they like with what they can do and what they want. This impassions their pursuits, heightens their motivation, and intensifies their commitment to succeed. Peak performers take charge each day by scheduling activities and time that maintain progress. They never lose sight of goals. They analyze and dissect their results with uncompromising precision and objectivity. They analyze reasons for outcomes and determine how plans and actions can be more effective.

Persistence of thought and action sets them apart. At first they don't appear different, more intelligent, or more successful. But over time their finely honed strategic and tactical adaptations to hundreds of thousands of environmental changes produce results that are truly remarkable.

Teaching for Survival

Children should enter school knowing what they like, what they can do, and what they want. Because once there, they must read, write, and compute. Those who have their own plans to achieve can cope. Past accomplishments and confidence will see them through. In fact, children who do anything at all very well can find a niche that makes their schooling experience positive, and maybe even fulfilling. Extracurricular activities offer opportunity for personal achievement as well.

The problem is that most children enter school *with no obvious talent or ability*. Worse yet, they have little notion of what they might like or what they might be able to do. So when they have difficulty with the academic option, they truly suffer. Figure 4 illustrates this problem. Youth who lack linguistic and logical-mathematical talent try to meet the "requirements." When they fail, they find themselves in special classes where they remain for years trying to improve. No one cares about what other things they *can* do, only about what they *can't* do. *Deficits get attention and strengths get overlooked.* These youngsters start doubting themselves and their abilities. And, as indicated in the diagram, they lose confidence, self-reliance, and self-esteem. They learn to depend on teachers and adults to do their thinking, deciding, evaluating, and adjusting. They practice "learned helplessness."

Emphasis on remediation excludes opportunities to learn mental self-management. The problem is pervasive. *All students* suffer equally because expectations at school—like those at home—require students to do what adults say. Teachers and parents decide what, when, where, and how. Students follow instructions. Independent, self-directed antecedent and consequent thinking doesn't occur. So youth never attach purpose or meaning to what they

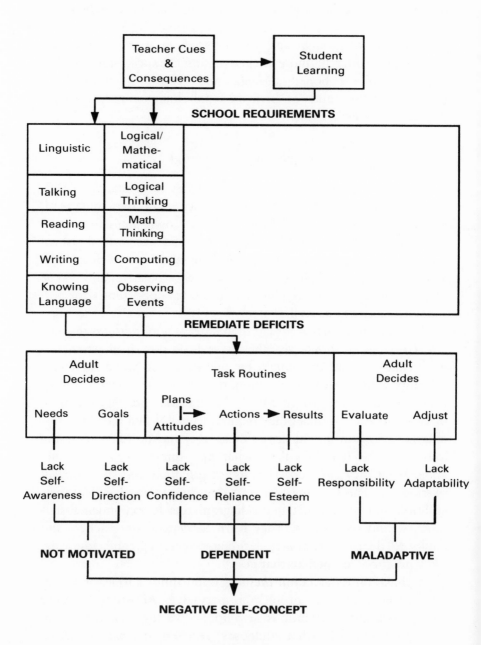

FIGURE 4
Teaching Survival

learn. Attending to the every thought and wish of the supervising adult drains them of their natural motivation to learn and their desire to achieve.

Youth who lack skills for mental self-management cannot analyze their behaviors and results objectively. Consequently, they learn to deny responsibility and look to others for solutions. Their failure to learn from mistakes maintains maladaptive responding. From a distance, they appear intelligent and on some paper-and-pencil tests maybe they are. But on the only test that counts—the ability to adapt to the environment—they fall flat. They don't even know what environmental cues *are* important after high school. Their teachers and parents always directed their course corrections. On their own, youth must self-direct and self-correct and they don't know how. Their unhappiness is no surprise. Lack of motivation, dependence, and maladaptive behaviors produce negative self-concepts that take years of therapy to remedy.

Drop-out prevention consultant Jerry Conrath says that "discouraged learners" quit because schools create too many opportunities for failure and not enough opportunities for success. Most slow-learning students blame their failures on luck and circumstance beyond their control. They never assume responsibility. Says Conrath, "They don't learn from their successes. They don't learn from their mistakes."[14] Hence they don't know how to adjust. They're victims of teacher judgments and school decisions that control their behaviors, their attitudes, and their lives. "If you want the student to take personal responsibility for mistakes, insist he take responsibility for his successes."[15] Placing students in "bonehead" classes only reinforces negative self-concepts. Conrath recommends accelerated classes to help them catch up. Educators agree: current practice doesn't work.

Special education students face the same problem. Teachers focus on deficits so completely that children believe that their most important attributes are *what they can't do*. Many students complete their entire school experience believing that completing a task without help is independence. It never occurs to them that their teachers decided which tasks to complete, when to complete it, how to complete it, what was wrong with it, and how to correct it next time. They have no idea that independence means *independent thinking and acting*. Special education instruction actually creates learned dependence.[16]

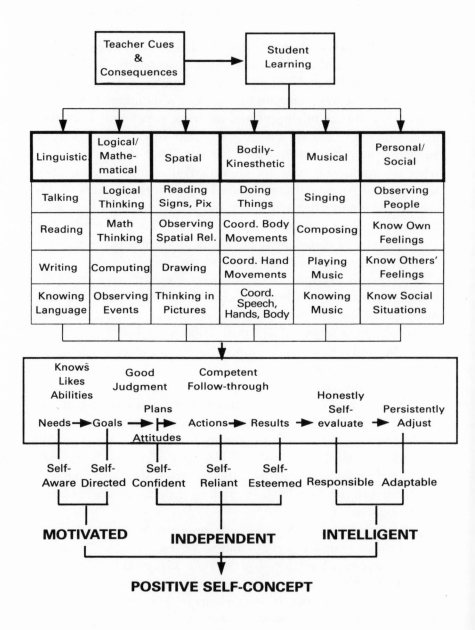

FIGURE 5

Teaching Achievement

Teaching for Achievement

All students must develop their talents and practice their indepen-dence. This means taking a chance, learning from failure, and striv-ing for success. Teachers and parents who prevent failure do more harm than good. Feelings of incompetence, inadequacy, and nega-tive self-worth are inevitable consequences of overprotection. Mak-ing the world special only postpones the inevitable question "Can I make it alone?" When young people enter the world on their own, they need confident strengths rather than remediated deficits. This is the primal source for intelligent mental self-management.

The achievement map in Figure 5 illustrates the ideal progression from competency development through mental self-management to the establishment of self-awareness, self-direction, self-confidence, self-reliance, responsibility, and adaptability. Level 3 achievers are internally motivated, independent, and intelligent. They secure op-timal fits with their environments. Their persistent, daily problem solving generates hundreds if not thousands of cumulative adjust-ments between specific behaviors and environmental consequences. They learn what works and what doesn't work, given their individ-ual needs, talents, and abilities. These thoughts and action patterns are the same "thinking skills" that educators recommend all teach-ers to teach.[17]

Steps to Personal Achievement

Achievement begins with competence. Everyone must learn they're good at something, and the earlier the better. By three or four most children walk, talk, feed themselves, and go to the toilet by them-selves. As they gain control over their bodies and their environ-ments, they discover ways they're different from others. Jenny learns what she likes and what she can do that others don't like and can't do. This sets her apart and gives her parents, relatives, and friends opportunities to praise her. Praise increases her confidence and self-esteem and fosters her belief that "If I'm good at this, I can be good at something else." She's on her way toward personal achievement.

During grade school Jenny develops her special abilities while learning to manage her behaviors intelligently. She formulates an-swers to the questions "What do I like?" and "What can I do?" In her talent area, she sets personal goals, develops plans to meet them, schedules her time and activities, and then follows through. She learns how to evaluate progress too, discovering for the first time how feedback helps her improve on her own. As she learns to self-manage, Jenny experiences the social consequences of competence. She notices that friends and teachers admire her talent even though it's not emphasized in the school curriculum. The principal allows her to leave early so she can work with her coach. Jenny discovers that *children with achievement potential receive support and attention*. Families, relatives, teachers, and friends welcome opportunities to help out.

By high school, more students discover what they can do. They explore the many options: track, cross country, soccer, tennis, golf, basketball, football, hockey, forensics, theater, band, chorus, science fair, math olympiads, writing contests, foreign language club, student government, and so on. Suddenly the achievement course is crowded.

Jenny learns the second lesson: *children who began their trek early are more competitive*. The advantage goes to those who've already mastered their talent area and established an achievement record. Support and recognition are in shorter supply. So she asks herself: "I have talent, ability, and opportunity. But it's not going to be as easy to get what I want. Should I stick with what I'm doing or can I find an easier way?" And her parents wonder, will she persist?

Figure 6 summarizes her steps to personal achievement. She knows her talents and abilities, step 1, and *how* to get where she wants to go, step 2. She sets goals, develops plans, takes action, evaluates, and adjusts. She's mastered the basics. Now she must persist, step 3. She must adjust and readjust again and yet again and as intelligently as possible, always checking the environment to discover what works and what doesn't. She solves three types of problems: needs-goal, goal-plan, and plan-performance problems.

Needs-goal problems emerge when Jenny's goals no longer match her needs, when she has new interests and different aspirations. What once was important no longer is important. So she reassesses her needs and sets new goals. *Goal-plan problems* occur when her plans don't work. Even though her work is excellent, it doesn't get her where she wants to be. There's something wrong with her strat-

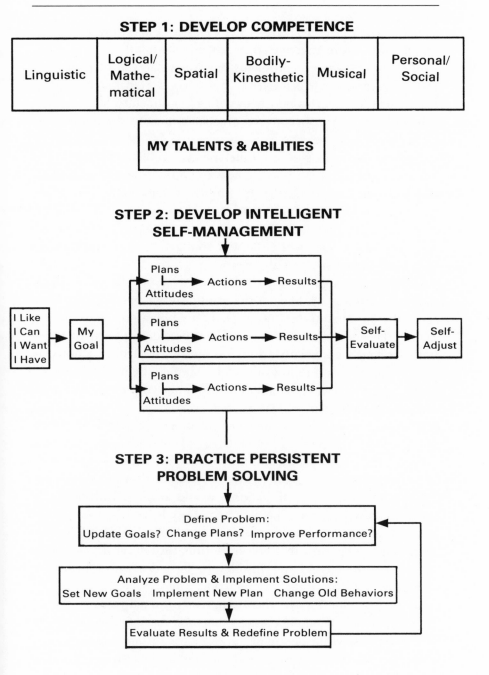

FIGURE 6

Steps to Personal Achievement

egy. What is it? Jenny reviews her plans and develops a different and possibly more effective approach. Maybe it will be more effective. *Plan-performance* problems develop when the plan requires tasks she cannot perform. Jenny has a good plan but it requires behaviors she performs poorly or with great difficulty. She can solve this problem with concentrated practice and skills development in those deficient areas.

Jenny spends most of her time solving problems like this. She takes lessons, receives advice on how to improve her techniques. By contrast, she works goal-plan problems only once every few months, and less often than that as she improves her self-management skills. She spends the *least* time with *needs-goal problems*. She solved most of those when she was younger. Now she knows her own needs, interests, and abilities.

Jenny doesn't spin her wheels deciding what problems are important and need solving. She has that routine down pat. First she identifies the problem type—needs-goal, goal-plan, or plan performance. Then she analyzes the problem, breaks it into manageable units, connects each with a solution option, sequences actions together logically, and follows through. Always, she monitors results and tracks progress. If her solutions work she continues. If not, she redefines the problem and starts over.

The three steps to personal achievement are: (1) *developing competence* based upon talents and interest, (2) *reaching personal goals* by using those talents and abilities intelligently, and (3) *persistently solving problems* that get in the way of achievement. It sounds easy, but it isn't. Otherwise, all children would achieve. Unfortunately, most don't make it past the first step. They leave school searching for themselves. Too bad they didn't start looking a decade earlier. By failing to negotiate that first transition, they never develop skills required at the second and third levels. They don't manage or persist. They just drift.

Those few who discover themselves early can tell you quickly and with conviction what they like, what they can do, and what they want. They may not be "right" in the sense of doing exactly what they plan twenty years hence but they don't have to. Self-direction is not being right. It's having the capacity to discover what's "right" at one's current level of awareness.

Achievement Roles for Parents and Teachers

Adults introduce children to the success principles by leading, mentoring, and befriending. They *lead* by demonstrating and persuading. They *mentor* by teaching and counseling. And they *befriend* by sharing, cooperating, and even competing. When they lead, they give children visions of what they can be and then set expectations and provide opportunities that encourage achievement. When they mentor, they teach and counsel how to become competent, intelligent, and persistent. And when they befriend, they share the benefits of personal achievement with their children.

Figures 7 and 8 show how these relationships change over time. Parents and teachers do more leading and mentoring in the early years and more befriending in the later years. This correlates with the three-step sequence illustrated in Figure 6. Leadership and mentorship are most important in the beginning when competence is most important. By adolescence, friendship increases in importance as youth learn how to self-direct their own problem solving. Figure

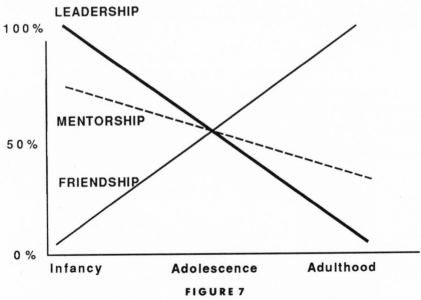

FIGURE 7
When Parents and Teachers Perform What

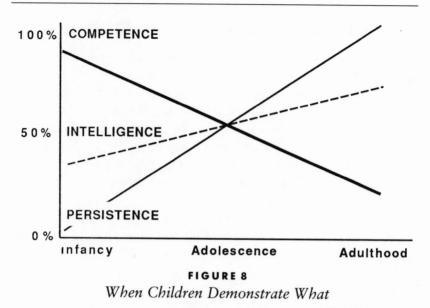

FIGURE 8
When Children Demonstrate What

8 illustrates how competency development declines while the intelligent use of that talent increases. Note also the steep increase in the importance of persistent problem solving. By adulthood persistence is most important, intelligence is second, and new competency development is last.

8

Competence

Art Buchwald epitomizes rags-to-riches achievement. He grew up in an orphanage and went on to win a Pulitzer Prize for journalism. Then, in 1989, he joined other notables in Washington, D.C., to receive the Horatio Alger Award, as *U.S.A. Today* reports:

> Tonight in Washington, D.C., the group honors a range of people, from basketball great Julius Erving to Sen. Daniel K. Inouye (D—Hawaii), who grew up in a Japanese ghetto in Honolulu, and restauranteur Truett Cathy who helped his mother run a boarding house.
>
> "I shucked corn and shelled peas," says Cathy, now chairman of the Atlanta-based Chick-fil-a restaurant chain. "I knew that if I had anything in life, I'd have to earn it."
>
> TV evangelist Robert Schuller paid his way through seven years of college and theological school waiting tables. Now he runs the Crystal Cathedral Church in Garden Grove, Calif., which draws 2 million viewers for its weekly television broadcast. "I've always had big dreams," he says.[1]

This special breed of trekkers (persistent, indefatigable achievers) combined "Pluck and Luck"—the title of an Alger book—to overcome impossible obstacles. James Mitchener fits the profile. He was a foundling at age two, adopted and raised with foster children by Mabel Mitchener and occasionally sent to the local poorhouse for support. "I never had skates, I never had a bicycle, I never had a wagon—nothing that the other kids had. Nothing. A guy said he could never figure out how I tied my shoelaces because they were all just knots. That was my background. . . . At 14, I left home with 35 cents in my pocket and hitched to Florida. It never occurred to me that I wouldn't make it. I think that before I was 15, I had been from Canada to Key West."[2] By age 82 James Mitchener had completed 37 books—translated into 52 languages, 9 movies, 4 television shows, and a musical. He has received a Pulitzer Prize and the Presidential Medal of Freedom.

Mary Kay Ash, chairperson and founder of Mary Kay Cosmetics, also started from scratch. From age ten, she was on her own, taking care of the house and her father while her mother worked: "Because she was the manager of the restaurant that she worked in, she was available to talk to me when I needed her. I would call her ten times a day and I'd say, 'Mother, I don't know how to do this.' And she'd say, 'Okay honey, now listen to me. Now you do this first and then you do this and then you do this. *Now you can do it, you can do it.*'"[3] Robert Dedman, founder and chairman of Club Corporation of America, an attorney with four degrees, and a philanthropist, with an estimated personal fortune of over $600 million, also began in "rags": "I was born to very, very poor parents, back in Rison, Arkansas. They were the living incarnation of the term 'too poor to paint but too proud to whitewash.' Their combination of poverty and pride caused them to have an attitude that the best place to find a helping hand is at the end of your own arm."[4] Karl Eller, chairman of Circle K convenience stores, got his start working in a boarding-house and delivering newspapers at 4:00 A.M. He never stopped working even at college: "I had to foot my own way through college. By that time my mother was living back in Chicago and I'd been sending her all my money from the days in the Army. So I had to support myself through school. I lived at a judge's house and did his lawn so I could earn my room. I ended up getting my board free from the scholarship deal, and all my books and tuition."[5]

The Price of Competence

Talent and potential are free gifts. But developing them requires time, energy, commitment, persistence, and tedious, painstaking, hard work. Most are not willing to pay that much so they never master the skills needed to succeed. Achievers are different. They invest in themselves, make the necessary commitment, and take the time to develop. Because without competence, they'll never make it.

> Competence—to use the language of logic—is not a *necessary and sufficient* cause of high achievement. That is, competence by itself does not always lead to success. There are other very important factors that are essential to high achievement. . . .
>
> But competence probably comes closer than any of the achievement factors as a *necessary* cause. *No one becomes a high achiever without becoming competent at something. . . . But all the high achievers know something well, or they learn to do something well.* [italics added][6]

Competence takes practice. In chapter 6 we learned that high achievers dedicate a minimum of ten years to accumulating knowledge and skills before taking the lead in their field. Even Jack Nicklaus, who played his first golf tournament at age ten, required a decade of practice before competing on the national circuit. At 20 he came in second behind Arnold Palmer in the U.S. Open. Was he simply more talented than his competitors? He thinks not. When Griessman asked him "if there are really talented golfers who never make it," Nicklaus answered: "Oh, hundreds of them. A lot of guys out there are more talented than I am, and through the years we've passed them by many times. You see guys and you say, 'Gosh, how did this guy not make it?' And then it's pretty easy to figure out why he didn't. *He had a lot of talent, but didn't have much dedication, wasn't organized, didn't know how to learn, didn't know how to comprehend what he was doing, didn't try to learn how to get better*" [italics added].[7]

Competence includes specialized knowledge, techniques, procedures, and methods that accomplish tasks effectively and efficiently. It's detailed, precise learning, quite different from general knowledge acquisition. W. Clement Stone, author of *The Success System that Never Fails,* calls it know-how and activity knowledge. Imagine analyzing piano playing through a microscope. You would see that it's more than just reading notes and pressing keys. You would discover that the force of the key press and the length of the key hold affect tone, rhythm, tempo, and amplitude. Pianists master these techniques to produce music. They have know-how and activity knowledge. Most world-class pianists play only the piano. Their expertise is targeted, specialized, and concentrated. This is the nature of competence, and, according to Stone, is why competent people become successful: "It takes less time to achieve success when you concentrate your thought and effort on learning a lot about a little and becoming an expert than when you dissipate your energies by trying to learn a little about a lot."[8]

Stone used this principle to sell insurance: "I learned almost all there was to know about that one policy. And I learned from experience what to say and how to say it—what to do and how to do it—to sell in tremendous volume." He practiced repeatedly, learning by trial and error what worked and what didn't work. "I gained activity knowledge and know-how. . . . In a sense, like a scientist, I learned from trial and error—trial and success. . . . In another sense, like an actor, I could put feeling, emotion, and timing into my memorized talk. . . . I changed the sales talk to meet changing conditions."[9] Jack Nicklaus uses the same approach: "I think the big thing about doing anything is striving to improve every day. I'm learning new shots every day. I worked on a couple of new shots yesterday—ones that I didn't have in my game. I spent about two hours working on a specific shot yesterday that I didn't have. I got it today."[10] Mary Kay Ash says: "Whatever I start out to do, I make it a point to learn everything I can about that. I knew nothing about the cosmetics business. I had no prior knowledge of that when I started this company, but today I think I rank up there with Estee or anybody else as far as cosmetics are concerned. So I would say I am very competent from the standpoint of whatever I undertake."[11]

Charles Schulz, creator of Charlie Brown and Snoopy, knows that other cartoonists draw better than he does, but he believes that he's the expert in the medium.

I don't know how *good* I am at drawing a comic strip, but I think I *know* as much about drawing comic strips, if not more, than anybody else. I think I'm very proud of what I've done, and I think I've created some of the best comic-strip characters that have ever existed. But this does not mean that I'm the best. Nobody is best at anything. That is a foolish, modern thought that there has to be a number one in everything. But I think I really understand the comic-strip medium.[12]

How did these successful people develop their talents? They worked at them. Listen to Andy Rooney: "I'm quite creative. I do not tend toward cliches with words. I have a quick flair for occasional humor. I work quite hard . . . that's one of the things I didn't know about myself until later in life . . . because a lot of things I do, I don't have much ability to stick at and finish properly. *But when it comes to writing, I work hard. I get in here early every morning and I stick at it.*"[13] The same is true for Charles Schulz who begins at 9:00 A.M. every day in his split-level studio where he draws pictures for more than 2,000 newspapers. He produces, corrects, and perfects continuously. James Mitchener, whose "life epitomizes . . . common sense, frugality, hard work and good old-fashioned American virtue, writes every morning from 7:30 to 12:30. 'I sit right here at this typewriter,' he says, demonstrating with two fingers. 'When I'm done with my draft, John reads it. See, everything here in pencil is his. Then I give it to my secretary and she puts it on the word processor. Can't work without it these days.'"[14] Louis L'Amour, author of 101 of the world's most popular westerns, wrote five pages every day, including Sundays and holidays. Science fiction writer Isaac Asimov says that the principal factors responsible for his success are *persistence* and *industry*.

Achievers work at their craft to perfect what they do best. Charles Schulz recommends that you "Just try to draw a good strip every day. You should start doing your great things right away. I think this is the secret in any sort of performing art—not trying to save yourself for the great day when you become famous, but just do the best you can each day."[15]

The Long Trek

Achieving competence is a long journey so it had better be enjoyable. People who complete the trip love their craft. It motivates and focuses. Even during unexpected detours and postponed arrivals achievers continue to build knowledge and skill. As Griessman notes, "Competence involves learning through diligent application until one has stored in memory literally thousands of patterns. And it involves practice—not just repeating mistakes (thereby converting errors into habits), but getting feedback from the best people available."[16]

Veteran Trekkers

W. Clement Stone started his sales career on the streets of Chicago.

> I was six years old and scared. Selling newspapers on Chicago's tough South Side wasn't easy, especially with the older kids taking over the busy corners, yelling louder, and threatening me with clenched fists. The memory of those dim days is still with me, for it's the first time I can recall turning disadvantage into an advantage. . . .
>
> Hoelle's Restaurant was near the corner where I tried to work, and it gave me an idea. It was a busy and prosperous place that presented a frightening aspect to a child of six. I was nervous, but I walked in hurriedly and made a lucky sale at the first table. Then diners at the second and third tables bought papers. When I started for the fourth, however, Mr. Hoelle pushed me out the front door.
>
> But I had sold three papers. So when Mr. Hoelle wasn't looking, I walked back in and called at the fourth table.[17]

By 16, Stone had sold his first insurance policy, and at 20 he established his own agency and created his own national sales organization. Since then he has been president of several insurance companies, editor and publisher of *Success Unlimited,* and director of Alberto-Culver Company. Stone attributes his success to lessons learned as a newspaper boy in Chicago. His *inspiration to action* came from being poor. When he tried and failed to sell papers on the street, he learned *know-how* by selling in the restaurant.

Mary Kay's competency journey also took the rugged route. She married after high school and soon had two children, no money, and no place to live. So she moved into her mother's house and worked seven days a week as a typist to pay the bills. After the third child arrived along with a divorce, Ash took a job as a dealer for Stanley Home Products and tried, unsuccessfully at first, to sell products through home parties. But she kept at it, setting her goal to be crowned "Queen" for selling the most products by the next national convention. She won the award. For the next 13 years, she perfected her sales techniques, and then, with help from her son, she opened her own business with a staff of nine and a single shelf of cosmetics. Now Mary Kay Cosmetics has 150,000 independent beauty consultants throughout the United States, Australia, Canada, West Germany, and Argentina.

Louis L'Amour's journey to success took him across the globe. He worked as longshoreman, lumberjack, elephant handler, fruit picker, and officer on a tank destroyer in World War II. He even spent time as a professional boxer, winning 51 of 59 fights. He circled the world on a freighter, sailed a dhow on the Red Sea, and was shipwrecked in the West Indies. But he never lost sight of his real goal. He wanted to write "almost from the time I could walk."[18] Finally, at age 45, he completed *Hondo,* his first western, and went on to become one of the most prolific and successful writers of our time. He was the first novelist to receive the Congressional Gold Medal, the same award given to Charles Lindbergh, Thomas Edison, and Dr. Jonas Salk.

Ray Charles's journey seemed ill-fated from the start. He grew up in abject poverty, lost both parents and a brother early, and went blind. But he liked music and learned to sing and play piano. By his teens, Ray attracted enough attention and praise to make him think he had "talent." Then when he auditioned for Luck Millinder's band, he was told "Ain't good enough, kid." Ray asked him to repeat. "You heard me. You don't got what it takes." How did Ray react to this rebuff? "It was the best thing that ever happened to me. . . . *After I got over feeling sorry for myself, I went back and started practicing, so nobody would ever say that about me again*" [italics added].[19]

Achievement takes time, effort, and practice, practice, practice. Interviews with superachievers document the prodigious effort required.

> The amount of time that really great performers, whether musicians or athletes, devote to practice is mindboggling. . . . Practice, for writers, means writing and rewriting. Albert Payson Terhune used to say that *an aspiring writer should write one million words and throw them into the wastebasket. Only after a million words is an aspirant qualified to make a beginning in the art of authorship.* The message is that any writer who manages to become successful prior to writing a million words is well ahead of the game. [italics added][20]

Lee Trevino started playing golf after leaving the Marine Corps at 21. His motto is "If there's sunlight, there are golf balls to be hit." Although he had talent, he knew he also needed skills and technique to tap it. So he committed everything to that goal: "I don't think success is very difficult to achieve. I think that when the good Lord puts you on this earth, you are gifted with some type of talent. *The biggest problem is that people are not willing to sacrifice what it takes to achieve their potential in the field they are talented in.*"[21]

Young Trekkers

Nadja Salerno-Sonnenberg, an internationally acclaimed violinist, began her trek at age five. In her autobiography *Nadja: On My Way*, she describes her start. "Mama had a friend who taught violin to beginners, so the violin was stuck under my chin when I was five and that was that." Given a choice, she might have chosen piano because when you "want an A, press down a key and there's A." Getting an "A" from the violin is more difficult. It requires "almost endless practice. But even then, the nightmare's just begun. Making music out of those tones is no spring picnic. For one thing, there are no frets on a violin fingerboard as there are on a guitar. A violinist has to memorize the notes by touch."[22] But Nadja wanted to make music, and was willing to sacrifice to do it:

> No matter how many musical ideas I have, if I didn't spend more than *twenty years* practicing, learning the craft of the violin, all those ideas wouldn't be able to come out.
>
> As a student, from eight to twelve o'clock every morning I did exercises, scales, etudes . . . basic things that train your fingers. It's like outfielders playing catch or taking batting practice. They are the rudiments of playing that warm you up and keep your muscles in shape. [italics added][23]

Unfortunately, technical proficiency is not musicality, the sine qua non of success in that field. You must apply technique to make music. This requires different strategies. Nadja breaks the problem into components:

> You analyze it harmonically, you analyze it melodically. Then you do a technical analysis, analyzing bow patterns, bow speed—everything you do can be analyzed. That's how complicated playing the violin can be.

Basically, you're breaking a complicated piece into fine details. Then, as you perfect each detail, you put it back together as if it were a model airplane.[24]

What's true for violin is true for all competencies. They begin with technique. Next comes analytical problem solving to apply technique to complete important tasks. Musicians like Nadja manipulate their instruments to produce different musical effects. Editorial writers sequence words in grammatically acceptable and understandable sequences for persuasive effects. And scientists master design and measurement techniques to observe significant effects between their variables of study. Competence begins with technique and ends with effects.

For 33-year-old world-famous cello virtuoso Yo-Yo Ma, *musical effect* is "when 1,000 people sit on the edge of their seats and breathe as one."[25] Yo-Yo Ma began his trek at age 4, tutored by his father who was a musicologist and violinist from Shanghai. By age 7 he performed in a Washington, D.C., concert conducted by Leonard Bernstein, and by age 9 he made his debut at Carnegie Hall.

For eight-year-old Bart Scott, *athletic effect* is winning the ten-year-old singles championship in the Colorado State Junior Open. Scott's technical moves that mixed baseline bashing with near-the-net volleying won the match. Now Scott is adding emotional control to his game. Although technically capable of beating players much older, Scott had trouble *applying* technique during championship matches. He loses control. Scott describes his own weakness: "I played better than average today. I never beat anyone 0 and 0. Once, I was about to, but I got real mad and started hitting the ball way too hard. I got pretty happy because I was going to win, and then I started wailing on it, and I missed them all. He got two games."[26] Scott began playing tennis with his father, a teaching pro and high school tennis coach.

Unfortunately, most children don't experience these effects because they have no competence. Some may even feel like young Steven Spielberg who once considered himself a "dork"—incapable of doing anything well. He recalls his ax-sharpening demonstration in front of 500 fellow Scouts. "On the second stroke, I put the blade through my knuckle."[27] Earning the canoe merit badge was a disaster too. Instead of swimming under the canoe and flipping it over his head, "[the canoe] came down on my head. I had to be pulled out of the water." Spielberg confesses that when called on to build a cooking fire, "I dropped my mess kit into the mud. Couldn't get the fire started. I was hungry and also very tired and instead of putting the canned food into a pot, I forgot and put the cans unopened on the fire. They exploded, sending shrapnel in all directions."[28]

But Spielberg was ready for the photography merit badge. He won it with a three-minute epic, "Gunsmog,"—a parody of the then-popular *Gunsmoke,* featuring fellow Scouts, a stagecoach holdup, sheriff, and an outlaw. "He and his actors and his dad and his cliff-hurtling dummy trooped out to the nearby desert, and Spielberg made the movie for about $10 (not counting mileage). He showed it at the following Monday night's troop meeting, and thus was launched a career as teen movie-maker, Hollywood Boy Wonder and, at 41, The Most Successful Movie Director ever."[29] Spielberg had discovered his talent. "I sort of called myself a visual scribe," making movies, showing them to the troop, and then watching "everyone come out of their seats, partly because they were in the picture." He learned what worked, what didn't, and he finally discovered what he liked and what he was good at. "[Making] boyhood movies . . . helped him develop the self-confidence to barge into the movie business as a young man."[30]

Robert Penn Warren also started young. Instead of joining Scouts, he got sick with the flu and his father read poetry to him. Since then, he says, "I've had a very bad flu for the rest of my life. Poetry is an illness." By his early 20s, Warren was an established poet. Later he became the first American writer to receive Pulitzer Prizes for both poetry and fiction. He also received the National Medal for Literature, the National Book Award, and the Presidential Medal of Freedom, and he became the country's first poet laureate. Warren recalls his early start: "Sometimes I found it a lonely life, trying to write. . . . I spent most of my childhood in a lonely way; spending most summers on a remote farm with an aging grandfather was a big asset. He was full of poetry and history. [He was] made for a young boy to talk with."[31]

Nadja Salerno-Sonnenberg, Yo-Yo Ma, Bart Scott, Steven Spielberg, and Robert Penn Warren started trekking *early.* They got a head start on the training time required to achieve excellence. Salerno-Sonnenberg made her debut with the Philadelphia Orchestra at age 10, Yo-Yo Ma made his Carnegie Hall debut at age 9, Bart Scott won the Division Championship for 10-year-olds at age 8, Steven Spielberg landed a 7-year contract with Universal Studios at age 21, and Robert Penn Warren made his mark as a poet in his 20s. They achieved these remarkable results because (1) they discovered what they loved, (2) they pursued it with passion, and (3) they received help.

How Children Become Competent

Today's parents want their children to succeed and many are willing to do what's necessary to help them. The trend began in the mid-1980s when the country rediscovered success. Parenting goals shifted from concern about creative experiences in expressive environments to early achievement in super preschools. Instead of picketing schools for better books and newer classrooms, "[parents drilled] tots with flashcards and [spent] thousands of dollars to put children into private schools to get a leg up on the future. Teens [were fretting] over admission to the right university, and college students [were agonizing] over grades and job interviews."[32]

Programs like Glenn Doman's Better Baby Institute in Philadelphia and his early learning seminars on "Eighty-nine Cardinal Facts for Making Any Baby into a Superb Human Being" were created in response to the new trend. Infants and young children studied flash cards, read words, did math problems, and recited facts. Meanwhile parents afflicted with this "start 'em-as-early-as-possible" syndrome attracted attention. Susan Reed writes: "Recently, a woman called one of the tonier private schools in Chicago requesting a kindergarten application. When asked the child's age, she replied, 'Oh, I don't have any kids yet. But I'm thinking of getting pregnant.'"[33]

Some experts say too much instruction too soon will only produce hurried children "pushed" earlier and earlier to do more and more. But many boomer parents are not convinced. They *believe that's exactly what their children will need to succeed.* And if the future is anything like the past, they may be right. Foreign achiever-countries like Japan, Korea, and West Germany may well jeopardize how much we can guarantee our children. Boomers haven't forgotten what happened to them. They want their children to be ready. The permissive parenting practices of past decades didn't work and public schools don't graduate self-directed achievers. It's time parents took charge and made a difference.

Boomer parents realize that young people must learn to rely on themselves to get what they want in life, that there are no guarantees like those promised in the 1950s. So why not give them a head start—an early start? Child development experts can say all they want about "pushy" parents. The fact is that today's youth need more than what they've received. Decades of declining youth achievement should be sufficient evidence that we can do better. Furthermore, where *is* the *evidence* that early intervention doesn't work?

In *The Too Precious Child*, Williams, Berman, and Rose describe parents "who are more than just 'concerned' about their [children's] psychological needs; these parents are possessed by a vision, often a very competitive one, of doing everything perfectly, following an ideal sequence of steps that will lead to a 'successful' child."[34] Williams, Berman, and Rose claim that "The more you care about your children and the more you may worry about their lives and futures, the greater may be your temptation to overprotect or to push them into too early acquisition of skills."[35] According to these experts, "good" parenting is a balance between "too much" of this and "too little" of that. But isn't this another "Catch-22"? If we overinvolve ourselves with our children we risk the too-precious child syndrome and if we underinvolve we get declining achievement. There must be a third option. And there is. A few parents still manage to raise talented, intelligent, and persistent achievers. Whether by design or fortuitous circumstance, they combine the right mixture of leadership, mentorship, and friendship to maximize their children's potential. Their emphasis on hard work and achievement actually *increases* their children's mental health.

Performing tasks well makes children feel good about themselves. It builds confidence and self-esteem, which in turn reinforce motivation to achieve. The process and outcome become intrinsically reinforcing. These effects are independent of native intelligence but not independent of family influence. Some families consistently raise successful children. The reason is family culture.

The Power of Family Culture

I saw family culture at work as a freshman in college. I had two roommates, John from my hometown, Spokane, Washington, and Steven from Waterbury, Connecticut. John's brother also attended Dartmouth and Steven's brother went to Harvard. Their fathers were Dartmouth alumni. Later, John earned a graduate degree in business from Stanford and Steve received a medical degree from Harvard. My other Dartmouth classmates had similar backgrounds, with brothers, sisters, and parents all graduating from prestigious schools. Their values and aspirations matched the family's success profile.

The family influence I noticed was not the result of "pulling strings" to make things easier. That couldn't explain the success of my classmates. No, John and Steve were at Dartmouth because of *ability*. I was convinced of that. I lived with them, observed them, and respected them. They were talented *and* hard working. I always thought that what I lacked in intelligence I could make up for with hard work. Well, most of the time that was true. But at Dartmouth many of my classmates were willing and able to work just as hard, and sometimes harder.

Family culture includes *values, expectations,* and *behaviors* that each member lives by in order to adapt. Our *values* are what we like and want, and our *expectations* indicate our feelings about the probability of getting what we like and want. When I *expect* a new car by next year what I really mean is that I feel good about the probability of getting a car by then. Parents who *expect* their children to do well in school have positive feelings about those outcomes. When they communicate their feelings their children usually try to oblige those expectations. Expectations are equally powerful in school. Research on effective practice consistently finds that teachers who expect high achievement beget high achievers, while teachers who expect low achievement beget low achievers. It's a frightening self-fulfilling proposition that negative expectations are as powerful as positive ones.

Behavior patterns are the repetitive ways family members respond to different problems. Some families interact adaptively to resolve difficulties and meet family goals. Others are maladaptive;

they compete and fight with each other and become mutually destructive. Their behavior patterns add to the family's problems.

Achievement-oriented families value "doing one's best," "striving for excellence," and "trying harder next time." Competition-oriented families teach children to "always be the best," "do anything to win," "be first," and "be number one." Altruistic families encourage children to "help people who are less fortunate," "be considerate of others," and "cooperate and share." In his book *Raising Your Child to Be a Mensch*, Neil Kurshan argues for raising such children.[36]

The point I wish to make is that all families are intergenerational transmitters of the adaptive code. Whether they know it or not, they communicate or fail to communicate the how-to's of getting what one wants and needs in life. Some codes produce unintended dependence, personal maladjustments, and social deviance. Parents on welfare transmit attitudes of helplessness; parents who are alcoholic, drug addicted, and physically abusive pass on codependency; and parents with histories of crime teach their offspring how to survive by exploiting others. Dependence begets dependence, addiction begets addiction, and crime begets more crime. Today's social problems are intractable because they reflect these powerful forces.

Adaptive cultures perpetuate themselves too. Think of the millions of immigrants who have come and continue to come to this country with nothing. A few generations later, some of their descendants are on top. Today, the "Asian invasion" illustrates the process, as New York high school math teacher Frank Halloran notes: "I don't know why. But I do know that most of our Asian students see homework and school as their job . . . *For most of our Asian kids, who (it's true) come from achiever families—executives with Hitachi and so on—school is their job number one. They are not nearly as distracted by all of the other things as our native kids.*" [italics added][37] What's happened to the American family's achievement culture? Was it lost when both parents started working? Or have parents simply replaced "earn-get" achievement principles with "want-get" indulgence? Teachers want to know, if parents don't: "Many teachers feel that today's children have higher and higher expectations but are willing to exert less and less effort: kids expect to be rewarded with high grades and lavish careers, but they do not want to work for them. There is a tendency to believe that 'thinking makes it so,' or 'I tried, and therefore I should be rewarded.'"[38]

Not all American families have lost the will to achieve. Some still pass on traditions of excellence. They perpetuate their brand of achievement in spite of declines throughout the rest of the country. Such families are so unusual by today's standards that *U.S. News & World Report* featured some of them in "Amazing Families: Why Gifted Parents Produce Gifted Children."

> [T]he Barianos family of Rockville, MD . . . preserved their skills as master craftsmen from the Greek island of Rhodes for four generations, and [restored] marble columns, mosaic floors and gold-leaf ceilings [that] adorn nearly every monumental building in the nation's capital from the Washington Cathedral to the White House. "Our family's understanding of this trade is part of a treasury," says John, 54, who runs the family business today with his 30-year-old son, Vasilios. *"We receive the gold; we protect it, and we give it to our children."* [italics added][39]

Obviously, Vasilios understands intergenerational transmission. "We receive the gold, we protect it, and we give it to our children." And the "gold" he's talking about is not money, VCRs, color televisions, designer clothes, sports cars, or ski vacations. It's values, expectations, skills, behavior patterns, know-how, activity knowledge, specialized knowledge, and everything else necessary to succeed at the profession. Each generation inherits it, adds to it, and bequeaths it.

Pulitzer Prize–winner Russel Crouse, coauthor of such hit plays as *Life with Father* and *Arsenic and Old Lace,* has a daughter, Lindsay Ann Crouse, who starred in the film *House of Games,* and a son, Tim, who staged his original script for *Anything Goes* on Broadway. Russel transmitted the "gold" in special ways.

> [Tim] remembers the word games their father played with him as a child in the Upper East Side townhouse. A dinner-table sport was "Pick the Lead," with Russel, a former sportswriter, telling jumbled stories over the evening meal, then challenging Tim to state the most important point. Neighborhood strolls often ended with father asking son to describe the shoes and neckties of friends they had just seen on the street. Years later, the quizzes paid off. Tim became first a reporter and then, at 25, the author of *Boys on the Bus,* a bestselling book on press coverage of the 1972 presidential campaign.[40]

Rick Rominger and his brothers, Charlie and Bruce, follow traditions started by their grandfather in the 1930s. Rick, a former high school valedictorian, college honor student, and accomplished athlete, works with his brothers on 6,000 fertile acres 80 miles north of San Francisco.

> The Rominger grandchildren learned early that work was the source of life's greatest pleasures. . . . At the age of 9, they were gathering walnuts and picking honeydews, corn and figs. As teenagers, they put in full days on harvesters and plows.
> . . . Success of the family is itself the Romingers' ambition. "Our goal in life is not to go out and make a lot of money, to see how big a house or fancy a car we can have," says Rick. "It's just to be farmers, to work and to be with our family."[41]

Lee Petty began stock-car racing in the 1940s, and by 1954 won a national championship. His son, Richard, joined him on the circuit while other boys in Randolph County milked cows and plowed fields. Says Richard: "I don't guess I ever thought about doing anything else." With his father's support, he won 200 races, 7 NASCAR championships, and the title "King Richard." Twenty years later, Kyle, Richard's 19-year-old son, took over. "When I was 9 years old, if he [Richard] could hit a 50-foot jump shot, then I got out and practiced until I could hit it, too. I thought that if I could beat him at what he was doing then I'm going to be pretty good at it." The Pettys transfer the "gold" by immersing the family in racing and intergenerational competitions. Says Richard's wife Lynda, "At meals, they talk about the cars. And after a race, they talk about what happened all the way home."[42]

The Power of Achievement Parenting

Some parents still pass on excellence to their children, in spite of 40 years of television, fractured family structures, and declining youth achievement. They do it by giving children opportunities to learn *what they have to teach.* Russel Crouse entertained associates like Irving Berlin, Richard Rodgers and Oscar Hammerstein, Ethel Merman, and Edna Ferber, yet still had time to transfer the "gold." Grandpa Albert Rominger transferred golden California farmland to Rick, Charlie, and Bruce. Lee Petty passed on stock-car racing to his son Richard who, in turn, gave it to his son Kyle. How did they do it? They led, they mentored, and they befriended.

Leadership

Parents lead by demonstrating values, communicating expectations, and providing opportunities. They *demonstrate* with achievement-oriented actions and behaviors. They *set expectations* by announcing what they hope to achieve, what they hope their children will accomplish, and how they expect their children to behave. And they *provide opportunities* for themselves and their children by seeking new opportunities for the family, moving to new cities, buying houses in good school districts, finding good teachers, taking children to lessons, and helping with assignments, projects, and hobbies.

My parents were leaders though they never thought of themselves as such. They both worked. When I was young, my father had two jobs, his regular 8:00 to 5:00 job as an accountant and an evening bookkeeping job. By the time I was eight, my mother worked too. She started her own retail clothing store, unusual in 1950 when most mothers stayed home. My sister and I became "latch key kids." We loved it. We had the house to ourselves, although the neighbors watched and reported any suspicious activity. Nothing went unnoticed. Daily telephone chats with mom kept us in line. Later, we learned that her customers watched us too. We thought we were "on our own" but we weren't quite.

It didn't matter much because by then we were well along on our competency trek. We had been taking tap dancing since 1945 and had just started piano. Expectations were always in effect. Our parents insisted on *practice first*. If we didn't practice, we didn't get to take lessons. We were to work, improve, and do our best. It was a simple, understandable, and irrevocable policy. My father always said "Do the best with what you have." He told us repeatedly: "I don't care what you decide to do when you grow up. Just be the best you can be." We performed publicly almost as soon as we started lessons. We were available for any group in need of after-dinner entertainment. So we had ample opportunity to check our progress. If we made mistakes, no problem. We practiced harder and tried to do better next time. We were our only competition.

At first, I thought all children grew up the same way. But a few years in school changed that view. Hardly any did. Since then I've learned that these childhood experiences were not entirely unique. In *Developing Talent in Young People* Benjamin Bloom describes how other parents stumbled onto the same approach as my parents. Consider Kathryn Sloane's analysis of the values expressed by the families of these talented youngsters: "The parents organized their time and established priorities as a means of pursuing a variety of activities while expressing the belief that *'if it's worth doing, it's worth doing well.' Work was completed before play.* Wasting time or idling away the hours was cause for disapproval in these homes, as was doing a sloppy job or shirking responsibilities."[43]

In *Vivian Ayers-Allen: On Raising Creative Kids,* Ms. Ayers-Allen describes how she raised her three children: Phylicia Allen, who plays the lawyer-mother on *The Bill Cosby Show,* Debbie, an award-winning dancer and choreographer, Tex, who has his own jazz band, and Hugh, who just received an M.B.A. from Duke University. "I didn't whip or lock them into closets. *I tried to marry them into a reward system—if you do this, you get this. And I had them highly programmed, with no time for incidents.* Our struggles were in pulling together and feeling a sense of abundance in the face of scarcity" [italics added].[44]

Mentorship

But leadership alone is insufficient to build competence. Children also need instruction. I vaguely recall the first dance lessons my sister and I took. We were in a class with other children. The teacher stood with her back to us demonstrating steps that we tried to copy. My sister picked them up right away. I didn't because I was usually looking somewhere else. That's the trouble with learning to dance: you have to observe the teacher carefully, remember the moves, and then repeat them on your own. If you miss the demonstration, fail to remember it, or stumble in its execution, you're lost. I got lost a lot. So, I watched my sister instead of the teacher. My mother saw what was happening and decided we were too young to learn in large groups. So she arranged for us to take private lessons. That was better. If I didn't understand, I got another chance.

Still, I had to memorize the movements quickly in order to repeat them after the demonstration. Learning dance is not like learning piano, where you can return to the music if you forget. Opportunity to learn begins and ends with what you see and remember. During those early lessons mother was my teacher. She knew I wouldn't learn much on my own so she learned the steps herself and then practiced them with me at home until I learned them. I can still remember her favorite phrase: "Just one more time, then you can play." It always worked too, even though I knew she would repeat it again and again and again. There was always "Just one more time."

For many years she supervised us and helped us practice, setting up the schedule, specifying the amount of time expected, and, when necessary, helping us learn. She taught us to "overlearn" routines before performances. This was our hedge against jitters. Other parents report similar stories, as Kathryn Sloane notes:

> The parents learned that to advance in a talent field, daily practice was important and not to be neglected. In sports, practice at the swimming pool or tennis court was scheduled and supervised by the coach. The parents arranged the family's routine to conform to this schedule. . . . When practice was in the home (especially in music), the parents helped the child schedule and plan practice time. They scheduled a regular time and made sure other family activities did not interfere.[45]

We never had a choice about practicing. It was a "nonnegotiable" activity like brushing our teeth, cleaning our bedrooms, and doing chores—part of the routine of growing up. We were too young to argue anyway, so we accepted it. In retrospect, I realize we learned more than dance and music. We developed discipline for hard work. Concentrating at school, completing homework on time, and getting good grades was just an extension of our parents' basic expectation: "Do your best." By then, no one nagged. We knew how to work and wanted to achieve.

During their early years children need instruction and intervention from their "adjunct teachers" at home. Says one mother of a tennis player, "We sat there . . . while he took a lesson, so we learned as well as he did, and then you know what to look for." A parent of a swimmer recalled that "I think I learned everything I know about it from [my child's first coach]. . . . I just remember all the instruction—how to hold your head, how to put your arms in the water, your kick, your breathing."[46]

Later parents shift roles, focusing more on reinforcing work habits, monitoring progress, and advising about what to adjust. Our mother monitored progress closely. When the hometown teacher no longer challenged us, she found another in a town 50 miles away. She made sure that instruction maximized our potential. One young pianist recalls his father's role in his success: "I got to the point (about age eleven or twelve) where I wasn't making any progress at all, and my father felt that if he's going to be paying for the lessons, even if it's not going to go anywhere, I've got to be doing better than I was doing. I needed somebody to teach me how to practice, for example. [So my father found a new teacher]."[47]

Friendship

When we started lessons we never thought about the work and dedication it would require or the thousands of hours of instruction it would involve. From the beginning, the opportunity to perform in front of people was positive. As we progressed, we received abundant rewards for our work. Performing for local groups and organizations, we were rewarded with applause, accolades, and attention. At family reunions, our relatives asked us to perform. Even cousins treated us special. We entered talent shows, which were popular then, winning trophies, ribbons, and certificates. The results were reported in newspapers and spread our "reputation" around town. At school, teachers expected us to do well and we usually did. The positive achievement cycle accelerated. By the mid-1950s, we were featured regularly on a local TV talent show, winning our share of the competitions. In high school some friends and teachers even became "fans." The psychological effects were more significant than any actual talent we had. Our confidence increased as did our desire to achieve. Soon we believed we could excel at anything. And this perpetuated the cycle. In high school, my sister became head cheerleader and prom queen (several times), and I was elected student body president—all directly attributable to that early start.

My point is that children with competence experience tangible benefits that more than outweigh early sacrifices. These rewards add to the support they regularly receive from parents, teachers, and coaches.

> The children learned to feel special in their homes, at first. But soon their sense of being special was reinforced by responses from people outside their homes. Many of the pianists reported being told by their teachers that "I was her favorite student" or "I was his best pupil."
> . . . The children were invited to play at elementary school assemblies. They earned distinction among schoolmates.[48]

Peer support for talent is a powerful reinforcer. I've seen it work hundreds of times. It's not just limited to talent shows either. "As the youngsters' art interests became more widely known, they were identified as 'the class artist' . . . or 'the artist of the family' . . . They were referred to as 'Rembrandt II' or 'poet and artist' in the school yearbook. The power of the special label seems enormous."[49]

> "I had a special thing I could do" . . . we heard again and again. "Art was the one thing I could do and [my sister] couldn't" . . . "When I found I could draw really well, nobody could beat me in that, . . . I really pursued that" . . .
> The parents of one of the sculptors gave their child private lessons expressly because they wanted him to be able to feel the power of being able to do something that his brother could not do.[50]

Friendship means sharing in the child's abilities and accomplishments. It begins in the family and spreads to the classroom, the school, and eventually the community. As recognition and appreciation develop, children understand the significance of what they can do now as well as their potential for the future. Their talent has a purpose, a justification for those years of sacrifice and hard work.

"Giving the Gold"

My wife and I transferred the "gold" to our four children. Our purpose was not to establish specific career paths or to prepare them for elite, private schools. This was not the "gold." We wanted to establish a sense of achievement and confidence that comes from doing something well. The tasks and talent areas we chose matched our interests and abilities because we knew we could help them most in those areas. At age three, each child started piano, accordion, and dance for a few minutes a day, pressing a few keys in sequence, learning a "shuffle step," and pointing a toe. Practices were short and enjoyable and within a few months the child could play melodies and perform simple routines independently. By age 5 the child took lessons with teachers while we practiced with him or her at home. The benefits for their work came early too. At family events they showed what they could do, which generated much recognition and attention. There were regular recitals. This was fun too, but a bit more demanding. They went fully prepared. Afterward, regardless of how well they played, we were happy because they had done their best. We wanted them to enjoy performing, not fear it. So all performances ended positively, with a stop for ice cream afterward. The approach was simple and consistent. Go to lessons, practice for perfection, perform as well as possible, and then enjoy the results: applause, attention, congratulations, and, of course, ice cream.

We shifted roles routinely from leader to teacher to friend. During performances we were their friends, sharing the excitement and satisfaction of the performance. But during daily practice and weekly lessons, we were leaders and teachers. And the cycle repeated. They learned new material at lessons, practiced rigorously during the week, and then performed for special events. Although it was fun, it was also hard work. Cathy and I didn't always like driving to lessons and monitoring practice schedules. And the children didn't always feel like concentrating, working, and learning. Sometimes it was a drag, for everyone. But we knew the total effort was important, the price we paid for giving and receiving the "gold."

By high school, our children knew they were special. They didn't need us to tell them, to build up their self-esteem artificially. They didn't expect our constant praise. *Their confidence was based upon a decade of personal achievement,* involving hundreds of performances, wins, losses, and comebacks. Their performance booty—trophies, ribbons, certificates, and plaques—reminded them of the good times, when everything fell their way. They understood the risks too. Things did not always turn out well. Hard work and excellence are *necessary* but not always sufficient to succeed. Sometimes you lose even with your best effort. But veteran achievers return again and again, and by high school our children were veterans.

Recently, my wife and I attended an annual talent program at the high school. The announcer introduced our youngest child, Dustin, reminding the audience of the eight-year span of Mithaug performers. Dustin extended the tradition. He also inherited a "reputational advantage" because he followed his brother and sisters. He felt pressure to perform well too. And when he did, he suddenly appeared more talented and capable than he actually was. He became more confident, set higher expectations, and invested more time and energy into his pursuits. The positive success cycle accelerated. Studies of young talent call this process "accumulating advantage." Lauren Sosniak describes how the positive cycle begins and then accelerates with input from parents and teachers:

> Feelings of specialness and competence seem to play significant roles not only in keeping the youngster at the piano but also in ensuring optimal instruction and further opportunities in the process of learning. It seems that the more special and accomplished the pianists felt themselves to be, the more willing they were (often even eager) to invest time and emotional commitment in musical activities. Similarly, the more special the parents and teachers thought the child to be, the greater their investments toward the students' eventual accomplishments.[51]

Clearly, the first success is the most difficult. The energy, industry, and tenacity required to practice hours each day year after year are too much for most young people. But each succeeding success demands less. Our children didn't stop with music and dance. In high school they achieved in theater, yearbook editorship, debates, cross country and track, writing, and science fair. This list makes them sound like they're gifted but I assure you they're not. They mastered a few competencies early which gave them strong starts on mastering other competencies later.

Figure 9 illustrates what I mean. Learning a new competency is like climbing a mountain. It's slow, tedious, and difficult on the way to mastery at the top, but from there performance proficiencies accelerate and learning takes less effort and discipline. The downhill

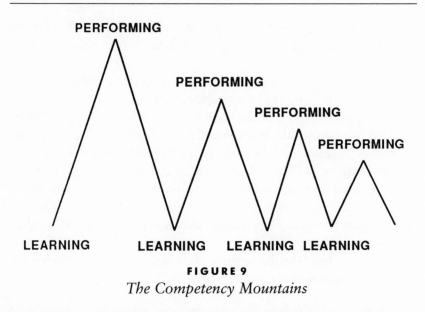

PERFORMING

PERFORMING

PERFORMING

PERFORMING

LEARNING   LEARNING   LEARNING   LEARNING

FIGURE 9
The Competency Mountains

trek gathers momentum and accumulates rewards. The next competency is less difficult and the trek shorter. Some trekkers get on a roll building skills, confidence, and self-esteem at incredible rates. Achievement reinforces achievement, confidence builds confidence, and self-worth adds to self-worth. Self-actualization seems like it's but one trek away.

Intelligence

Competence is necessary *but not sufficient* to succeed. The world is full of competent, knowledgeable, and talented people who fail to reach their goals. Each year, colleges and universities graduate thousands with degrees to certify their achievements. Does this guarantee success? No. Even graduate work may lead nowhere. To be successful, you must *use* your talents to get what you want from environments you like. Achievers act intelligently *by matching their talents with environmental demands*. They accomplish this in three steps. *First,* they set goals commensurate with their strengths and weaknesses. *Second,* they find environments that value what they have to offer. And *third,* they *adapt* by responding to environmental demands *in return* for the opportunity to accomplish their goals. They strike a deal with the environment, an exchange that maximizes returns at both ends.

In *The Triarchic Mind: A New Theory of Human Intelligence,* Robert Sternberg says that "Intelligence involves the ability to adapt to one's environment. . . . [It is the] purposive adaptation to, selection of, and shaping of real-world environments relevant to one's life and abilities."[1] In *Frames of Mind: The Theory of Multiple Intelligences,* Howard Gardner notes that intelligent adaptation involves *profitable exchanges* with the environment: "An intelligence is the ability to solve problems, or to create products, that are valued within one or more cultural settings."[2] And in *Law of Success,* Napoleon Hill reminds us that "Success in life, no matter what one may call success, is very largely a matter of *adaptation to environ-*

*ments in such a manner that there is harmony between the individ-
ual and his environment"* [italics added].[3]

Intelligent Self-Management

Imagine yourself a budding pianist who started early, practiced diligently, competed successfully. Now it's time to choose a career. You
review your options, consider other talent areas, but always return
to piano. There's nothing you like more or can do better. So you
decide to continue. You apply to the best schools, audition, get accepted, and make your choice. You'll attend Juilliard, get a degree,
and become a concert pianist. Everything is set: New York, competitions, concerts, fame, fortune. Finally, the hard work will pay
off. Right? Well . . . maybe.

Again, no guarantees. Your talent may not be enough. Why? Because important *nonmusical skills* are also necessary to succeed in
the music community. You must meet those demands too. You'll
need help from music colleagues, professors, competition judges,
critics, concert promoters, symphony advertisers, patrons, orchestra
conductors, agents, recording studio executives, concert goers, and,
of course, the listening public who buy records, cassettes, and CDs.
These people decide your future. If they think you have talent, want
to help, *and* enjoy your music, you have a chance.

This is the other side of the success formula, the one that *builds
a match* between what you can offer and what the environment will
pay. It requires more than playing well and winning a competition,
as virtuoso violinist Nadja Salerno-Sonnenberg explains:

> So time learning an instrument isn't the only factor in the business of
> music. . . . *If you have that talent, and you have determination to
> succeed, you're more than halfway to the goal.* . . .
>
> Competitions are one way of testing appreciation. If you win, you
> get a lot of recognition overnight. But a competition will only give
> you initial debuts in various cities. Winning a competition, and initial
> debuts, do not mean success. You have one chance in a city. If they
> like you, they'll rebook you. That's business. And it's the rebookings,
> reengagements, that mean a career. [italics added][4]

Intelligent competency management requires *passion, direction,
organization, action,* and *reaction.* People who manage their skills

intelligently begin with an energy source I call "passion." It's the internal motivation that drives achievers to act and react, again and again until they accomplish what they set out to do. The second component of competency management is *direction*. Intelligent self-managers focus their passion on goals and objectives that are compatible with their needs. They don't waste time on activities that are counterproductive or that distract them from what they need and want. The third component is *organization*, the effective and efficient allocation of time and resources to important goals. Achievers "have their acts together." They set priorities, schedule tasks to complete each day, and then follow through.

The fourth component is *action*. Passion, direction, and organization are worthless unless you act and act competently. The performance must get the job done, complete the task, or accomplish the objective. In school, students meet teacher standards; on the job, workers meet supervisors' expectations. But in mental self-management, *you meet your own standards*. You're no longer content with pleasing others. You want to please yourself instead, comparing what *you accomplished* with what *you expected to accomplish*. Mental self-managers monitor their behaviors and results continuously to keep themselves informed about the effectiveness of their performance.

The fifth component is *reaction* to positive and negative feedback. What happens when your actions don't meet expectations? Do you blame others, make excuses, and avoid the truth? Or do you analyze the situation, identify possible causes for failure, and correct your actions? Effective mental self-managers react adaptively to positive and negative feedback. When results meet expectations, they continue doing what worked; when results fall short, they consider alternatives. They analyze causes, propose solutions, and they try them out one at a time to find out what works best. They react by adjusting goals, objectives, plans, and actions repeatedly over time. Their route to succeeding is a series of successive approximations to what they want to achieve.

Successful people have all five of these self-management characteristics. Their passion for achieving their goals is exceptional. On the surface they look like everyone else but underneath they possess fire, drive, ambition, and a seemingly boundless supply of energy and optimism to achieve what attracts their interest. This is a major reason for their success. Children with passion are easy to spot because they pursue tasks and activities with unusual interest, concentration, and commitment. Sometimes this alone accounts for why they succeed and their brothers and sisters who have more talent and ability do not. Sloane observed this pattern too:

> The child who "made it" was not always the one who was considered the most "talented." Many parents described another one of their children as having more "natural ability." The characteristics that distinguished the high achiever in the field from his or her siblings, most parents said, was a willingness to work and a desire to excel. *Persistence, competitiveness,* and *eagerness* were other often-used terms.[5]

Passion

When I ask my children what they like, what they can do, and what they want to do, they can answer me without hesitation. They've thought about it before. Years of developing their competencies, trying them out, modifying them, and discovering their benefits have transformed their emotional and psychological needs structure. They're no longer happy doing just anything. They feel compelled to express what they do best. Their long track record on the achievement trail has been sufficiently rewarding to convert "likes" into "passions." They're addicted to maximizing their potential. They have what W. Clement Stone calls "inspiration to action."[6] Passion yoked to need equals *internal motivation.*

Harvard psychologist David McClelland and his team of behavioral scientists have identified what they call "achievement motivation." They test and train people who are motivationally deficient. One of the tests for achievement motivation asks participants to choose the distance from which they will toss a rope ring over a spike. Some nonachievers choose distances so close that they can place the ring every time while others stand so far away that they never throw a ringer. People in these two groups lose interest and quit early because the task is either too easy or too difficult. Achievers, on the other hand, stand far enough away to make the task challenging. *They stick with the task.* They're hooked on "accomplishment feedback," which is satisfaction for receiving a continuous stream of short-term successes.[7]

Children develop internal motivation the same way. They accomplish small tasks first, enjoying immediate rewards for achieving modest goals. Over time, repetitive accomplishments add to their motivation and desire to achieve. By the time they ask themselves "what do I like," "what can I do," and "what do I want," they have answers.

Successful people *use* their passion to propel themselves forward and to sustain their commitment to long-distance treks. Passion grows with need—the greater the need the greater the passion. Conversely, the greater the unmet need, the greater the passion to reduce it. W. Clement Stone calls this "inspirational dissatisfaction." "All the world's progress in every field of activity has been the result of action by men and women who experienced *inspirational dissatisfaction*—never by those who were satisfied. For dissatisfaction is man's driving force."[8] Listen to Eugene Griessman, author of *The Achievement Factors:*

> At the personal level, powerful motivation by itself does not always lead to high achievement. *But, when combined with even modest ability, the results are often astonishing.*
>
> Paul "Bear" Bryant once told me, "I'm a poor coach of great players. I'm a good coach, I think of that ordinary guy. . . . People that win the most are the people who can recognize those players who are not winners but don't know it. The walls of my office are loaded down with championship pictures of people who didn't have the ability to win, but didn't know it" [italics added].[9]

Direction

When passion finds purpose, the effects are awesome. But channeling that energy requires self-knowledge. What do you like and what can you do? If you can answer these questions you can decide what you want to do. You can set your life's mission. English author Edward G. Bulwer-Lytton wrote: *"The man who succeeds above his fellows is the one who early in life clearly discerns his object and toward that object habitually directs his powers"* [italics added].[10] Would you have your children grow unconsciously into genius? Attorney John Foster says that "One of the strongest characteristics of genius is the power of lighting its own fire."[11]

Passionate achievers harness interest and ability in pursuit of goals. They seek *harmony* between feelings, thoughts, behaviors, and their environments. Children who find themselves early have time to develop the talents and interests they most enjoy. They can practice, test, and refine their prowess for years before setting out on their own. By adulthood they've mastered the fundamentals. Their self-awareness, self-direction, self-confidence, and self-esteem set them apart. And all of this because they started early. Griessman's interviews with high achievers confirmed this advantage:

> There are advantages for the individual who makes an early choice and stays with that choice. Those individuals who learn the vocabulary of a field can use it throughout their careers, adding knowledge as their chosen field develops and changes. . . .
>
> *Most of the high achievers I interviewed were well on their way in their chosen careers by their thirties, many by their twenties, and a surprising number had begun to make a mark in their teenage years.* [italics added][12]

Aaron Copland discovered music standing beside the piano listening to his brother and sister play piano-violin duets. Later he announced to his father, who owned a department store, that he intended to compose concert music. Grammy Award–winner Emmylou Harris sang country music on the side, while pursuing a career in acting. When she examined what she really wanted to do, she discovered that "The love that made me want to go that extra step beyond was music." Helen Gurley Brown, editor of *Cosmopolitan,* took longer to find her path. At 31, with 17 secretarial jobs under her belt, Brown found she had a "feel" for what people wanted to read. She had discovered her niche. "I am still uneducated and not a heavy thinker. . . . It's such a small talent, really, 'feeling' one's way through a piece of writing, but it began when I was young. That specialty—feeling—isn't much, is it? But it was enough."[13]

Vincent Van Gogh was exposed to art as a child by visiting his favorite uncle who owned a chain of art stores in Europe. He didn't discover his talent for painting until he was 26, after failing as a lay preacher because he was a poor public speaker. Four years later, he wrote his brother: "In my opinion, I am often rich as Croesus—not in money, but (though it doesn't happen every day) rich—because I have found in my work something which I can devote myself to heart and soul, and which inspires me and gives a meaning to life."[14]

Isaac Asimov earned a doctorate in chemistry from Columbia University and planned a career in teaching and research until he discovered that writing science fiction was more fun. At 37 his department issued an ultimatum: no more science fiction writing on university time. So he took a leave without pay that lasted three decades. Since then he's published 364 books, and now writes a book a month. He discovered his niche: "As a researcher, I can do a creditable job, but I am merely adequate—no more. As a science writer, on the other hand, I am one of the best in the world, and I intend to become *the best*."[15]

It's not easy finding that niche: what you like, what you can do, and what you want to do. Figure 10 illustrates what's involved. The three circles represent activities you like, can do, and want to pursue. Note that only the shaded segment is common to all three. That's your compatibility zone: the heart of natural inclination and seat of latent passion. Note the large areas of likes and abilities that don't intersect. "I like more than I'm good at," and conversely, "I'm good at more than I like." Van Gogh and Asimov chose activities

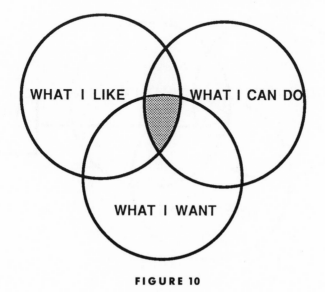

FIGURE 10

they liked but weren't good at. Van Gogh was a terrible public speaker and Asimov was a mediocre researcher. Brown and Harris made opposite errors by choosing activities they were good at but did not like. Brown was tired of secretarial work and Harris was not passionate about acting. Few of us are like Aaron Copland who announced what he wanted to do as a child and then proceeded to fulfill that destiny. At age 44, he won the Pulitzer Prize for musical composition.

Figure 11 illustrates the connection between a goal and the compatibility zone. *This is what maximizes motivation to achieve.* Claude Bristol, author of *The Magic of Believing,* says "If you have definitely determined what you want and have fixed a goal for yourself, then consider yourself extremely fortunate, for you have taken the first step that will lead to success."[16] W. Clement Stone says: "All personal achievement starts in the mind of the individual. Your personal achievement starts in your mind. *The first step is to know exactly what your problem, goal, or desire is.* If you're not clear about this, then write it down, and rewrite it until the words express precisely what you are after" [italics added].[17]

The first step in Norman Vincent Peale's "Eight Steps to a New Life" is to "*Pinpoint your primary goal in life.* It's not enough to

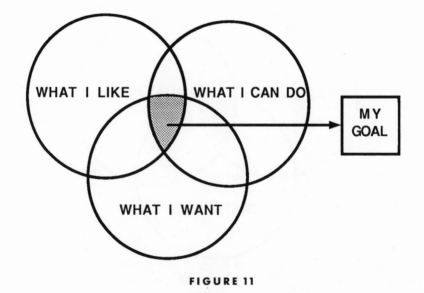

FIGURE 11

say, 'I want to be happy' or 'I want to make money' or 'I want to be a better person.' You must determine *exactly* what you want, and when. You need to say, 'I intend to be a registered nurse in three years,' or sales manager of this company . . . in four, five, or six years."[18]

Over half a century ago Napoleon Hill studied the careers of more than 16,000 men and women in an attempt to evaluate their success and determine factors that were responsible for it. He discovered "that ninety-five per cent of all who were analyzed were failures, and but five per cent were successes. (By the term 'failure' is meant that they had failed to find happiness and the ordinary necessities of life without struggle that was almost unbearable.)" When he investigated reasons for those differences, he discovered that "the ninety-five per cent who were classed as failures were in that class *because they had no definite chief aim in life,* while the five per cent constituting the successful ones not only had purposes that were definite, but they had also *definite plans* for the attainment of their purposes." Hill also discovered an important relationship between job satisfaction and success: *"the ninety-five per cent constituting the failures were engaged in work which they did not like, while the five per cent constituting the successful ones were doing that which they liked best"* [italics added].[19]

Organization

Intelligent self-managers use five strategies to maximize effectiveness. *First,* they establish priorities to guide their behavior. *Second,* they identify environmental demands they must meet to get what they want. *Third,* they make plans to meet those demands. *Fourth,* they maximize their strengths and minimize their weaknesses. And *fifth,* they act and react with confidence.

PRIORITIES. Our most important resources are time and energy. Organized effectively and expended intelligently, they maximize results. Successful people eliminate time spent on dead-end activities. They have goals and know how to "hold a point"—a term used by Clifford W. Rackley, former president of Tenneco Oil Company. Like good hunting dogs who hold their position (the point) until the bird flies, successful people demonstrate constancy of purpose, always keeping sight of their objective regardless of the confusion and distraction that surrounds them.[20] In *Having It All,* Helen Gurley Brown says that the number-one secret to success is *priorities.*[21] Time management experts agree. In *Working Smart,* Michael LeBoeuf says that the first step to significant accomplishment is to specify what is most important to accomplish each day.[22] Griessman's interviews with top achievers validated this advice: "When we say that high achievers have priorities, we mean that they have rank-ordered their goals—they have decided to give more emphasis to some goals, less emphasis to others."[23]

DEMANDS. The second step in self-organization is to know your environment. What does it demand? What will it require to meet your goal? No one gets something for nothing, a stunning discovery for youth expecting the world to give as noncontingently as mom and dad do. All environments drive hard, nothing-for-nothing bargains. Mike Hernacki, author of *The Ultimate Secret to Getting Absolutely Everything You Want* says that "In order to accomplish something, you must be willing to do whatever it takes to accomplish it."[24]

Next, determine the exchange rate. Exactly what does the environment want for you to achieve your goal? Are you willing and able to pay the price? Dr. Robert Anthony explains:

> Positive self-motivation begins with changing your awareness. To make a constructive change in your life, you must evaluate the potential benefits for any given action. Then *you must convince yourself that the benefits will justify or outweigh the price you have to pay for them.* Others may inspire or even threaten you to make such a change, but it is YOU who must motivate yourself by means of "profit and loss" comparison. To some degree, you have been doing this all your life only, now, you can make certain that the process will work *for* instead of *against* you.[25]

Successful people figure transactions daily by calculating the exchange rates for different achievement options. Then they direct themselves for maximum gain.

PLANS. John Noe, author of *Peak Performance Principles for High Achievers,* says that peak performers distinguish themselves by setting "high goals" and "no small plans." Making no small plans "starts with getting control of little choices such as: 'How are you going to spend this day? What do you do when you're bored? What do you do that you don't have to do? What do you do when you don't have to do anything? What do you do first, second, and third, today?'"[26] Plan to reach your goal by breaking it into bite-size morsels for quick and easy consumption. This gets you going and encourages you to continue. To master a complex skill, learn one behavior at a time, gradually combining them in a sequence. Unfortunately, this is not how most people try to reach their goals. According to Noe, "The failure to achieve high goals is, in most cases, due not so much to a lack of ability as to an unwillingness to prepare. It is always easier to rationalize your failures away than to go through the struggle of preparation."[27]

STRENGTHS AND WEAKNESSES. People who act intelligently know their strengths *and* weaknesses. They maximize what they can do and minimize or neutralize what they cannot. This, according to Sternberg, is the cultural definition of "intelligence."

> Intelligence is essentially a cultural invention to account for the fact that some people are able to succeed in their environment better than others. . . .
> . . . what does seem to be common among people who master their environments is the ability to capitalize on their strengths and compensate for their weaknesses.[28]

Unfortunately, the reverse principle operates in public schools. Children who don't meet reading and math requisites quickly learn about their limitations. Students in special education classes spend most of their time in remediation. Is it surprising that they leave school without discovering their strengths? Why not reverse the sequence, identifying strengths, building upon them, *and then* minimizing deficits?

No one succeeds by thinking about what he can't do. Nevertheless, 250,000 special education students graduate from school each year knowing more about their deficits than their strengths. No wonder only 30 percent find full-time work and 70 percent return home to live with parents.[29] This makes no sense when the alternative is so powerful. Every day we read a success story about someone with a presumed handicap. We can learn from these remarkable people and their ability to concentrate on *abilities* not *dis*abilities.

My father always said "Do the best you can with what you have." He was a good model because when he lost his left arm at 14 (he was left-handed), he left the farm in Montana to learn bookkeeping—a skill consistent with his potential *abilities*. He enrolled in a business school in Spokane, Washington, and commuted from Montana riding the train on top of box cars because he couldn't afford the fare. Imagine hitching to a moving train, swinging up with one arm, and then holding on for hundreds of miles! He did. He also did anything else he wanted to do: fly fishing, horseback riding, baseball, and golf.

People who appear to have limitations succeed by focusing on what they can do and by developing methods for getting around what they can't do—the same strategy used by all succeeders. My father plays golf as well as most men. He doesn't hit the ball exactly like others but he often gets it there in fewer strokes and that's what counts. He also plays a good game of pool. But again, he doesn't hold the pool stick and shoot exactly like other players. He builds upon his strengths. This is what all children and youth must learn. They must find what they do best and then maximize this ability. At the same time they must develop strategies to compensate for what they don't do as well. In *The Triarchic Mind*, Sternberg says successful people know their strengths and weaknesses and adjust to the environment accordingly:

> The most successful individuals are usually not ones who are stellar at everything they try; rather, they are people who know their strengths and weaknesses, making the most of their strengths while finding ways around their weaknesses. At the same time, there are potentially excellent performers who do not perform up to their abilities because they capitalize on the wrong ones.[30]

Jim Abbott was the California Angels's eighth pick in baseball's 1988 amateur draft. "They talked to me about my situation, having one hand. They said it didn't matter to them, that they just needed a left-handed pitcher."[31] Abbott was born without a right hand. So he learned to balance his glove on the nub of his right wrist during the windup and throw. As the ball speeds 90 mph toward home plate he jams his left hand into the glove to field a possible hit. (My father used a similar method when pitching softball.) Does he have a handicap? "I don't think people should make too much of it. I was blessed with a good left arm and a not-so-good right one."[32] In 1987 Abbott won the Sullivan Award as the nation's top amateur athlete and carried the U.S. flag at the opening ceremonies of the 1987 Pan Am Games in Indianapolis. Abbott focuses on strengths. "I don't think of myself as different. I don't think of myself as courageous. *I grew up learning to do things within my capabilities.* I've had a good time doing what I've done." And that's enough to succeed.[33]

At 16, LaShawn Brown helped the North women's basketball team win the gold medal shooting with a hand that had virtually no fingers. Brown lost all but her thumb and a portion of her index finger in a lawn mower accident when she was seven. So she learned simple tasks all over again. "I had to learn how to write left-handed. Tying shoes, that took me a while. After a couple of weeks, I finally got it. I had to practice like I was a little kid."[34] Julie Wallace, raised by an uncle in Japan until she came to the United States at age 14, is a fourth-degree black belt in karate, third-degree black belt in judo, swimming record setter in the 200-meter butterfly at the World Military Games, and 1984 Ironman Triathlon participant; she also has a bachelor's degree in chemistry and journalism. But when she contracted leukemia, she lost her vision and was paralyzed. She's since recovered and now, though still blind, is up every morning at 5:00 for three hours of swimming and another three of bicycling. Her goal is head-to-head competition against sighted athletes and to become the first blind person to swim the English Channel. Recognizing her health risks, Wallace says "I have to capitalize on as much as I can because life is so short for 'somedays' and 'maybes.'"[35]

Former *Chicago Sun-Times* reporter and editorial writer Cecil Neth spends four to five hours a day on a specially designed computer that allows him to finish a book on how families can deal with ALS, amyotrophic lateral sclerosis—also known as Lou Gehrig's disease. The 64-year-old reporter was diagnosed with the disease four years ago and time is running out. The average ALS patient lives three to five years. The untreatable disease destroys muscle after muscle in its inexorable, lethal progression. Neth's only remaining movement comes from one eyebrow connected to a switch attached to a headband connected to a computer system. Neth writes for hours each day to finish his book in time.[36]

Another victim of this disease wrote *A Brief History of Time*, which explains how we can travel forward and backward through time. Now confined to a wheelchair, Steven Hawking, the Lucasian professor of mathematics at Cambridge University in England, uses a computerized voice synthesizer to lecture on the nature of the universe. When asked "Has being confined to a wheelchair, constantly within yourself thinking, affected the way you approach problems as a physicist?," he answered "I don't think so. *My illness is really not very much on my mind.*"[37] Of course, he's too busy solving the great cosmic puzzle.

The superachievers in Griessman's study also played to their strengths. "Many of the high achievers mentioned points of weakness. But they refused to dwell upon them, and they avoided building a case against themselves. Instead, they confronted their weaknesses and tried to eliminate them. Or they sought ways to circumvent them, seeking situations or careers where they could capitalize upon their strengths."[38]

Multitalented Steve Allen is an actor, singer, song writer, lyricist, comedian, talk show host, jazz pianist, and more. His compositions include such hits as *Impossible* and *This Could Be the Start of Something Big*. Is there anything he can't do? Yes, *he can't read music!* "I started out the right way. . . . I took those old John M. Williams first-year piano lessons. But right from the start I had an ability to create my own things, and *that ability soon outdistanced my halting ability to read,* so I got impatient, and I didn't have a piano for a few years, so I lost the ability to read altogether" [italics added]. How does he compose? With a tape recorder. Then he hires someone to transpose the song into musical notation for him.[39]

CONFIDENCE. Confident people have positive expectations. They believe in their plans and *feel good* about following through on their prospects. They get their thoughts, feelings, and actions "in sync" because thinking positively makes them feel positive. This helps them act effectively, which in turn produces positive results. And positive results feed back to reinforce confidence. Figure 12 illustrates the cycle.

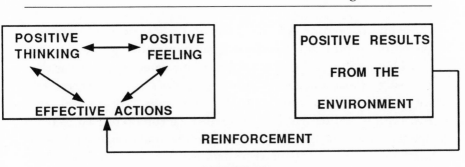

FIGURE 12
The Confidence Cycle

It has a reverse gear too, when negative thoughts about a plan generate negative feelings that disrupt performance, reduce expected outcomes, and decrease confidence. Ask peak performers for the most important ingredient for effective action and they'll say "confidence." You must believe in what you're doing and that you can do it well. If not, forget it. You'll fail. Feelings and thoughts produce positive or negative expectations. When they're positive, you do well. When they're negative, you don't. This is the principle behind Norman Vincent Peale's positive thinking philosophy. And according to Dr. Herbert Benson, author of *Your Maximum Mind,* "In many ways, the positive-thinking attitude is the *sine qua non* of any successful self-improvement effort. In other words, you must *think* you can achieve a self-help goal before you can expect to reach that goal."[40]

Actions

We've just seen how intelligent adaptors use *passion, direction,* and *organization* to get what they want. *Passion* is the energy source, *direction* focuses that energy, and *organization* coordinates resources toward single-minded outcomes. Achievers build up their organizational capacity by setting priorities, assessing demands, planning actions, maximizing strengths, minimizing weaknesses, and becoming confident in their abilities to achieve.

Passion, direction, and *organization* account for 60 percent of effective mental management. The remaining 40 percent translates those internal resources into *actions* and *reactions*. Every day people enroll in programs to lose weight, quit smoking, get in shape, learn new skills, change jobs, or start new careers. As long as they receive guidance and encouragement, they're okay. But left on their own, their interests wane and old habits return. These people lack the passion, self-destruction, and self-organization needed to manage their own change. They depend on the "fad" program to stimulate desire and discipline their actions. But when they must call upon their internal resources to maintain their program—an inevitable requirement for reaching their goals—they're back where they started, eating the wrong foods, missing workouts, and gaining weight.

Initiative and accomplishment require passion, direction, and organization. Our youngest child, Dustin, passionately wanted his own identity in high school—an identity separate from the one established by his brother and sisters who preceded him. He decided to start by earning a varsity letter in cross country his sophomore year. He knew he would have to get his act together to do it. He would have to organize himself, set priorities, and so on. He would have to work out during the summer too. So he developed a plan to get up at 4:30 A.M. and run every day. He asked me to join him. I agreed, if *he* woke *me*. This placed responsibility for the plan with him. I didn't expect it to work. But every morning he woke me at the scheduled time and we worked out together. I rode a bike, he ran beside me. The plan worked and he earned his letter that year. Would Dustin have been as successful if *I* had told him to try for the letter, if *I* had given him the plan, or if *I* had woke him up every morning to run? It worked because Dustin did it. He used his own inner resources—passion, direction, and organization.

The first step in any new action sequence is the most difficult, especially for young people accustomed to having someone else initiate and direct their activities. Successful people master start-up obstacles early. They begin new activities regularly, learn from them, and then incorporate what they've learned into their daily lives. They don't wait for the mood. They do it now! W. Clement Stone taught himself to sell insurance that way. He knew he could find excuses for not calling customers. He too was afraid of rejection. So he acted immediately.

Fortunately, I struck upon the self-starter: *Do it now!* Because I had learned the value of trying to establish the right habits and the harm of acquiring wrong habits, it occurred to me that I could force myself to action as I left one office if I would rush quickly into the next one. Should it occur to me to hesitate, I would use the self-starter *Do it now!*—and immediately act on it. This I did.[41]

Reactions

The last of the five intelligent adaptations is *reaction* to feedback about what works and what doesn't. There are five components to intelligent reactions: (1) accurately monitoring and recording results, (2) objectively comparing results with expectations, (3) logically concluding about progress toward goals, (4) rationally deciding what to change, and (5) effectively following through with change strategies.

Dancers and athletes are consummate adaptors. Their agile adjustments on stage and on the playing field thrill and astound. They speed up the adjustment cycle 100-fold, pivoting in space with actions and reactions that we can hardly trace. As they perform they monitor; as they monitor they evaluate; and as they evaluate they adjust—almost simultaneously. It's magic, a precious moment in time when planner, performer, and adjuster are one. How do they do it? They spend years reading results, judging causes, making decisions, and adjusting in time to be effective. This is intelligent reaction.

We all do some of this. And we all can do more. But we don't have to do it so quickly and in front of audiences. We only need do it for ourselves, the only audience that counts. We can even take days, weeks, months to figure out the most effective adjustment. One of our country's most famous adjusters made a career of trying, failing, and adjusting. In 1832 he lost his job and was defeated in a run for a state legislative seat; in 1833 he failed in business; in 1835 his sweetheart died; in 1836 he had a nervous breakdown; in 1838 he was defeated in an election for Speaker of the House; in 1843 he was defeated in a bid for Congress; in 1848 he lost again in a bid for a congressional seat; in 1849 he was rejected for land officer; in 1854 he was defeated in a bid for a Senate seat; in 1856, he lost the nomination for vice president; and in 1858 he was defeated once again in a Senate race. But in 1860, Abraham Lincoln became the 16th president of the United States.[42]

Adaptable people accept responsibility for failure by using their experience to discover a better way. Ralph Waldo Emerson said "A man's success is made up of failures, because he experiments and ventures every day, and the more falls he gets, he moves faster on."[43]

Children don't learn how to succeed until they learn how to fail. Unfortunately, many never get that chance because their parents protect them. They believe failure is harmful. They're wrong. It's the only teacher we listen to. It spells out our shortcomings and gives information about our strengths. But that's not how young people see it. For them failure is the ultimate negative sign, ranking equally with peer disgrace, loss of car privileges, and loss of weekly allowances. Fredelle Maynard, author of *Turning Failure into Success,* agrees with me: "Most parents work hard at either preventing failure or protecting their children from the knowledge that they *have* failed. . . . The trouble with failure-prevention devices is that they leave a child unequipped for life in the real world."[44]

How Children Become Intelligent

Youth who score okay on paper-and-pencil *I.Q. tests* may still fail the nuts-and-bolts *reality test*. If they lack passion and commitment, don't know where they are headed, or how to organize their resources, they'll never even take the reality test. They'll never try to succeed. And if they avoid responsibility for their actions and ignore the feedback that helps them improve they'll fail the reality test every time they try. To pass, youth need to learn "life smarts," the essentials of intelligent mental self-management. They need help from their leaders, mentors, and friends.

Leadership

Kids from successful families have more opportunities to learn intelligent self-management because their parents use the same skills to succeed. By watching parents achieve goals and think through problems, children learn the principles of mental self-management. Successful parents are powerful role models for achievement. As

Developing Talent in Young People indicates, Bloom's researchers found that parents of talented children demonstrated what they expected.

> These parents were *models* of the "work ethic" in that they were regarded as hard workers, they did their best in whatever they tried, they believed that work should come before play and that one should work toward distant goals. They expected their children to learn the same values. They taught these values to all their children and reminded them frequently when they strayed from these values.
>   . . . The family routines, including meals, bedtimes, family interactions, and recreation, were structured to give the children appropriate responsibilities and to help them become "self-disciplined." When a child became interested in a talent field, he or she was expected to make use of the same values as they applied to the particular field. *To excel, to do one's best, to work hard, and to spend one's time constructively* were emphasized over and over again.[45]

Children learn intelligent self-management when (1) they *see* self-management at work, (2) they have parents who *expect* them to manage themselves intelligently, and (3) they have *opportunities* to practice these skills. Leadership begins with demonstrations. Children must observe their parents set goals, make plans, take action, evaluate results, and adjust to change. It's not enough to tell them what to do. Demonstrate, practice what you preach.

Parents must also expect and encourage independence, initiative, and responsibility for personal achievement. This is easier said than done, especially with the first child. Derek, our oldest child, always demanded more independence. Ultimately, he trained us to respond appropriately. This made life for his sisters and brother easier. They assumed responsibility earlier for setting their own goals and developing their own plans. Dana, our second child, stepped out of the Mithaug music-dance-drama tradition her sophomore year when she came home with a cross country uniform and announced she had joined the team. Later that year she earned a varsity letter and became team captain.

Children who mature as their talents develop also learn mental self-management. As they go to lessons and develop practice routines, they learn to set goals, develop plans, follow through, evaluate, and adjust from one week to the next. Weekly exposure to intense, direct, uncensored feedback about what was good, what wasn't, and what to improve teaches them how to think and analyze, what skills to improve and what behaviors to adjust. Gradually they assume responsibility for directing their own learning and development. At first they depend completely on teachers and coaches to decide what they will learn, when, and how much to practice. But as they advance they learn about themselves: what they can do, how long it takes for them to learn, and what types of outcomes are likely. At advanced levels, their teachers expect them to make major decisions affecting long-range outcomes.

Mentorship

Parents of successful youth also *teach* intelligent mental self-management. They catalyze youth passion, provide start-up directions during early years, organize activities and timelines, teach competent actions, and mentor positive reactions to negative results. Achievement-oriented parents leave little to chance.

PASSION AND DIRECTION. Parents help children develop passion by shepherding them into competency areas that are compatible with their interests, their abilities, and their family's values. Recall the "Amazing Families" described in chapter 8 and how children and parents shared common talents from the categories illustrated in Figure 13.

Nadja Salerno-Sonnenberg's family was very musical so it's not surprising that Nadja pursued that interest too. "My mother, Jose-

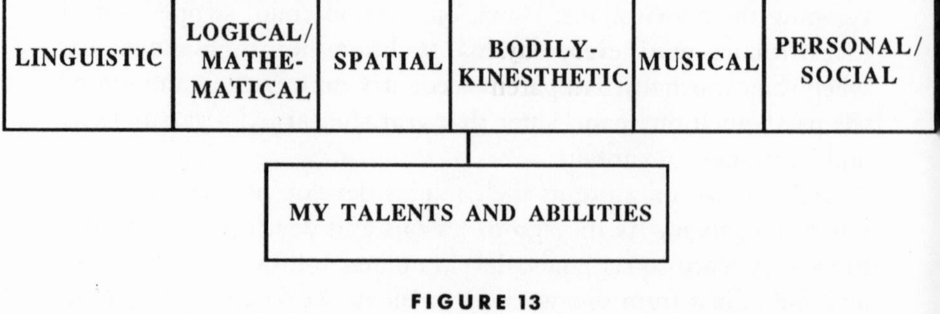

LINGUISTIC	LOGICAL/ MATHE- MATICAL	SPATIAL	BODILY- KINESTHETIC	MUSICAL	PERSONAL/ SOCIAL

MY TALENTS AND ABILITIES

FIGURE 13

phine Salerno, played piano. My brother Eric sang. Grandfather John Salerno (always known to us as Papa John) was a trumpet player. Nanny, grandmother Rose, cooked and played kazoo."[46] The choice of violin, however, was somewhat arbitrary. "Mamma had a friend who taught violin to beginners, so the violin was stuck under my chin when I was five and that was that."[47]

My wife and I chose the performing arts for similar reasons. Cathy is an actress and plays piano. Her mother is a music teacher and her father played piano and was an opera singer. My father sang and my grandfather played piano. According to one of Bloom's studies,

> At first it was typically the *family interest in their activity* that kept the young children engaged. *The decision to begin piano lessons, and to practice daily in preparation for the weekly lessons, was made for the pianists by their parents.* Parents took the children to and from lessons and made sure the children practiced every day. Whether or not the pianists enjoyed studying and practicing, *they really had little choice in the matter at the start.* [italics added][48]

Children are easily influenced by the passionate interests of those around them. They see the pleasure the activity elicits and want to share in it. It's no surprise that passionate families raise passionate children. Emotion is contagious. It infects impressionable minds and creates desire to excel. It is also important during the early stages of competency development when children start their proficiency climb to mastery. Most children usually want to quit after a few miles.

I taught music lessons during graduate school; after working with about 50 students, I began charting the quitting cycle. The average student lasted six months. By then the honeymoon was over and the novelty had worn out. Students realized that learning to play required hard work every day. Those who survived the six-month drop-out test usually had parents who came to lessons and listened to them play. In these early stages, *parents provided the passion and interest that their children lacked.* But after a few years, accomplishment feedback kicked in to fuel their passion to improve.

On the other side of the competency mountain, young trekkers developed a sense that what they were doing was important. Sosniak noted how young pianists developed a feeling of competence as well. "As months and years passed, the pianists found that playing was no longer simply fun, it required a lot of work. The work, however, was becoming much more than a requirement or an obligation the pianists might have had to fulfill for their parents. The pianists began to realize that they were becoming skilled at music making. It was something they could do, and do well."[49] As one student put it, "I just remember being aware of . . . this sense of mission as it were . . . some role that I would play, important, significant role in musical terms. That *I* would have something special to say with specific works."[50]

Not every child reaches this level of competence. But all children can achieve *in some area of interest*. They can learn what they like and what they can do so they can direct themselves to maximize those outcomes. Parents jumpstart the process by initiating and maintaining their children in competency development until *acquired* passion and self-direction take over. Parents of superachievers don't wait for some mysterious and inexorable unfolding of their children's latent talent. They use a simple, commonsense approach. They lead, expect, and provide, and then they intervene, direct, and correct. They're modelers and interveners.

ORGANIZATION. Passion and direction alone are insufficient for intelligent self-management. Children must also translate their achievement drive into concrete, everyday action. How do they do this? They learn to set priorities, meet demands, plan their actions, maximize their talents, and believe in themselves. They master the art of organizing thoughts, actions, and feelings for maximum effect. Some call this self-discipline, self-control, and self-reliance. But it's more. Self-organization is the maximization of personal resources. It connects daily actions with passion and purpose.

Priorities. Children learn priorities by watching their parents and by fulfilling expectations. When mom and dad demonstrate consistent patterns of choosing and acting, children learn what's important. Parents who always finish their work before watching television or going to a movie communicate the value of work. Parents who organize evening meals, holidays, and vacations so everyone can be together demonstrate the importance of family. And parents who discuss their personal goals and accomplishments with their children communicate the value of personal achievement. In time, children absorb these observations into their own value structure.

Parents also teach priorities directly through use of the contingency principle. If competency development is a priority, it should fall under the jurisdiction of the practice-*then*-play rule. I learned to value competence that way, as did my children. Bloom found that successful parents "organized their [children's] time and established priorities as a means of pursuing a variety of activities while exercising the belief that 'if it's worth doing, it's worth doing well.' Work was completed before play. Wasting time or idling away the hours was cause for disapproval in these homes, as was doing a sloppy job or shirking responsibilities."[51] Compare this orientation with how most American youth spend their time today. Television and hanging out at the mall compete equally with homework and self-improvement. No wonder most children have no sense of direction. They have no priorities.

Demands. The work-then-play contingency also introduces children to environmental demands. In fact, it *is* a demand. Each day, children must accomplish something important before play. During the early years, they may follow the rule because there's little difference between performing (a competency) for "fun" and for "work." It's all the same. But as lessons progress, demands for time and energy increase. Children learn that in order to achieve, they must work hard and practice diligently even when their friends don't. If they want to *become special* they must *be special* which means taking the time and making the effort to improve. Their performance must meet increasingly demanding expectations.

Contrast this with what teachers say about today's students who expect more rewards for less effort.

> Many teachers feel that today's children have higher and higher expectations but are willing to exert less and less effort: kids expect to be rewarded with high grades and lavish careers, but they do not want to work for them. There is a tendency to believe that "thinking makes it so," or "*I tried, and therefore I should be rewarded.*"[52]

Achievers are different. The older they get, the more self-demanding they become. While the rest of American youth contribute to the "more reward–less work" trend, achieving youth expect fewer rewards for more work. Sosniak found that young pianists faced increased work and performance demands *as they became more proficient:*

> The master teachers assumed that their pupils were serious and that nothing would stand in the way of their studies. They assigned an enormous amount of material and they expected it to be learned to the high standard they set.[53]

Plans. Young children are usually poor planners. They don't think before they act, which often gets them into difficulties. Gradually they learn to anticipate the consequences of different actions and to develop plans to avoid those that produce unpleasant experiences. By school age they think ahead well enough to adapt to different environments. They listen to teachers, memorize rules, and then think ahead to avoid dangerous actions.

In addition to thinking ahead, young children have a remarkable capacity for shaping their own thoughts and actions into complex competency patterns. But they don't usually fulfill this potential unless they receive *one-on-one* instruction. That's why they begin school at age six rather than at age three or four. When they're older they can concentrate sufficiently to master the school curriculum during *group* instruction.

Children who receive *individualized* instruction and training master complex skills and demonstrate remarkable proficiencies at astoundingly early ages. Their teachers and coaches break skills and tasks into small, bite-size learning units to match their learning capacity. Teachers with a flare for "task analysis" can teach nearly anyone anything at nearly any age, as Howard Gardner discovered on his visit to China:

> I had not anticipated that children as young as four or five could draw, sing, dance, tell stories, and perform dramatically as well as does the average Chinese child. Yet, once one has encountered virtually identical ink-an-brush paintings of chickens, or renditions of a folk song all over the country, the Chinese feat at least becomes explicable.
>
> *The Chinese have dissected virtually every desirable behavior, broken it down into the tiniest possible elements, and developed a teaching regime that proves effective with nearly every child.* [italics added][54]

Individualized task-analytic instruction is standard practice in the teaching of music, dance, and many sports. The teacher breaks a skill into units and teaches them one at a time. In tap dancing, instructors show the target step and then break it down into toe taps, heel taps, forward and backward toe brushes, jumps, and hops on each foot. Piano teachers break a line of music into a sequence of key presses for each hand. Children receiving instruction like this learn more than just the skill. They also learn *how to teach themselves.* They learn to think systematically, breaking problem-tasks into smaller units, rearranging them in learnable sequences, and mastering parts in isolation. Then they reassemble and practice the completed unit until they can perform the routine proficiently. *This is the essence of* planning *and* problem solving.

Children exposed to competency development improve their analytical capacities without knowing it. The process is natural and functional. At advanced levels performers develop their own strategies for analyzing what they want to accomplish. Recall Nadja Salerno-Sonnenberg's description of the virtuoso's approach to mastering a new musical work:

> Learning a piece can be cut down to different levels. Everybody has their own system for doing this. First, many violinists will learn the notes in a very basic, technical, rudimentary way. Just the notes, figure out the fingerings, what fingerings are good for you, figure out the bowing, and all of that. . . . [then you] analyze it harmonically, you analyze it melodically. Then you do a technical analysis, analyzing bow patterns, bow speed—everything you do can be analyzed.[55]

Strengths and Weaknesses. Achieving youth know their strengths. They have a self-image that differentiates themselves from others. Parents, teachers, and peers reinforce this self-image with names like "the athlete," "the scholar," "the artist," "the musician." Achievers easily identify discrepancies between their talent and nontalent areas. This helps them maximize what they can do. Some may participate in extracurricular activities to showcase their abilities. After all, school is an *opportunity.*

Nonachieving youth don't see the world with such clarity. For them, it's all the same. Their lack of ability and interest dampens passion and expectations. They don't see opportunities, only requirements. So they avoid work, minimize effort, and seek obscurity. Even extracurricular activities have lukewarm appeal. Their drab, laid-back, noncommittal attitude shows up vividly against the achiever's enthusiasm for the big questions: "What do I like?" "What can I do?" and "What do I want?"

Superachievers know themselves *because of their differential experiences* with talent and nontalent areas. This helps them self-direct. A successful tennis player illustrates the self-direction process: "[I was] better at tennis. . . . I knew I'd be a good professional in tennis. Whereas in basketball . . . I wasn't physical enough. Those guys, they're big. They're physical. . . . They were bigger. I was maybe smarter. But I didn't have the raw physical assets."[56]

Achieving youth also recognize strengths and weaknesses *within* their competency area. Tennis players know what part of their game is strongest, swimmers know what strokes they swim the fastest, and runners know which distance produces their best times. This doesn't mean that they neglect subareas that cause problems. On the contrary, competence in any field requires work on weak areas to minimize their effects.

When I taught music lessons I was surprised to find all my students avoiding weaknesses and persevering on strengths. Musical sections they learned quickly received attention while difficult sections were ignored. The results were uneven to say the least—clipping along at an acceptable tempo for a few seconds and then grinding to a halt for what seemed like hours. Left on their own, I was certain they would play like that forever. Every teacher and coach knows this problem. It's one of the first obstacles achievement trekkers overcome to perfect their talents. Usually the best procedure is surgery. Isolate and remove the faulty part, pummeling it with repeated practice until it's strong, and then reinstall it into the main routine.

Confidence. Achievers maximize results by "psyching" themselves with positive thoughts and feelings about their performance. They avoid thoughts and feelings that scuttle confidence and immobilize action. Worry destroys concentration. Achievers replace it with practice, preparation, and rehearsal. I've prepared my own children for hundreds of performances. Before the event, we always talked of positive actions and feelings. I kept worries to myself. The time to deal with them was during practice. The best chance for success now is to feel good, think clearly, and act confidently.

When achievers suffer from sagging confidence, they focus on images, thoughts, and feelings from past accomplishments. They recapture that "successful" posture, tone of voice, movement style, and regain control. Of course this capacity doesn't develop overnight. It takes years of competency development and hundreds if not thousands of performances before achievers *know* what actions, attitudes, and thought patterns work. This means real-life accomplishment feedback from many environments and people, not just from mom and dad.

Unfortunately, this principle eludes many parents who think that telling children they're "good," "competent," and "unique" makes it so—*that it increases confidence.* Not so. Children are bright little scientists who demand to see for themselves the basis for these accolades. Second-hand compliments are only effective when paired with first-hand experience. Children need to experience the connection between what they do and the feedback they receive. Results must be specific to performance. Then it's "accomplishment feedback." And it must come from multiple sources. Children with fawning parents at home may get different results at school and on the playground. Simply put, there's no shortcut to confidence. *It begins with competence.*

ACTIONS. *Passion* motivates, *direction* targets, and *organization* maximizes. But only *action achieves.* Sounds simple enough and 40 years ago it was. But today, action has a powerful competitor: inaction. Television has invaded our homes, captured the minds and hearts of our young people, and usurped their priorities. When there's a choice between television and productive initiative, youth choose the box. Thousands of hours of talent development have lost out to sitting and viewing. Forget complaints that children view too much of this and too little of that. The real issue is time. When can they develop skills, pursue interests, and kindle passion? Reinforcement for inaction builds contrary habit strength. Watching three to four hours a day from preschool on takes its toll on initiative, hustle, and resourcefulness. The more youth watch, the more they want to watch. Inaction breeds inaction.

Compare the schedules of tube-viewers with those of achievers. You would think that one group is on vacation and the other is in a labor camp. The first group enjoys the life of the child. The second learns the life of an adult. Too bad for the second group—missing all that fun! That's what "experts" say about that so-called pressure. Why not ask achievers? They'll explode a few myths fast. For them, couch-potato behaviors are boring and dead end. The most powerful reinforcer comes from personal challenge.

Achievers and couch potatoes are on different trajectories. And they're likely to stay on them. It's as difficult for couch potatoes to become achievers as it is for achievers to become couch potatoes. Each passing year their paths widen. Who's responsible? Parents are. Left alone, children end up in front of the television. It's too seductive to resist. Achiever parents intervene by insisting that their children be productive. Bloom's successful parents "wanted to be involved in something, learning about something, working on something, as often as possible. . . . Work was completed before play. Wasting time or idling away the hours was cause for disapproval in these homes."[57]

If you want children with initiative, resourcefulness, and hustle, encourage action on important tasks. Expect accomplishment. Action habits are easy to establish *early*. But after a decade of passivity, youth have 3600 plus days of habit build-up to break down.

Initiative is only part of the action equation. Youth must also respond with purpose and direction. Random, improvised behaviors are usually ineffective and a waste of time. Youth must learn actions that produce predictable effects. This requires discipline and practice. It requires competence. Time and again, I see opportunities for exceptional results squandered, not because the original plan was bad, but because its execution was. Those in charge of getting the job done failed to prepare. They just walked "on stage" and "winged it." Preparation, rehearsal, and practice make the difference. Youth with histories of competency development understand what this involves. Unfortunately, they're a minority. Most youth don't have a clue. They find incomprehensible Lee Trevino's statement that "You hit so many golf balls that your hands get blistered and crack and start bleeding."

REACTIONS. Achievers use their results to learn and improve. They compare outcomes with expectations, identify discrepancies, and then search for what works, what doesn't, and why. They expect praise *and* criticism from others. General appraisals like "good job," "well done," or "you're great" don't help. Achievers want specifics, the details that will improve their performance.

When our children were young, we gave them "good job" feedback after each performance, saving the details for practice sessions at home. As they learned to evaluate themselves objectively, they asked questions about specific elements of their performance. They wanted details, comparisons, descriptions, differentiations, shadings. What was especially good, what not so good, why was one element better this time than last, what needs work, where can I improve, and, of course, what was excellent? General feedback no longer helped. When high school productions ran several evenings, they requested that we attend each night so we could give feedback in time for improvement the next night. School officials thought we were great supporters, attending all those shows. But we had no choice.

Today's youth avoid feedback because it might be negative and that makes them feel bad about themselves. Parents and teachers avoid giving negative feedback for the same reasons. They praise instead, even when performances are inadequate. Unfortunately, no one improves by means of praise alone. Positive *and* negative feedback are necessary. Denying this fact only stunts growth, perpetuates mediocrity, and fosters immaturity. Lacking the capacity to deal with negative feedback, youth blame parents, teachers, schools, and society for their disappointments. But the problem is theirs. All youth must learn to self-correct. If they don't learn how now, they'll end up insecure, defensive, and unhappy later on.

Teach your children to adjust when they're young. Deliver specific feedback after each performance and discuss the benefits of adjusting. This will teach them to use results to get what they want. Starting early acclimates them to adjusting and readjusting. They never expect perfection the first time. Accomplishing an important goal requires change, adaptations, refinements, and, most of all, time.

Friendship

Achiever parents are leaders, teachers, and friends. They raise their kids by *demonstrating* self-determined behaviors, *teaching* self-determined behaviors, and as a consequence of that leadership and instruction, *interacting* with *self-determined behaviors*. Mind you, we're not talking wimp behaviors here. We're talking about young people who have the wherewithal to get what they want out of life—tough-minded, self-directed, rugged individualists who expect a say in decisions and a share in actions. So, if you raise self-determined children, plan to be their friends (because you won't win as their enemies). Interact with them so they can learn the adjustment skills necessary for family, peer, and school environments. Give them a chance to practice self-determined behaviors to achieve social as well as personal goals.

Parents teach social adaptation by helping children discover mutually satisfactory solutions to joint problems. In the 1970s Dr. Thomas Gordon introduced an intelligent approach to solve what he called "conflict-of-needs situations":

> The parent asks the child to participate with him in a joint search for some solution acceptable to both. One or both may offer possible solutions. They critically evaluate them and eventually make a decision on a final solution acceptable to both. No selling of the other is required after the solution has been selected, because both have already accepted it. No power is required to force compliance, because neither is resisting the decision.[58]

To be an effective mutual problem solver, you must know your own needs. What do you want to achieve? What problems are in the way? Who can help clear that way? This is the first step toward effective self-advocacy. Awareness of your needs also helps understand what "Other" needs. How can you help "Other" so he, in turn, will help you? Answering these questions leads to joint planning, follow through, results monitoring, and evaluation of effects. Your next negotiation with "Other" refines your mutual pact to improve outcomes. The diagram in Figure 14 illustrates this method from "My" point of view.

Achieving youth are good negotiators. They know themselves well enough to identify their own needs and goals. At the same time, they're realistic. They don't blame others, or feel that they've been treated unfairly when they don't immediately get everything they want. Years of competency training has taught them that problems can be solved.

Nonachieving youth don't have these experiences. They spend most of their time waiting for someone to decide what's wrong with their performance and how they should correct it. They rarely identify problems or construct solutions on their own. When they leave school, they expect authority figures to define what they need to do

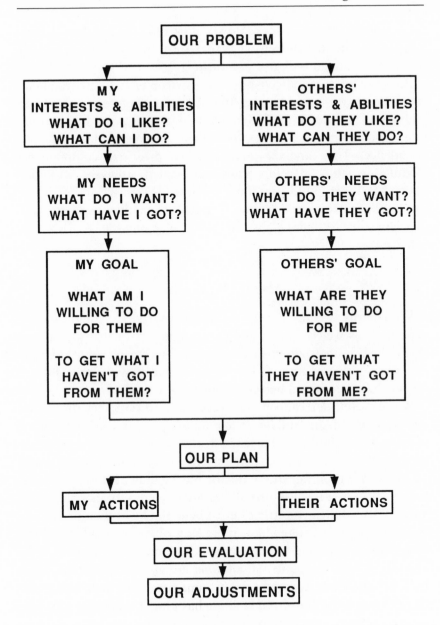

FIGURE 14
Mutual Adaptations

to get ahead. No one does. Slowly they discover they need help negotiating the fit between what they have to offer and what the social environment will give in return.

People who move effectively from environment to environment encounter many opportunities to match their interests with their abilities. They don't need therapy to learn how to find happiness. Their happiness comes from their self-knowledge and self-confidence. They analyze goals quickly, prioritize components, identify demands, develop plans that match strengths with demands, and then build emotional support for positive action. They focus, concentrate, and follow through. Then they evaluate and problem solve to remove obstacles in the way of what they want to achieve.

Use It or Lose It

When Deirdre was in high school she discovered she could excel in academics as well as music and dance. Like her older brother and sister, she was an accomplished pianist, with a strong record of honors in various competitions. But her natural forte was dance. By age 16, she had committed herself to pursuing it seriously.

But even self-determined achievers run into obstacles that force adjustments. In the middle of her junior year, one of her ankles swelled. The condition persisted for several weeks. At first we thought it was a chronic dance-related injury. Then another joint acted up. We took her to the doctor but he didn't know what was wrong. Within a few months all her joints were seriously impaired and she had difficulty getting out of bed. She lost range of motion in her elbows and walked like an old lady. She was unable to sit for long periods, and had to leave class when the pain became severe. She didn't want to go to school, was moody, and depressed. She was not the same spirited person we knew. Within a few short months her mental and physical health were at rock bottom. She couldn't dance, study, or participate in school functions. All she could do was apply ice packs to painfully swollen joints. Finally her doctor diagnosed the condition. She had juvenile rheumatoid arthritis. Within six months she had surgery on one knee to relieve swelling. Doctors thought the other knee would need it too. She was on heavy doses of steroids and other medications. It was one of the worst conditions of arthritis for a girl her age the rheumatologist had ever treated.

One day waiting for her at the doctor's office, I picked up a book entitled *Use It or Lose It*. As I skimmed through it, I realized that Deirdre's recovery *was her responsibility*. It depended on her attitudes and actions. If she could recapture that belief in herself and increase her activity level, she might be able to establish some control over the disease. But she had to do it herself. No one could do it for her. I talked with her doctor and he agreed. On the way home, we discussed how she might learn to manage the condition and become healthy again.

We started swimming together to get action back in her routines. Gradually her spirit returned. By spring quarter senior year, she had improved. She told me she had a new goal. She was going to be dancing again by summer. And she would enroll in the dance program at the university in the fall. I was hopeful.

What happened over the next year is still hard to believe. By April the following year I watched her perform once again, this time at a University of Colorado dance concert. A week later I received this note in the campus mail.

Dear Dennis:

I just came from a dance concert where your daughter was the star, playing both the piano and accordion while obviously also being a very talented dancer. I thought you should know of the great job she is doing at the University. And, only a freshman!

Cordially,

E. Gordon Gee
President

A year later symptoms were gone and she was free of medication. Deirdre was back on track pursuing goals she had set for herself at sixteen. She gave new meaning to the phrase "Use it or lose it." Doctors don't know why she recovered so completely. When I ask her she says "*I did it!*" Apparently her habit-strength for achievement overpowered that disease.

Persistence

The third factor needed to succeed is persistence. Successful people get what they want in life because they: (1) *develop their talents;* (2) *adapt intelligently* to environments they like; and (3) *persist* at removing obstacles in the way of their goals. They are competent, intelligent, and persistent, as illustrated in the formula below.

COMPETENCE

+

INTELLIGENCE = SUCCESS

+

PERSISTENCE

Most people think competence and intelligence are enough. But they're wrong. No one succeeds without persistence, as Hill pointed out half a century ago: "Lack of persistence is one of the major causes of failure. Moreover, experience with thousands of people has proved that lack of persistence is a weakness common to the majority of men. It is a weakness which may be overcome by effort. The ease with which lack of persistence may be conquered will depend entirely upon the intensity of one's desire."[1]

Persistent Achievers

Persistence is the journeyman of the success team. While talent rests for its next award-winning performance, persistence is at work ferreting out another opportunity or developing a new solution. Persistence pushes the cause forward, inch by inch, unceremoniously but relentlessly. It's the Rodney Dangerfield of success, never getting much respect. I remember reading copies of letters of recommendation written about me by former professors. Instead of frequent references to my brilliance and intellectual insight, I found comments about my capacity for hard, sustained work. That discovery disappointed me at first. But now I depend on that capacity to accomplish difficult projects.

Steve Jobs

Steve Jobs is our contemporary hero of persistence. He did for the personal computer what Henry Ford did for the automobile. He fixed on a single unifying mission—to put cutting-edge technologies to practical use—and then delivered the personal computer to the masses.

Jobs is the historical stepchild of Thomas Edison whose three months of formal education outproduced and outinvented scientists with broad academic backgrounds. Today, Steve Jobs is the technological guru for the world's brightest computer science Ph.D.'s— yet he dropped out of college after one semester. How did he do it? With single-minded dedication, and persistence. At age 12 he got a job at Hewlett-Packard, and at 15, he teamed up with neighbor and friend Steven Wozniak who had read a magazine article about "phone phreaks" tapping into AT&T's long-distance switching equipment with electronic "blue boxes." Wozniak, the electronics genius of the duo, built a state-of-the-art blue box that he and Jobs sold door-to-door in Berkeley.

In 1976, Jobs, now 21, and Wozniak founded Apple Computer. Wozniak designed and built the prototype and Jobs promoted it, introducing the word "personal" and setting accessibility and mass marketing goals that rivaled Ford's during production of the Model T. Nothing would stand in his way. When his fledgling company needed money, Jobs approached legendary Don Valentine who refused him unless he hired a marketing expert. Jobs asked for a recommendation, but Valentine refused. Jobs persisted. *He called three and four times a day for a week,* until Valentine finally suggested Mike Markkula, former marketing manager for Intel. Jobs persuaded Markkula to visit his garage where Wozniak was building the prototype. Markkula joined the group. He developed a business plan, arranged for a Bank of America credit line, invested $91,000 of his own money, and became the chief executive.

Within five years Apple was a billion-dollar company and needed a chief executive with marketing talent. So Jobs went after the most successful CEO in corporate America, Pepsi Cola president John Sculley, who had just beat Coke in the trenches with the Pepsi challenge. Sculley refused Jobs's offer. Finally Jobs issued a challenge: "Do you want to spend the rest of your life selling sugared water or do you want a chance to change the world?"[2]

Sculley was up against relentless, single-minded persistence. Jobs always got what he wanted: "Steve showed no sign of disappointment in my reply. *He didn't know the word 'no.' It never meant anything to him. No is just a temporary hurdle that Steve always seems to surmount.* He had an uncanny ability to always get what he wanted, to size up a situation and know exactly what to say to reach a person."[3] Sculley finally accepted. Two years later he did the unthinkable: he kicked Jobs out of Apple.

Jobs was finished with Apple, but not with computers. While reading in biochemistry a few months later, he got an idea for a new venture. So he called Stanford's Nobel Prize–winning molecular biologist Paul Berg. Jobs saw connections between biochemists' needs for computer-simulated experiments and students' needs for computer-simulated science lessons. "If we could just bring some computational horsepower to this problem, and some software, there could be a revolution. The field would explode. All these graduate students and undergraduates would get to participate in state-of-the-art research, not just a few specialists off in a corner somewhere."[4] He was back at age 35, taking NeXT to the cutting edge. "What we want is to create the next computing revolution."[5]

Robert Swanson

Robert Swanson founded Genentech a year before Jobs and Wozniak started Apple Computer. Now Genentech is America's premier biotechnology firm. The company's 21st century "gene doctors" cloned human insulin for diabetics in 1978, duplicated cancer-fighting gamma interferon in 1981, created a blood clotting factor to aid hemophiliacs in 1984, and marketed the world's first growth serum,

Protropin, in 1985. Now about a quarter of a million American children who might never have grown taller than five feet can expect to achieve a normal adult height. By the year 2050 Genentech scientists expect to isolate the gene responsible for aging and have a bead on prolonging life to 125 years.

Swanson's family background is modest too. No one before him finished college. Swanson's father was a union man, an electrical maintenance foreman at Eastern Airlines, and his mother was a homemaker. Swanson learned how to achieve from them. In school he worked hard for good grades. If he was not the brightest and quickest in class, he was the most dedicated and disciplined. He knew what he liked, what he was good at, and how to channel his energy and talents to those ends. He learned focus and strategic thinking from his parents who encouraged him to strive to be the best: "Swanson's parents taught him not only to aspire to be the best, *they showed him* how *to be the best*. Any hurdle could be overcome with patience. It was all a matter of step-by-step planning and thorough preparation. Nothing must be left to chance" [italics added].[6]

That's how he got to MIT—with systematic planning, persistent follow through, and energetic hustle. At MIT, Swanson set goals, identified steps to achieve them, and followed through. He was not brilliant, receiving C's and D's his freshman year, but he was effective and persistent. He completed his chemistry degree in three years and enrolled in the Sloan School of Management as a senior where he took an entrepreneurial course on venture capital and how to start a company. It was exciting.

After MIT, Swanson joined Citibank in New York, rose to middle management, and was offered a Far East job with opportunity for promotion. Instead, he accepted a position with Kleiner and Perkins, a prestigious venture capital firm in the San Francisco area. The job didn't last. He wasn't cut out to be a venture capital partner. Swanson picked himself up and went back to the drawing board. He sorted out his options, set his goals, and proceeded once again.

Swanson learned about gene-splitting while at Kleiner and Perkins. Recombinant DNA could start a new industry. So he decided to use recombinant DNA to start a new pharmaceutical company. With help from Herbert Boyer, who co-constructed the world's first clone, Swanson formed Genentech. Boyer set up the labs and Swanson found the money, organized the business, and directed the company.

Ted Turner

"Captain Outrageous" Ted Turner is founder of CNN and TBS, owner of Atlanta's baseball and basketball teams, and winner of the America's Cup. Recently he acquired the MGM film library. He's also another paragon of persistence. He learned it from his father who demanded A's not B's, work that was "perfect" not "okay." Nothing was ever good enough, no matter how hard Ted tried. Friends worried he would be scarred by self-doubt, feelings of inferiority, and insecurity. His father wasn't. He believed insecurity was the best motivator for achievement. He wanted Ted insecure enough to compete for greatness. Ted learned the lesson well. The day he arrived at Georgia Military Academy he beat up the biggest of his roommates to prove who was boss.

He graduated from the academy and enrolled at Brown. During his senior year the university expelled him for having a girl in his room. He returned home to divorced parents and a failing business. His father was overextended and wanted to sell. Ted objected. How could he quit? What about that "survival of the fittest" routine? Then his father committed suicide, leaving the business to Ted— provided that he sell it. He refused. "I came out of that tragedy the same way I've come out of every other. *I didn't quit.* [italics added]"[7] His father's will required Ted to sell the business to prearranged buyers. But he threatened to ruin it first. That scared them off and gave Turner a chance to turn the business around. He did. Remarkable! A college dropout succeeds again—with persistence: "*The secret to my success is that I never quit.* Winners never quit, and quitters never win. You might go bankrupt, you might lose everything, but as long as you're out there still dukin' back, as long as you haven't given up, you're not beaten" [italics added].[8]

How Children Become Persistent

Jobs, Swanson, and Turner achieve and succeed through *persistence*. It's their way of finding happiness and fulfillment. After reaching one milestone they move on to the next, always stretching themselves. They believe in themselves when others don't and keep the faith when others give it up. They succeed because they refuse to lose. Setbacks are temporary obstacles to renewed opportunity. They're passionate, single-minded, and committed to realizing their full potential.

Persisters don't get confused about what they should do and when they should do it. Their riveting focus on what's ultimately important allows them to recognize opportunity and then act quickly and decisively to seize it. Persisters "hold a point." When you observe them at six-month intervals you see a logical progression from where they were to where they are. The cumulative effects of their sustaining efforts are awesome. Every day they're at it, working at tasks and solving problems that move them forward. Michener writes every morning from 7:30 to 12:30; Louis L'Amour wrote five pages a day, including Sundays and holidays, Isaac Asimov writes a book each month, and Andy Rooney says "when it comes to writing, I work hard. I get in here early every morning and I stick at it."[9] Now you can see why persistence is the last of the success factors to consider. Competence and intelligence are prerequisites. Without competent performance, persistence looks like stubbornness, and without intelligence it seems like mindlessness. But yoked with these powerful allies it builds empires, moves mountains, and reaches for stars.

Children develop persistence as they become talented and intelligent. Parents encourage it just like they promote competence and intelligence. They *lead, mentor,* and *befriend.* When they *lead,* they model and expect persistence. When they *mentor,* they teach concentrated, dedicated problem solving. And when they *befriend,* they nurture sustained performance during wins *and* losses.

Leadership

For children to persist, parents must persist. At first when my children observed me working at home, they thought the "boss" made me do it. They didn't understand I did it because I wanted to. That didn't match their idea of fun! They thought work and fun were at opposite ends of the pleasure scale. I've since straightened out that confusion. Now they understand that I enjoy my work and would rather do it than watch television (unless it's Bronco football). I've also shared my goals and plans with them as well as the actions I've taken to accomplish them. Periodically, they ask about my progress to check *if I'm persisting.* I tell them I am. Kids need to see what persistence looks like and that important people—like their parents—practice persistence all the time.

Cathy and I tried to encourage persistence, too. I recall Derek's passion for puzzles when he was young. We matched puzzle size with his ability so he could complete them independently. Even then he occasionally quit before he finished. We encouraged him to continue and were enthusiastic when he did. We wanted him to feel good about task completion.

I was a task-completer early on and received much notice and recognition for it. I overheard comments like "He always completes what he starts" and "He can do anything he sets his mind to do." My mother opened her clothing store when I was in grade school and printed thousands of advertising flyers to drop on doorsteps around town. She hired me and several of my friends to distribute them. Our instructions were to place one on each doorstep. I had several hundred, and I didn't finish until late into the night which sent my parents out searching. I didn't understand the fuss because it took me that long to place *one bill on each doorstep.* I wasn't about to return until the job was done even though I suspected everyone else had quit hours earlier. For me, completing the job was the deal. My parents were worried but also proud that I didn't quit. They told that story many times and I loved it! It was powerful reinforcement for persistence.

Parents who *expect* persistence must provide *opportunities* to persist. This too goes against popular notions, especially in a culture that uses entertainment to combat boredom. Many parents think that they must find ways to relieve their children's boredom. How often have I read the same article at the end of the school year: "How to relieve your child's summertime boredom?" Children who complain they have nothing to do don't need entertainment, they need challenges. Theirs is an *internal* problem, not an external one.

Parents provide opportunities by setting expectations and then backing them with tasks and activities *that require continuous effort over time.* This is important because it may be their only opportunity to become persistent. Schools certainly don't teach it.

Dana, our older daughter, completed a term paper in American history that was supposed to require an entire semester of independent work. She finished it in a weekend and received an "A." So much for persistence training. Teachers expect less because students sustain less.

So where *do* they learn persistence? Youth on fast-tracks to personal achievement build persistence as they develop their talent. Consider pianists who start with one half hour a day of practice and gradually increase to three, four, and five hours a day. Don't think that doesn't require self-discipline, because it does. These kids know what it means to dig their heels in and master their assignments. There's no time for passive entertainment *or* getting bored during the summer. They're simply too busy.

Mentorship

The first step to persistence training is *starting a challenging task*. The second is *to stay with it* day after day, week after week, and month after month. This tests everyone's persistence—yours as well as your children's. At first, teaching it is like starting a car with a weak battery in subzero weather. After a jumpstart and a warm-up, the car runs fine. Young children need the same boost. Their batteries are not strong enough to self-start. I was the family starter for years. Derek, Dana, and Deirdre were three years apart so I got them up at the same time each morning to start their lessons before I left for work. At night I worked with them on their dance before they went to bed. It was a standard routine. Dustin, who came along several years later, was up at 5:00 A.M. and off to the ice rink. That was the greatest challenge and nearly drained *my* battery. Of course, you don't have to be *that* committed to teach persistence. But remember: to raise a persistent child, you must be a persistent parent.

PERSISTENCE TRAINING. You can teach persistence using any task or activity. The only requirements are that they be completed every day and that they increase in difficulty. Pick one that's interesting and work on it with your child for short periods every day. Follow a daily schedule of learning and practice. I prefer morning sessions before school so the work is out of the way after school. At the same time focus on the mechanics: *concentration, task completion,* and *problem solving.*

Start with *concentration.* We encouraged focused work by leaving our children alone when they found interesting activities. Our rule was "Never interrupt them while they're thinking." If a task absorbed them in our presence, we left quietly. Remember, most infants and young children prefer playing with mom and dad. We can be major distractors to focused thought. The "never interrupt" principle minimizes these effects and prepares children for more structured learning. Observe the length of these "thought episodes" to determine how much time your child spends. Start there and gradually increase session length as concentration develops and tasks become more challenging. Schedule sessions each day and follow through consistently. Daily learning and persisting are as important as picking up toys after play and brushing teeth after meals.

Next emphasize *task completion.* Specify the amount of work to be completed each session and reinforce the real achievement of getting work done rather than the false achievement of merely putting in time. The difference is important. Children are more willing to work when they know exactly what to accomplish in order to finish. Also it encourages them to monitor progress by *what they do* rather than by how long they take. When my children practiced music lessons, I outlined what music they were to play and how many times they were to play it. If they could not play an entire piece, I found a section or measure for them to work at and master with repeated practice. This taught them to stay on the task until they completed the required repetitions, or mastered the task, whichever came first.

The final phase is *problem solving.* For every lesson, children must observe their teachers and coaches as they: (1) *identify* the task component that impedes learning (problem identification); (2) *breakdown* components into small, easy-to-learn units (problem analysis); (3) *arrange* units into learnable sequences (planning); (4) require *practice on the sequence* (solution implementation); (5) *evaluate* performance the following week (solution evaluation); and (6) *rearrange the sequence* for the next week's work (adjustment). Eventually children adopt the routine for their own use. They become persistent architects of their own competence, building skills from the ground up, brick by brick, layer by layer until the resulting structure is a competent, reliable performance.

PERSISTENT SELF-MANAGEMENT. Persistent youth also learn to tackle problems that get in the way of their goals, as Figure 15 illustrates. Intelligent mental managers set goals, develop plans, follow through, self-evaluate, and self-adjust. Their goals, plans, and actions satisfy important needs. When they don't, there's a problem. The goal may be misdirected, the plan poorly developed, or the follow-through inadequately executed. Persistent problem solving comes to the rescue with a new round of problem identification, solution development, implementation, evaluation and adjustment, illustrated in the second half of Figure 15. Persistent youth recycle the routine, updating goals, changing plans, and improving performance until they find ways that satisfy needs.

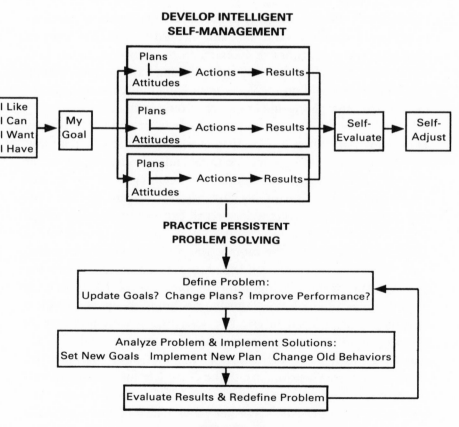

FIGURE 15
Self-Management and Problem Solving

Friendship

Persisters who master the self-improvement struggle are ready to compete among equals; this is the third and final phase of persistence development. Will they hold their own with peers? Are they prepared to compete for limited resources? Or will they withdraw from the challenge because they may not win?

COMPETITION FOR OPPORTUNITY. Competition for opportunity is the first law of social organization. It occurs on the playground, in the lunchroom, and in the boardroom. Newly forming groups proceed through the same stages. Members meet and display what they can do by showing their full range of skills and abilities. A division of labor emerges, with positions allocated according to members' abilities to advance group goals.

Remember those elementary years on the playground? I do. My friends and I spent a good deal of time demonstrating how good we were at everything: running, hanging from parallel bars, catching and throwing baseballs and footballs, sinking baskets. You name it, we showed we could do it. We let it all hang out, continuously, for weeks. After that, everyone knew who could do what.

In my class there were two standouts, especially for softball. Those kids were better hitters, throwers, and catchers than anyone else. So they were always the captains and they usually chose the best players first. Kids who couldn't do anything were chosen last. Friendship wasn't a factor because the stakes were so high. The team with the best players won. I recall expressions on the faces of those who went last in the "draft." Lucky for me, I was just good enough to go in the middle rounds. But it was tense.

Kids who couldn't play well ended up in positions that minimized damage. This meant playing in the out-out-outfield, far beyond the batting power of any hitter. Poor batters found themselves last in a lineup that overlapped recess. I've seen this process hundreds of times since, in meeting rooms instead of on playing fields. Participants are older, more sophisticated, but the routine is much the same. First there's tension, while the chair sets the agenda, defines the problem, and opens the discussion. Then comes competition. Each participant presents his or her views. The group considers and reacts, giving approval for some while politely ignoring others. In a short while it's all over and everyone now knows where the real "power" is—with the participant who communicated the best solution most effectively. Now the group makes plans and takes action, assigning tasks and roles according to ability and willingness to contribute. The solution-giver becomes the informal leader and receives differential respect and status from the other group members.

Competition for opportunity is functional. It helps groups to succeed and organizations to survive. We understand its principles in our professional lives yet fail to appreciate them in our children's lives. We kid ourselves into believing they won't have to compete for opportunity until they graduate from high school or college and find a job. Wrong!

Children must compete the first day they step out of the sanctity of home and onto the playing field with their friends. Competition for opportunity occurs at all ages and in all groups. Children who understand the process prepare themselves by matching their interests and talents with the needs of the groups they wish to join. If a group can benefit from Jenny's contributions, her prospects are good during those competitions for opportunity. But she must demonstrate her potential value to the group. She may need to *persist*. Others may offer equally valuable contributions. Sometimes it takes *repeated attempts* to meet group requirements and gain acceptance. Few get what they want the first time.

COMPETITION WITH PEERS. Competition decides who performs what roles and who gets what jobs. High school graduates compete for entrance into colleges and universities, college graduates compete for admission to graduate school or for jobs, and employees compete for promotions on the corporate ladder. Competition sorts and matches talent and ability with needs and opportunities.

Successful people persistently pursue competitive opportunities even though they don't get what they want every time. Nonsuccessful youth can't stand the uncertainty. They expect the same guarantees and entitlements they receive at home. Recall Todd from chapter 1 who received funds from his parents to start a limousine service and then demanded to operate it from their home.

Parents who worry about the "harmful" effects of competition should consider the consequence of its alternative, guaranteed opportunity. The Eastern Europeans tried that system and it collapsed! Our social structure *rewards* competence, intelligence, and persistence. It *ignores* incompetence, ignorance, and capriciousness. People who have no skills, don't know how to maximize their strengths, and lack resolve in directing their lives, don't find success, happiness, and fulfillment.

Fortunately all children at least *start out* competing, even if it's only with siblings and friends in the backyard. They discover they don't get everything they want every time they try. Sometimes their best efforts don't impress either. After all, it's the occasional win that is most motivational. Continuous success is as boring as continuous failure is discouraging.

Youth with competition experience leave school and home knowing what to expect. They won't get what they want just because they work hard and deserve it. That was true for every contestant they faced in past competitions. Only a few win. Competition for afterschool opportunity operates the same way. Many are qualified but few are selected. When persisters are among the "left out," they learn from their results, adjust their approach, and try again—like this young swimmer who found a way to gauge his progress against veterans: "It was just the fact that I was swimming with senior swimmers—national swimmers—my own age. Frankly, it was they who pushed me along in the freestyle. . . . Working out with them everyday, [I] *proved to myself* that I could keep up with them, beat them. [That] gave me the confidence that I needed . . . that was my first big breakthrough" [italics added].[10]

In the small town I grew up in during the 1950s talent shows were big events. Everyone attended. The contestants included instrumentalists, dancers, vocalists, jugglers, comedians—you name it. My sister and I entered at young ages and won often. Eventually we were regulars on a local TV talent show called "Starlit Stairway." We did well there too. The last year we won the grand prize, the result of a series of "playoff" competitions held over several months. We had tried twice before but came in second both times. We never considered quitting. We figured the probabilities and stayed with it.

My kids logged their share of competitions too: piano adjudications, accordion competitions, figure skating competitions, talent shows, track and cross-country meets, science fairs, forensics/debate meets, gymkhana (western horse, barrel racing) and horse shows. Needless to say, they didn't win all the time. There was a healthy win/loss ratio. During the early years winning was easier because they competed against children who were less serious and less well-prepared. Each year they accumulated more trophies and ribbons. These were exciting and powerful experiences.

As they advanced in their talent areas, the level of competition did too. Now only the serious contenders were still taking lessons, working, and improving. The children's early and relatively rich win/loss records helped them through those leaner times. Derek, our oldest, did particularly well. His talent on the piano attracted so much attention that teachers recommended he consider it seriously. He played with community orchestras and won acclaim at local adjudications. It was great but I wondered how he would do when the ratio leaned out permanently. Would he persist?

I recall taking him to a university competition where he went against college students. He was 12. He played beautifully. Afterward we waited with other contestants for the results. By that time I was incapable of objective judgment. He had won so often, why not this time too? But he didn't win, not even an honorable mention. That was his first lesson in diminishing returns. After that he knew it wouldn't be as easy. There were too many talented people out there working just as hard for the same opportunities. In order to make it, he would have to go the extra mile. And, as he later learned, that would require more than just working hard. He would have to put out enormous effort, persistence, *and* courage. Now we call it . . .

True Grit

Shortly after his seventeenth birthday, Derek became seriously ill. He developed acute lymphocytic leukemia. The disease is most lethal for males his age. His chance for survival was in the 20–30 percent range. Aggressive chemotherapy began immediately. After a year he no longer looked the same. He lost his hair, much weight, and his strength. Steroids bloated his face. With help from a home tutor, he continued school. His senior year, while still on chemotherapy, he auditioned for a school talent production. The opportunity to perform gave him a much needed goal. He was accepted into several numbers provided he agree to wear a wig during performances. He did. I even joined him in one act, a fast, energetic tap duo to "Dueling Banjos." He survived the many weeks of rehearsals by saving his strength during the day so he could get through practice at night. By show time, he was virtually indistinguishable from the rest of the cast. His wig, the makeup, and costumes worked miracles. His performances were memorable too. He graduated with his class and enrolled in the state university the following year.

He continued chemotherapy as a freshman, losing and regrowing his hair once again as he endured yet another aggressive cycle of treatment. It was hard and periodically he talked about quitting treatment and taking his chances. But he persisted, completing the full five years. At 21, he celebrated the end of treatment by winning competitions that allowed him to play with the Denver and the Fort Collins symphonies. Now he's in New York studying at Juilliard with a "healthier" perspective on what it takes to succeed. He writes about "True Grit" in the *Juilliard Journal,* the school's monthly newspaper.

True Grit

By Derek Mithaug

Recently, 19-year-old Aleksei Sultanov won the Eighth Van Cliburn International Piano Competition. On the same day, 17-year-old Michael Chang won the French Open Tennis Championship, the youngest ever to win the title. Earlier, Arantxa Sanchez, also 17 years old, won the women's title. These young people are in a class by themselves. Their achievements reflect their talent, discipline, and hard work.

Do you find yourself discouraged when faced with such awesome achievement? If so, you're not alone. I've always admired those brilliant individuals who possess such gifts. They seem to have that royal flush dealt to them from some higher force. How else could such talent and achievement be concentrated in one place? I envied their success and became discouraged. Then, my father introduced me to real heros.

Wilma was born prematurely and contracted double pneumonia, scarlet fever, and polio which left her leg crooked and her foot twisted inward. She wore leg braces until she convinced her doctor she didn't need them. At 12, she tried out for the school basketball team. She made the team as a chaperone for her older sister. But Wilma wanted to play. One day, she approached the coach. "Well, what do you want?" he asked. "If you'll give me ten minutes of your time, and only ten minutes everyday, I'll give you in return a world class athlete." He laughed. "I'll give you the ten minutes you want, but remember, I'm going to be busy with real world class athletes, people who are getting scholarships and going off to college."

That ten minutes was all Wilma needed. A track coach spotted her running up and down the court and asked her to join the team. He saw her potential. At 16, she qualified for the 1956 Olympic team and won a bronze medal in the 400 meter relay. But Wilma was still disappointed in herself and decided to go for the next Olympics.

In the 1960 summer games in Rome, Wilma walked to the field with 80,000 fans cheering wildly. She won gold medals in the 100 and 200 meter dashes, and the 400 meter relay. She was the first woman to win three gold medals in record breaking times! From a little crippled girl nobody believed in, Wilma Rudolf became a three-time Olympic gold medalist.

Wilma is a real hero! But she is not alone; they turn up everywhere. In business and industry, superachievers come from nowhere and demonstrate the same "true grit."

Alfred J. Roach, founder of a $40-million American Stock Exchange Company, says, "There's a poem by Edgar Guest that I used to like when I was a boxer that exhorts you to 'Keep going, keep going because the other fellow's getting tired too.' This is exactly how I fought: I was knocked down on occasion but never knocked out. I always got up, because I knew that if I kept going, the other guy would get tired and I would eventually win."

Another businessman, Marion W. Isbell (founder of the Ramada Inn chain), says, "When I was in school, I could see clearly that so many of the kids were much smarter than I was. I don't know whether this was because of my poor nutrition or something else, but reading and remembering were extremely hard for me. I just didn't seem to catch on as quickly as the other youngsters. Then, when I moved to Chicago at 16, I figured that I might at least be smarter than these dumb Yankee's. But I soon learned that the folks in Chicago were not so dumb. It hit me that I would never be able to outsmart anyone, so I decided to outwork them. This, I soon realized, was not too difficult to do."

When I was 13, I saw a TV special on The Juilliard School. I dreamed of the day when I could go to New York and study there. I practiced and attended concerts in our small town. Like most high school students, I planned to audition in the spring of my senior year. My dreams were cut short at 17 when I was diagnosed with leukemia.

For the next three years, I gave up my Juilliard dream to concentrate on my battle with cancer. I spent months in the hospital undergoing intense chemotherapy. I lost my hair and weighed under 100 lbs., too weak to get out of bed. Somehow, with the help of my parents, I graduated from high school and enrolled at the state university, still undergoing treatment. I began practicing again and slowly regained my health. During the spring of my junior year, I flew to New York and auditioned. Now I'm here.

I don't consider myself exceptionally fortunate or gifted. But I am learning about the "grit" it takes to make it. When my friends and teachers gave up on me, I kept working. I have not lost sight of my goal. Now, I'm not discouraged by those superachievers. You shouldn't be either. Like them, you have the power to succeed. A lot of it has to do with will. Every day, each of us must face personal challenges, those opportunities to improve ourselves. On days I have difficulty facing mine, I think of my father's favorite saying, "It's a nine inning ball game and some of us are only warming up."

So, hang in there![11]

11

Finale

As school opened to introduce the last decade of the 20th century, the Department of Education reported that academic performance of American school children stayed persistently poor over the past two decades. Education Secretary Lauro Cavazos called the findings "a compendium of disappointment."[1] Describing a "bleak portrait" of student achievement, the report said: "large proportions, perhaps more than half, of our elementary, middle school and high school students are unable to demonstrate competency in challenging subject matter in English, mathematics, science, history and geography. Further, even fewer appear to be able to use their minds well."[2]

In the 1980s, the percentage of nine-year-olds with basic reading skills decreased from 68 to 63 percent. Forty-two percent of all 13-year-olds could not interrelate ideas and make generalizations, and 58 percent of all 17-year-olds could not find, understand, summarize, or explain relatively complicated information. Less than 5 percent of our 17-year-olds read at the advanced levels necessary for work in professional and technical environments. What can we do to reverse these ominous declines? Many still believe more money for education is the answer, even though it hasn't worked in the past. From 1963 to 1982 spending per pupil doubled in constant dollars while pupil-to-teacher ratios plunged from 24:1 to 19:1. *At the same time average combined verbal and math SAT scores declined from 980 to 890.*

Do we really believe we can buy our children the desire to aspire, the willingness to work, the initiative to achieve? Can more talented teachers make a difference when students don't know how to concentrate, don't want to work, and see no reason to learn? Will new textbooks, better science equipment, and more computers make a difference when students want to spend their spare time at the mall, using drugs, and watching television? How will money engage disengaged minds and inspire uninspired spirits?

We seem to be asking the wrong questions. It's not what we can do for youth, it's *what youth can do for themselves.* Let's figure out how youth can get themselves started and keep themselves going. Reports have us believe that our youth need to learn to read better, write better, spell better, add better, and do everything else better. But in fact, academic deficiencies are symptoms of deeper and more insidious problems.

American youth *don't believe they need to achieve in order to succeed.* They expect results without work and success without challenge. Personal accomplishment is foreign currency in the marketplace of immediate highs. Youth only work to get by, doing the minimum necessary to earn passing grades. They place no value on learning for self-improvement or practicing for self-mastery. The future is now. Today's valuables are immediate, tangible, and consumable.

How long will we continue raising generations of couch potatoes who expect life to get easier and easier while they get lazier and lazier? At what point will we run out of producers because everyone's a consumer? Will youth from other countries continue to save us by enrolling in our graduate schools, learning our technologies, and becoming our producers in science, business, and industry? What happens when they leave to produce for their own countries?

Since 1987 foreign students have comprised nearly half of all doctoral candidates in areas such as cognitive science, artificial intelligence, computerized expert systems, software engineering, and nonlinear mathematics. From 1963 to 1983 foreign-born Ph.D.s in industrial engineering increased from 7 to 68 percent, in electrical engineering from 23 to 55 percent, in chemical engineering from 22 to 52 percent, and in civil engineering from 37 to 63 percent. Of the 300,000 foreign students enrolled in American universities, nearly two-thirds are in technical and scientific fields.[3] Schlossstein sees a connection between this dependence upon foreign "intellectual capital" and the nation's future: "As these *capable and hardworking* foreigners increasingly return home, they produce a "negative brain drain" and deprive America of their valuable talents and skills (though their native countries benefit, as well they should). The problem is not that America has too many foreigners mastering these technical subjects, *but too few Americans*" [italics added].[4]

When was the last time anyone described American youth as *capable and hardworking*? How can we compete in the world marketplace when we don't have anyone who can make the team? Life in this country has become so easy that youth expect less work for more results. No longer is it necessary to stand in line for groceries because supermarkets and convenience stores are open 24 hours. We even change TV channels with the press of a button from the comfort of our chairs.

Our convenience store values demand more efficiency, never less. Our children expect the same. The only difference is our saved energy at home translates into creative and productive energy at work. We're part of the economic evolution from physical to mental productivity. As long as future generations convert "freed up" physical energy into focused, creative mental energy, everything will be fine. But what happens when young people don't know how to use their mental powers, when they inherit convenience and reciprocate consumption? Then we have a problem.

Today's challenge requires that youth manage their mental powers in ways never before required. It's no longer essential that they pull their weight planting crops, milking cows, and feeding chickens. The change from agrarian and industrial-based economies to an information society reduced demands for *physical* labor. Future generations must prepare their minds. The jobs they see today will be obsolete tomorrow, so they must learn to achieve, adapt, and persist *in any situation*. This requires that they: (1) discover their talents and interests, (2) develop their competencies, (3) maximize their "fit" with the changing needs of our culture, and (4) persist with mutually beneficial exchanges with their communities. This is how youth today can succeed in the world tomorrow.

The Case for Achievement

Personal achievement is the first step toward a renaissance for American youth. It requires that they focus their minds, channel their energies, and develop their talents. Unfortunately, youth have little interest in anything that smacks of self-mastery. Why should they look to themselves for happiness and fulfillment when they're happy the way things are? And they have a point. Most kids from middle-class America lead the good life. There's sufficient wealth from the two-income family to maintain kiddie living at levels that are downright affluent by most nations' standards. Youth already have what they need to be happy: unrestricted TV, ample spending money, designer clothes, well-furnished bedrooms, cars, and free time. What a way to grow up! What could be better? Bigger TVs in bigger bedrooms? More spending money? Another car? Fancier clothes? Less hassle and more freedom?

Who among them is crazy enough to choose that other path to happiness, the one paved with work, sacrifice, discipline, risk, and possible failure? Why should they give up daily joys in favor of Spartan programs of thinking, working, and persisting? Our afflu-ent, entitlement culture discourages self-awareness, self-direction, and self-reliance. Youth see no need to hustle and achieve. They have a skewed sense of how the world works and what it takes to achieve success. Each generation of affluently spawned youngsters swims to sea with a useless set of naive expectations. Then they discover life out there is choppy, unpredictable, and even dangerous. So they return home to calm and safe waters.

Many parents are culpably misguided. They believe that "Chil-dren should be children, enjoying life and having fun. There's time later to get a job, earn a living, and be unhappy the rest of their lives." There's some truth to this belief. Youth specializing in good times during the early years *do find* disappointing times during their later years. There's no way around the basic choice: "Play now, pay later; or pay now, play later." Youth who *pay now* choose the road to fulfillment. They sacrifice some good times today in favor of dis-covering their interests, developing their talents, and learning to think. Their purpose in life is to find that harmonious "fit" between what they have to offer and what the environment has to give.

How to Teach Success Principles

Parents can help children find their path to personal achievement by introducing them to the success principles. Too bad we didn't have this opportunity when we were their age. Instead, we learned these principles the hard way—through life's labyrinth of trial and error. Our children can take a more direct route by learning to apply all three principles as they grow up. No more choosing competence over intelligence or intelligence over persistence. They can master all three at once and maximize their effects now.

The Competency Principle

The competency principle describes the relation between ability and results. In general, the more capable you are in a competency area, the more likely you'll achieve positive results and positive self-evaluations. Good results and good evaluations, in turn, increase confidence and self-esteem. Competence starts a positive chain reaction: positive results beget self-confidence which builds self-esteem.

The Competency Principle

THE GREATER THE COMPETENCE,
THE MORE POSITIVE THE RESULT.
THE GREATER THE SELF-CONFIDENCE,
THE MORE POSITIVE THE SELF-ESTEEM.

All people who succeed are competent. They achieve positive results because of what they do, not who they are. They have skills and knowledge that generate accomplishment feedback that starts them on a "roll." Accomplishment feedback reinforces performance which generates confidence and increases self-esteem.

The Intelligence Principle

Successful people are intelligent adaptors. They maximize matches between: (1) what they like and what they can do, (2) their performance and environmental demands, and (3) their contributions and environmental rewards. They solve several adjustment problems at once. *First,* they match their interests and abilities. They achieve harmony between mind, body, and spirit by doing best what they like most. They yoke *intrinsic* motivation with *natural* ability.

Second, they find environments that want what they have to offer and then match their abilities with those environmental demands. If the environment doesn't need their skills, they change the environment by creating a need for their services, they develop skills the environment does want, or they find a new environment.

The *third* match is between results and evaluations. Intelligent adaptors monitor their behaviors and record their results accurately and objectively. They compare expectations with results and identify what produced what. Did they get what they wanted? If not, why not and what needs to change next time: plans, attitudes, or actions? Adaptive achievers match, compare, evaluate, and adjust continuously to fine-tune their adaptive fit and maximize their environmental exchange.

These three match strategies produce intelligent, harmonious fits as indicated by the intelligence principle:

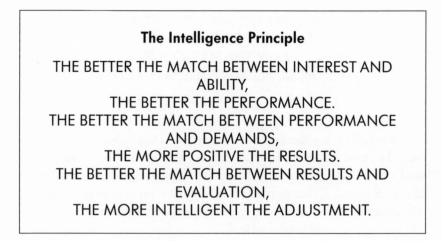

The Intelligence Principle

THE BETTER THE MATCH BETWEEN INTEREST AND ABILITY,
THE BETTER THE PERFORMANCE.
THE BETTER THE MATCH BETWEEN PERFORMANCE AND DEMANDS,
THE MORE POSITIVE THE RESULTS.
THE BETTER THE MATCH BETWEEN RESULTS AND EVALUATION,
THE MORE INTELLIGENT THE ADJUSTMENT.

The Persistence Principle

The persistence principle states that continuous, focused problem solving increases the chances of reaching a desired goal. Persisters work on important problems long enough to find solutions. They do it by means of *focused* trial and error, working one problem at a time, systematically eliminating what doesn't work while keeping what does. This is similar to the scientist's use of the Scientific Method. Edison's incandescent bulb resulted from systematic trial-and-error problem solving. Persisters solve all their adjustment problems by comparing what they expect with what they get. They learn from experience systematically. They are relentless pursuers of solutions that move them toward goals.

The Persistence Principle

THE MORE PERSISTENT THE SOLVING
OF PROBLEMS IN THE WAY OF A GOAL,
THE MORE LIKELY THE ACHIEVEMENT
OF THAT DESIRED GOAL.

Parenting Success Principles

Parenting success principles can be broken down into ten steps. As you read them, you'll think they're so obvious that you'll remember and apply them easily. I agree. They are logical and common sensical. But take my word, they're not easy. I've been working on them for over 20 years and I am still learning when and how to perform the roles they require. The steps operationalize the premise that parents and teachers must *lead, mentor,* and *befriend* if they're to influence children and students to achieve and self-actualize. But it's a whole lot easier to *understand* these roles than it is to *perform* them. The leadership role requires behaviors that are different from the mentorship role. And the mentorship role consists of behaviors not included in the friendship role. Yet, all three are necessary to start youth on that path toward personal achievement. Mind you, I deliberately wrote *start,* not get them there or guarantee their arrival there. We *start* them. They do the rest. They choose their own path, follow its course, adapt to its changes, and enjoy its rewards.

We use our most powerful tools to teach them to develop their talents, maximize their intelligence, and persist at their goals. This is all we can do. But, to borrow a phrase from A. L. Williams, "All we can do is all we can do, but all we can do is enough."[5] The trick, of course, is knowing when to perform which role and for what purpose. The ten steps that follow will help you answer these questions *for yourself*. They are guides to enhance your own style of parenting. They're not the usual cookbook "do's and don'ts" for raising obedient kids. Rather, they specify how each parenting role helps youth learn a principle of success.

Step 1. Parent for Success

When Joey was born, his parents immediately checked developmental charts to see where he was in height and weight. Was he at the 10th or the 90th percentile? A year later they consulted the charts again, this time to see if he should be crawling, standing, or walking. At two years, they counted his words and compared his vocabulary with that of the neighbor kids and child development guidelines. When he "beat" the norms, walked more and talked better than the rest, they felt great. They knew someday he would be a president, scientist, world-class athlete, or best-selling author. Anything was possible.

By school, they were hooked again. What percentile, stanine, or grade equivalent was he at now? Still ahead, or did something happen between age two and age six? Suddenly, they no longer hoped for the presidency; normal development would be fine, especially when teachers started talking about "special classes." Expectations changed suddenly. Now, year after year, they watched for signs. How did Joey compare? They checked norms once again. What was the answer?

Unfortunately, there are no answers. All parents can learn from the process of comparing Joey with his peers is that on the day of the test, he performs X, Y, and Z tasks better than, as well as, or more poorly than others his age. That's all there is. But they want more. They want to know if Joey will be successful. They don't understand that *no test predicts the future.*

If they want Joey to succeed, they need to ask different questions. "What does Joey like to do?", "What *can* he do?", "How can Joey make his own, unique contribution?", "And how can he maximize his strengths and minimize weaknesses in order to make that contribution?" This is the first step toward success parenting: thinking about Joey's *potential* for fitting into present and future environments.

Step 2. Demonstrate Competence

Children learn much by observing and imitating. When they see parents perform tasks well, they want to do the same. And when parents talk about "doing things well," children aspire to master and perfect. It's no accident that achievement runs in families. Leadership in competency development builds on that natural desire to do what mom and dad do.

Share your abilities and interests with your children. Engage them in the same activities. Encourage them to try. At the same time, communicate positive expectations to achieve. If you like reading poetry, playing cards, building bird houses, jogging, or whatever, demonstrate your skills and expect your children to participate at their own level. At the same time, watch their responses. Some activities will turn them off. Children are great: when they don't like something they fall asleep or walk off. That says enough. Note which activities stimulate their interest and tap into their abilities. This helps when making a decision about what competency to introduce.

The chart in Figure 16 will help too. It provides four sample behaviors in each of the six talent categories: Linguistics, Logical-Mathematical, Spatial, Bodily-Kinesthetic, Musical, and Personal-Social. For each sample behavior ask yourself "Do I like to perform this behavior?" and "Am I competent at it?" Next, review the chart again and identify which talent area(s) produce the most "Yeses." Now ask "Does my job match my interests and abilities?"

Next look at the chart in Figure 17 which lists sample occupational roles for the six talent categories. In the Linguistic category, for example, poets, writers, public speakers, scholars, and interpreters usually have sample behaviors listed in Figure 17—talking, reading, writing, understanding language. Contrast these competencies with what sculptors, painters, architects, geographers, and decorators need—the Spatial category in Figure 17.

What are your interests and abilities? Do they converge on one or several talent categories? And does your occupation match those preferences? Ask your spouse to conduct the assessment too and

LINGUISTIC	LOGICAL/ MATHE- MATICAL	SPATIAL	BODILY- KINESTHETIC	MUSICAL	PERSONAL/ SOCIAL
Talking	Logical thinking	Reading signs, pictures	Doing things	Singing	Observing people
Reading	Math thinking	Observing spatial relation- ships	Coordinated body movements	Composing	Knowing own feelings
Writing	Computing	Drawing	Coordinated hand movements	Playing music	Knowing others' feelings
Understanding language	Observing events	Thinking in pictures	Coordinated speech, hand, and body movements	Knowing music	Knowing social situations

MY TALENTS AND ABILITIES

FIGURE 16
The Talent Categories

then compare results. This exercise narrows the range of possible competencies for which your children may show interest and aptitude. Select one or two and test them. Expose your children to a competency and observe their responses. Then decide. Don't be surprised if you select competencies similar to those of other family members. Remember the "Amazing Families" in Chapter 8. Interests and competencies run in families. Parents with a musical bent

LINGUISTIC	LOGICAL/ MATHE- MATICAL	SPATIAL	BODILY- KINESTHETIC	MUSICAL	PERSONAL/ SOCIAL
Poets	Mathe- maticians	Sculptors	Athletes	Singers	Teachers
Writers	Accountants	Painters	Dancers	Musicians	Therapists
Speakers	Scientists	Architects	Actors	Conductors	Counselors
Scholars	Statisticians	Geographers	Mechanics	Composers	Salespersons
Interpreters	Economists	Decorators	Inventors	Music critics	Coaches

FIGURE 17

The Talent Categories & Occupational Roles

are more likely to have children who become violinists than quarterbacks.

Step 3. Mentor Competence

Leadership gets children interested and motivated but it doesn't get them started and keep them going. Direct intervention is necessary for that. During the early years, you'll be the driving force for new learning. Regardless of the talent area, daily practice will be necessary to build competence and deepen interest. The three phases of competency development are acquisition, practice, and performance. During *acquisition,* children work with teachers or coaches to learn the technical skills required for various tasks and routines. During *practice,* they work semi-independently to eliminate errors and build proficiency. And during *performance,* they demonstrate what they can do for family, relatives, school, and community.

Require regular practice at home. I recommend the practice-before-play rule. It works well and eliminates problems later on. At first you may have to sit with your children as they learn how to practice. Often parents expect teachers and coaches to teach practicing skills. They don't. Their focus is on content. They leave the rest to you and your child. So be prepared to help. If the talent area is one in which you share interest and have ability, you'll know what to do. But don't worry if you don't know anything. You'll learn by sitting in on the lesson and taking notes. I remember when Dustin began learning figures in ice skating. At first I knew nothing. So I stood on the ice with his coach as she instructed him. After a few lessons I could offer suggestions that were helpful. But I never demonstrated!

As children become more proficient, they need less help every day. But they still need encouragement and supervision to stay on their schedules. Be prepared to enforce the practice-then-play rule throughout grade school. When they reach adolescence, they will have sufficient self-discipline to maintain a practice schedule on their own. Now you can "back off" and turn over practice/training responsibilities to them. You've just shifted roles from teacher/supervisor to mentor/advisor.

Step 4. Share Competence

Children are eager to learn when their efforts generate positive consequences. No one enjoys hours of practice that don't lead anywhere. Nevertheless, children and youth rarely maintain themselves in their talent areas *at first. Intrinsic motivation to improve only comes after years of work in the talent area.* Therefore, they need external reinforcement during the early years. They also need to see what others get from being competent. What *are* those benefits? Children in the performing arts receive inspiration from concerts, theater productions, and dance performances. They also discover that their own public performances generate positive recognition. Whatever your child's talent area, it must have a socially rewarding consequence that communicates its ultimate benefits. Share those benefits as early and frequently as possible.

Step 5. Demonstrate Intelligence

Demonstrate intelligence by showing your children how *you* maximize your strengths and minimize your weakness to get what you want. Parents who enjoy their jobs, are competent at their work, and receive rewards for their efforts are intelligent adaptors. If this sentence describes you, then let your children see that "you." On the other hand, if it's not yet you, if you're still working at "becoming," that's even better! Talk about what you're going through, how you're trying to match what you like most with what you do best in your career. This is a great opportunity for them to see intelligent adaptation in action.

I've used both approaches. I describe those features of my job that I'm ideally matched for, and I explain how enjoyable it is to be good at something that's both rewarding (financially) and fun. I also talk about the parts that aren't so great and my plans to change them. This shows them that adjustment is continuous.

A second component of leadership is *expectations*. Expect your children to improve their adaptations. If something isn't working, expect them to analyze what's wrong and take corrective action. Helpless resignation in the face of unsatisfactory adjustments is unacceptable. Expect solutions and improvements even if it means changing environments.

The third component of effective leadership is *opportunity*. Family problems provide excellent occasions to practice mutual adjustments. Parents learn to adjust their lives to meet their children's needs, and children in turn must learn to adjust their lives to meet their parents' needs. The normal give-and-take of living together provides rich opportunities for mutual problem solving. The division of household chores is a start. Distribute assignments according to preference and ability, taking turns on jobs no one wants. This is a nice demonstration of intelligent adaptation.

Whenever possible, encourage children to set personal goals as well as the usual ones that help with order at home. Next, have them develop plans and time lines. Then check periodically to see if they're monitoring and adjusting so as to maintain progress. This reminds them of your expectations that they keep thinking, planning, acting, and adjusting. Encourage the belief that they can achieve anything if they manage their personal resources wisely.

Step 6. Mentor Intelligence

Children learn competence and intelligence at the same time. As they become proficient in a talent area they also discover what they like and what they can do. This is their start on self-direction. Knowing something about themselves helps them set goals that match their needs, interests, and abilities.

At first, children's goals tend to be *exactly* what teachers and coaches expect. Their plans, actions, and evaluation methods match too. The weekly lessons and training sessions suggest what goals to set, how much practice time to schedule, and what actions to take each day. They also discover the consequences of not meeting expectations: teacher and parental disapproval and disappointment. Lessons provide feedback. Even "good" ones end with new expectations. There's no such thing as a finished, completed, perfected act. Youth learn to adjust one week to the next. There's always something to improve, another obstacle to overcome.

Figure 18 illustrates this process. Youth manage multiple tasks and performance routines. By evaluating and adjusting to results, they maximize strengths and eliminate obstacles. Teachers and coaches introduce daily planning by writing expectations and weekly assignments in notebooks children take home with them.

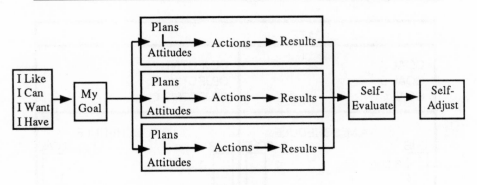

FIGURE 18
Intelligent Adaptations

Parents display practice schedules on charts for children to follow on their own. When they get older, they can use their own "executive planners" like those adults use to manage objectives, activities, and appointments.

Youth should master the daily planner in junior high school. Unfortunately, most students graduate from high school without even seeing one. Look at the sample planning sheet in Figure 19. You can use the format on any size paper. The top panel specifies three goals and three objectives for the day, the middle panel lists the time slots for activities and tasks for each objective, and the bottom panel evaluates results on the left side and indicates adjustments necessary for the next day on the right. Introduce this sheet, or one like it, in junior high or earlier if possible. The form allows youth to write their three most important goals each day, the most important being "Goal A" and the least important "Goal C." Next they specify an objective to accomplish that day *for each goal*. Then they list the tasks and hours for completing them in the middle panel. They indicate which tasks relate to which objective by recording an "A," "B," or "C" in the columns to the left of the hour times. This requires them to distribute their work between morning (AM schedule) and afternoon and evening (PM schedule).

They take their planners with them to remind themselves what they must do and when. After completing a task, they check the box to its right indicating "Done." At the end of the day, they *evaluate* their results, indicating "Y" for "Yes" and "N" for "No" for tasks assigned to each objective. And they *adjust* by deciding which

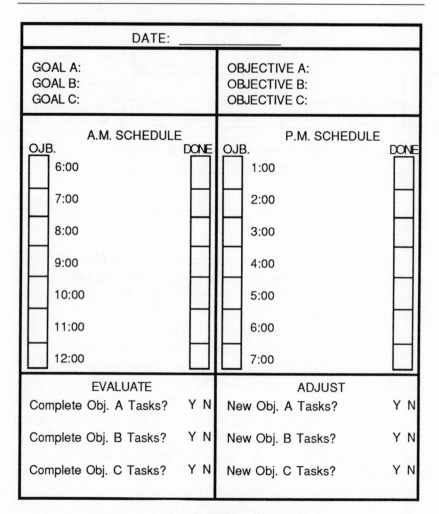

FIGURE 19
A Daily Planner

tasks to work on the next day. Do they need to assign themselves new tasks or continue working on the same ones?

Think of what it would mean to have a whole generation of youth directing themselves productively each day, intrinsically motivated and eager to learn, and seeking out challenging opportunities to stretch their capacities. Imagine what it would mean to parents, teachers, and the nation to have youth eager to achieve their own goals not just because of the external rewards that *might result* but because of the feelings of satisfaction and fulfillment that *would result*. This is possible when parents take a few simple steps on behalf of their children's self-direction.

Step 7. Cooperate Intelligently

Meeting the competency challenge also helps children solve interpersonal problems intelligently. Instead of viewing the world from the "me-first" perspective, they learn that exchange is a two-way street. If you want to get something from the environment, you must give something *first*. The same rule applies to interpersonal relations. If you want people to help you—friends, siblings, parents, teachers, and coaches—you must give them something they need *first*. This means understanding their needs, interests, and abilities as well as your own. What do they want from you? How can you deliver it?

It's unfortunate that so many children and youth grow up thinking that all they need is to satisfy themselves. Egocentric behaviors are natural and marginally amusing in childhood. But they're burdensome, if not pathological, later. Young people who understand reciprocity will find life much kinder and gentler in the long run. One of the best ways to teach this truth is through mutual problem solving in family and peer relationships. The diagram in Figure 20 summarizes its major features. Copy it and pin it to the refrigerator for everyone to memorize. Then when a problem arises, walk through the steps to find a solution that works for everyone.

This may be the single most important lesson children and youth can learn. Because without help from others it's nearly impossible to accomplish significant goals. Sure, there's much one can achieve alone. Self-discipline and self-mastery are powerful tools to employ against the challenges of the physical environment. But today's interdependent world presents as many social challenges as it does physical ones. Getting a job, keeping it, and earning a promotion are significant *social* adaptations.

Therefore, when you have disagreements with your children because they don't clean their rooms or do their homework, consider the cooperative approach to problem solving. What do you have to offer in return for the behaviors you want them to perform? Begin by identifying the problem and then reviewing respective needs.

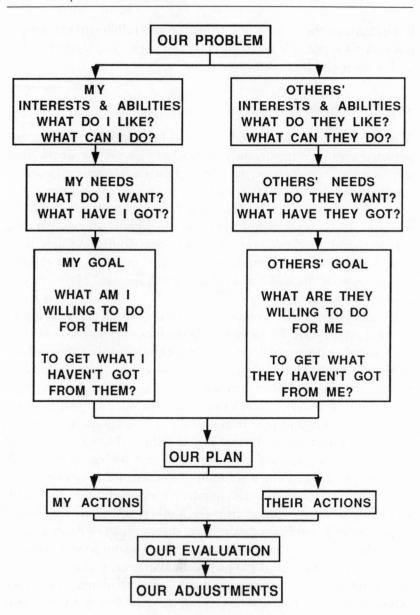

FIGURE 20
Mutual Adaptations

Then negotiate mutually acceptable exchanges. Let the diagram on the refrigerator guide your way. You may be shocked to discover how effective it is.

Step 8. Demonstrate Persistence

At first, young children have no conception of the sustained effort required to meet challenging goals. But you can introduce the idea by explaining how long it takes you to accomplish difficult tasks. Let them see you working on the same project day after day and tell them that you're *persisting*. Soon they'll understand that persistence is different from working for a long time during a single session. Persistence is coming back to the same task day after day, week after week—if necessary.

Expect your children to persevere and they will. Parents have a tendency to want to help their children through difficult problems. But that's precisely when they learn to persist. During high school my children came to me when they didn't understand math or science. I was delighted to help. Soon they asked questions I couldn't answer easily, so I asked them questions to understand the problems better. When they couldn't answer, I asked to see their texts. Sure enough, the answers they needed were right there. They hadn't even read the book! That was the last time I gave free answers.

Children are experts at minimizing effort. Remind them of the persistence principle and encourage them to stick with difficult problems. When answers don't come immediately or tasks take too long, it's time to review the principle. The times when they want most to quit are the times when they learn the most if they persist. Each time they stay the course, they build resistance against packing it in. Most people fail simply because they've never learned to hang on long enough. Don't let your children become members of this group.

The persistence lesson is useless, of course, if all tasks are easy and no goals are challenging. Children need *opportunities* to build commitment. Self-improvement provides one of the best ways I know of learning the principle. Sign up your child for weekly lessons in a skill area that requires regular study and practice at home. Then count the number of weeks before she no longer wants to practice and talks about quitting. It never fails: even gifted, talented, and seemingly self-directed children want to quit when novelty wears off and real work begins. Suddenly it's boring, difficult, and, of course, time consuming. Jenny wants something else, anything else. Every year parents get "conned" into believing that they picked the wrong talent area. When children complain, parents cave in, fearing grave psychological scars will blemish those young minds if their children are forced to continue. This belief is nonsense. But they believe it, carting Joey and Janey from one talent area to the next until finally they've tried them all. The only *sustaining* lesson learned from this process is that quitting is okay. That's the death knell for persistence.

Parents promote persistence by leading. They *demonstrate* their own persistence in the completion of their work and the accomplishment of their goals. They *expect* their children to persist at difficult tasks. And they *provide opportunities* for their children to work independently at self-improvement projects that stretch their concentration and build their commitment.

Step 9. Mentor Persistence

The leadership step gets children's attention. It lets them know there's more at stake than just learning a skill. It tells them that working through difficult problems has value in itself. The mental self-discipline required to concentrate on problems to the best of one's ability is worthy of praise, even if the ultimate solution isn't perfect. At his piano lesson, Rick gets a new piece. He likes it and wants to learn it. But when he gets home he discovers it's more difficult than he thought it was. So he waits until the middle of the week before starting. Finally he takes it out and begins. Suddenly he becomes so involved with figuring the notes and correct fingering that he forgets the time. Later he wonders why he waited to start. At his next lesson, he plays what he learned. His teacher helps him again, and he returns home, this time working on it immediately. Now it's less formidable and he enjoys it. By the third lesson, the piece has become Rick's favorite and he spends most of his time practicing it. But now he has another one he can't play. He repeats the scenario, avoiding the start-up as long as possible and doing the minimum just before the next lesson.

Slowly Rick learns to persist. Each week he solves a series of complicated reading and fingering problems that get in the way of playing what he wants to hear. He remembers the sounds but doesn't know which fingers produce it. So he breaks down the mass of notation into manageable units. He examines each measure, note by note, key by key, finger by finger. Slowly he puts the units together, practices them in sequence, and approximates the rendition heard at his lesson.

Rick's persistence consists of more than sitting at the piano every day and practicing previously mastered pieces. Rick spends time in deep, intense, concentrated problem solving. He breaks the music into learnable units, masters them in isolation, and then reassembles them into phrases. Week after week he follows the same routine. He's becoming a persistent *problem solver.*

Children in self-improvement programs build their capacities to concentrate as they improve. Their challenge is internal, as they try to advance themselves from where they are to where they want to be. They don't quit because they've learned that the longer they work, the better they become. Success is the reinforcement for persisting.

The persistence principle pays big dividends when combined with competence and intelligence. The diagram in Figure 21 illustrates this important point. First you identify problems that impede progress toward goals. You ask "Why don't I get what I want?, Have I set inappropriate goals?, Are my plans inadequate?, Is my perfor-

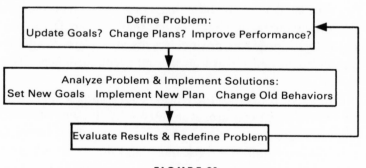

FIGURE 21
Persistent Problem Solving

mance effective?" Once you define the problem, you break it into components, rearrange its units, and implement the new approach. Then you observe and record results. Did the change make a difference? Have you met your needs, goals, and plans? Did your performance meet expectations? You repeat the process continuously. This builds competence and sharpens intelligence which, in turn, intensify and redirect problem solving.

Parents teach persistence by (1) giving children successively more challenging opportunities, (2) demonstrating how to break problems into do-able units, (3) setting schedules for regular, sustainable work, and (4) encouraging children to persist until they complete their tasks and meet their goals. The instructional process is so simple it's surprising that all children don't learn to persist.

If you analyze how persisters persist, you'll discover it's not because they chain themselves to impossible goals. Rather, they break them into possible, even probable, outcomes and then tackle them one at a time. Before they know it, they're close enough to believe they can go all the way. Their friends wonder how they do it. But it's easier than imagined. Persisters get "hooked" by early success which keeps them going. Share this secret with your children.

Step 10. Compete Persistently

The ultimate test for perseverance does not occur at home. It occurs in a world of equals, where competition for opportunity decides who fits and who doesn't. Young people who commit themselves to personal goals learn how to overcome difficult obstacles. That's only half the challenge. The other half comes when their best efforts fall short of giving them what they feel they deserve. Daily practice at home always produces positive results at lessons. Teachers and coaches evaluate and reward effort and accomplishment. They're *consistent*.

Unfortunately, the rest of the world is not so predictable, sending mixed messages that confuse, even discourage. It deals out rewards and opportunities competitively. Now results depend on who enters the piano competition, the track meet, and the tennis match. Will youth persevere under these conditions? Or will they lose interest and quit because winning is less certain?

I don't recommend competitions among siblings. But outside the family, they teach real-life win-loss ratios. Frequent competitions with peers adjust expectations for winning every time. Unless a child's competence is truly prodigious, he or she will learn what a 25 percent batting average means. You're four times as likely to strike out as you are to get on base. And in baseball—as in life— that's pretty good!

All children must practice going to bat and taking their best swing. If they don't get a hit the first time up, they must go back again, and again, until they get one. They must learn to analyze their performance. "Am I looking for the right pitches?" "Do I need to improve my technique?" Then they will learn how to avoid the same mistakes again.

Don't be afraid to encourage competition. You do your children no favors by sheltering them. So, if they must, let them choose challenges that best match their talents, interests, and abilities. Give them a chance to win their share of opportunities and the benefits that they bestow.

Success Parenting

If you want your children to succeed, prepare them to succeed. Don't leave it to chance. Schools don't teach success. And the university of hard knocks is painful and slow. Consider success parenting. It challenges you to look to the future rather than to the past. Why compare your children with their peers who aren't headed anywhere in particular? Better to focus on what works for adults who know how to get what they want from life. After all, that's where your children *are* headed—into adulthood. Then you can ask yourself: "How will they succeed, how will they be happy, and how will they find fulfillment?"

In this chapter, I reviewed three principles children must learn in order to succeed in life: the *Competence Principle,* the *Intelligence Principle,* and the *Persistence Principle.* I also reviewed three parenting roles to help them learn these principles: *Leadership, Mentorship,* and *Friendship.* Parents who teach these principles will help their children maximize their potential for success, happiness, and fulfillment throughout their lives.

	Leadership	Mentorship	Friendship
Develop Competence	Demonstrate Competence	Give Lessons in Talent Area	Share Experience in Talent Area
	Expect Competence	Reinforce Daily Practice	
	Give Opportunities for Competence	Require Regular Demonstrations of Competence	Share Rewards from Competency Demonstrations
Maximize Intelligence	Show Your Intelligent Adaptations	Teach & Mentor 1. Self-Scheduling	Demonstrate Mutually Beneficial Exchanges
	Expect Intelligent Adjustments	2. Self-Evaluation 3. Self-Adjusting	
	Give Opportunities for Intelligent Adjustments	4. Self-Awareness 5. Goal Setting	Solve Parent-Child Problems Cooperatively
Empower Persistence	Demonstrate Persistent Problem Solving	Teach & Mentor Goal/Task Analysis	Encourage Competition with Peers for Opportunity
	Expect Persistence	Single Unit Focus to Start	
	Give Challenges that Require Persistence	Task/Goal Synthesis to End	Establish Realistic Reward Expectations

FIGURE 22

Success Parenting Roles

The table in Figure 22 summarizes nine sets of objectives to strive for as you parent for success. Copy it and paste it in your daily planner, on the refrigerator, or on your nightstand to review daily until it's memorized. It will help you remember what roles and behaviors will help your child develop his or her competence, maximize his or her intelligence, and build his or her persistence. When children are young, you'll need more time leading and mentoring than befriending. Later, friendship becomes more important. Figure 23 illustrates these changes. Leadership and mentorship decrease as friendship increases.

Figure 24 summarizes the three goals: *competence* in a favorite talent area, *intelligent adaptations* across different environments, and *persistent* problem solving to meet goals. Although youth work toward all three at the same time, they make progress on each goal at different rates. Competency achievements occur relatively early in development. In fact, prodigious achievement often shows up as early as three and four years of age. It takes longer for mental agility to express itself across different environments. Persistent problem

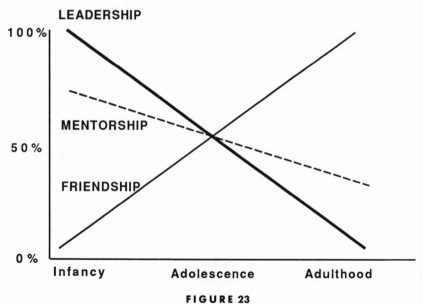

FIGURE 23
When Parents and Teachers Perform What

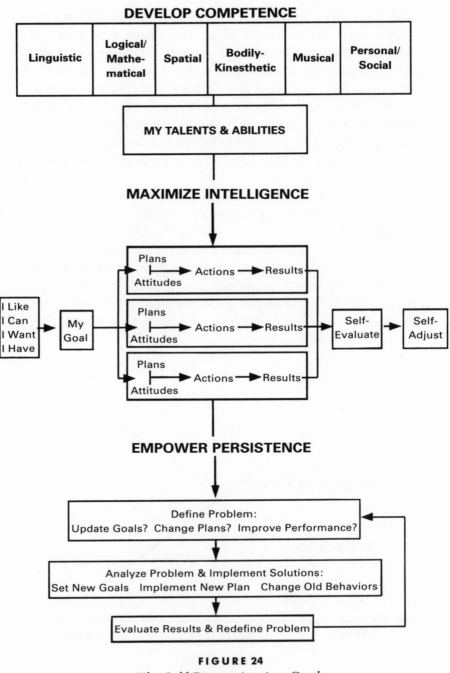

FIGURE 24

The Self-Determination Goals

solving may be the last to come of age, gaining the greater relative importance after adolescence and well into adulthood.

The chart in Figure 25 illustrates these different paths through the life span. During childhood, competence shows the greatest improvement, with intelligence second, and persistence last. After adolescence patterns reverse. Competence decreases in importance while intelligence and persistence increase. By adulthood, persistence dominates, intelligence is second, and competence takes third place.

Success principles apply to everyone. No one escapes their rule. Regardless of your station in life, natural gifts, or unfortunate liabilities, they'll work for or against you. People with abilities and disabilities alike must develop their competence, maximize their intelligence, and empower their persistence if they want to succeed. Personal achievement is the ultimate expression of this benefit. Regardless of Jenny's physical or mental gifts at birth, she still must make the most of what she has. Then she'll find success, happiness, and fulfillment.

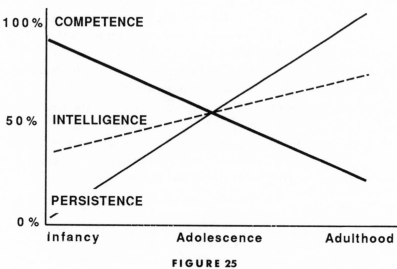

FIGURE 25
When Children Demonstrate What

Two Percent a Day

I've worked with hundreds of children, youth, and adults whose intellectual and physical skills ranged from severely limited to exceptionally gifted. Although unequal on comparative tests of ability, these young people were always equal on tests of personal achievement. Some of the most remarkable accomplishments come from persons who face the greatest challenges.

Ann Ruth was only five years old when she tried a stunt on a balance beam that left her with an injured spinal cord and permanent paralysis from the neck down. After ten hours of surgery and nine months in a California hospital, she returned home in an iron lung—against the advice of her doctors. Immediately, her father asked if she could breathe on her own. This was unheard of. According to doctors, it's impossible for patients with paralysis involving the diaphragm to breathe outside of the iron lung. But Ann's father was a "leader." If she could breathe just a few seconds on her own, why couldn't she learn to breathe for longer periods, he reasoned. He was right. She learned to use her neck muscles to breathe, which she controls voluntarily during the day. At night she uses the lung.

Ann's a superachiever. She refused special education classes, stayed with peers, and earned excellent grades. She was even elected class representative. She majored in sports communication at the University of Southern California and graduated with a 4.0 average. She planned a year of study in Spain and then graduate work at Cambridge University in England but won admission to an IBM nine-month training program on computers and took a job before finishing. Recently she jumped from an airplane at 12,500 feet for a 2 1/2-minute free-fall strapped in front of her instructor who pulled the rip cord. The instructor landed first, in time to catch her before she touched the ground. Ann's goal is to run her own greeting card business:

> I want to get my greeting card business going. When I was nine a friend of my mother's, Mrs. Thelma Steinberg, got me interested in painting. She is a talented artist. She began teaching me how to paint during my recovery, and she is still my teacher. [Annie paints with a brush clenched between her teeth.] I am doing oil painting and have

the illustrations put on greeting cards. I'm doing it to earn money but I also have a good time.[6]

Ann reminds me of our daughter Dana who, at age 20, suddenly had to switch her personal goals from studying economics in Lancaster, England, to learning to sort PVC pipe parts at home. After an especially difficult sophomore year, working two jobs, staying up late studying long hours, Dana returned home exhausted. She planned to rest before starting her summer job in preparation for a junior year in England which she had planned for years. This was her all-consuming goal.

Unfortunately, she became ill with an infection that settled in her cerebellum, the portion of the brain that controls coordination. Within two months, her condition deteriorated so badly she could not walk, talk, dress herself, or see clearly. A definitive diagnosis eluded neurologists. No one could say if she would ever recover or how long it might take. She returned home from the hospital, all the time assuring herself that the condition would abate in time for her flight to England in late September. The weeks passed and there was little change. Finally, in early August, she reluctantly decided to stay home. She was crushed. Not only was she unable to pursue the goal she had worked and planned for so long, but she wasn't even certain what was happening to her. She was frightened, disappointed, and depressed. How could things fall apart so suddenly?

Meanwhile, she lost strength as well as balance. She slept long hours and required assistance for the most routine personal care tasks. Every day her mother and I asked how she felt, hoping for some sign of improvement but also worried that additional symptoms might appear. At first she tried to be upbeat and tell us what we wanted to hear. But after a few weeks, even that was too much. In her difficult-to-understand, belabored speech, she just smiled and said: "The same." She was losing hope. Now we worried for her mental health. She needed to be positive to maximize her chances for recovery. She had to do her part. How could she regain hope?

Dana needed three things. She needed a new set of goals to replace the ones she had lost. She needed to take daily action toward achieving those goals. And she needed to see *daily progress*. Although the logic of this assessment was obvious, the "how to" was not. Dana and I talked about what she could focus on and considered many options. Unfortunately, there were too few tasks or activities she could actually do. Anything involving walking was out. She couldn't stand without assistance. Her hands were so uncoordinated that most fine, eye-hand activities wouldn't work either. Finally we decided to go with the simplest sorting task I could assemble. With three plastic bins in front of her—the middle bin containing 50 cpvc pipe fittings, 25 elbows, and 25 tees—she sorted the parts, placing the elbows in a side bin at the right and the tees in a side bin at the left. Meanwhile, I timed how long she took to complete the sorts.

Her new goal was simple. Decrease the time to complete 50 sorts—which meant increasing the rate of moving her hands and picking up and releasing parts. She took positive action each day by completing the tasks as I timed her. She followed her progress by comparing her times with the previous day's times.

When we started, she was more tolerant than enthusiastic. After all, sorting cpvc pipe fittings was not exactly her idea of high adventure, much less high achievement. Nevertheless, she did her best. Almost at once, we both realized how severely affected her movements were. During the first session her hands shook as she picked up one piece at a time, ever so slowly placing it in an adjacent bin. It was unbelievably slow. Could this be my same Dana who played piano with the Colorado Springs Orchestra in high school? Where were those fast and delicate finger moves?

After each session, I volunteered her times, indicating whether she was faster or slower than the previous day. At first, she gave no reaction. Sometimes, I wondered if she even cared. But after a few weeks, her attitude changed. She started to see improvement. When we reviewed where she was with where she had started and how much her times had improved, she knew she was getting faster. From then on, she *demanded* to know her times! She was hooked! She saw progress and found hope. Her confidence improved and her fear gradually disappeared.

Figure 26 shows her progress during those first five months. Notice the similarity between right- and left-hand performance. Sometimes we had contests to see which hand would win. At first her right hand was stronger, although she was left-handed. But later that switched. Later both hands performed equally well. As it turned out, this simple task became the barometer of her progress.

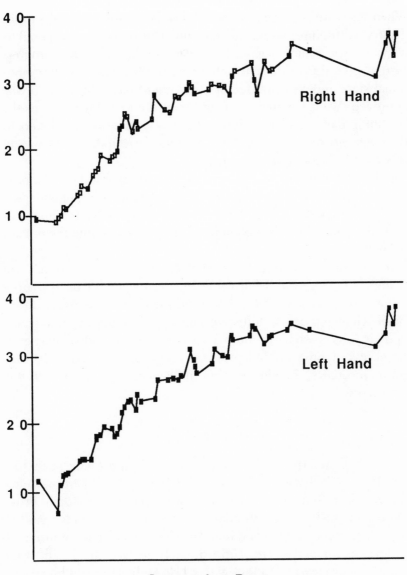

Right Hand

Left Hand

Successive Days

FIGURE 26
Dana's Sorts Per Minute

When she wasn't feeling well, we looked at the sorting results to see if she was still improving, and she was. The doctors couldn't tell us what to expect and suggested relapses were possible. But progress sorting pipe fittings lessened those fears. Regardless of her emotional state and all other factors that might have contributed, she improved. We calculated her gains from the first three days to the last three days at various intervals. Always she averaged *two to three percent gain per day*. That became our standard, our expectation in this time of uncertainty.

Dana still improves at the rate of 2 to 3 percent a day. And now she has more ambitious goals. She's set a date for walking independently and has reenrolled at the university. She still has significant challenges ahead but has confidence she will overcome them. And she will.

Dana reminds me once again that there are no "time outs" and "King's X's" in getting what we want. Even when life deals the occasional bad hand, we must do our best with what we have. If that means changing goals, adjusting plans, and taking on new goals, so be it. That's what we must do if we intend to follow that path to success, happiness, and personal fulfillment. We must develop our competence, maximize our intelligence, and empower our persistence.

A Nation at Risk?

It's too bad America's fast-track youth can't appreciate goals like Ann Ruth's "*inch by inch, life's a cinch*" or Dana's *2-percent-a-day* rehabilitation. But the thought of making microscopic, daily progress on any task is an unthinkable waste of time for kids who believe in shortcuts to the good life. American youth don't realize that *progress* is *an inchworm*. Unfortunately for us, the Pacific Rim countries have learned to follow that rule of the worm. While we've spent and consumed for over four decades, they have saved and produced. In 1945 Japan was in shambles and the United States basked in abundance. Forty-five years later, Japan has all the wealth and we have all the debt. What happened?

Six years ago we were the world's greatest net creditor, with an official $141 billion plus in foreign trade. Since then we've burned up $500 billion. We should heed the words of Scandinavian economist Staffan Burenstam Linder:

> No country has an entitlement to prosperity. No region has special privileges. Historically inspired feelings of superiority cause misunderstandings, and the ensuing inflexibilities are not affordable. Asian-Pacific competition now underscores this reality. It demonstrates that staleness is not tolerable. The virtue of the demonstration effect of Pacific dynamism is that it exposes the need for vitality and necessity to look for what can be achieved rather than for what can be maintained.[7]

American revitalization in the 21st century depends on our youth. Can they compete? Will they achieve? And do they want to? Answers to these questions won't be coming from our policy kingpins in Washington. They'll come from the American family and how it raises the 21st century's leaders and achievers. In the final analysis, the rise and fall of the American dream rests with none other than mom and dad.

Notes

Introduction

1. John Holt, *How Children Fail* (1964; reprint, New York: Dell Publishing, 1988).
2. Ann Landers, "Some Teens Face Difficult Problems," *Gazette Telegraph* (Colorado Springs, Col.), 15 December 1989.
3. William Dunn, "Mini-boom: Births at 25-year High," *USA Today*, 22 June 1989.
4. Office of Educational Research and Improvement, U.S. Department of Education, *Youth Indicators* (Washington D.C.: 1988), 70–71.
5. Ibid.
6. Ibid., 86–87.
7. Louis Harris, *Inside America* (New York: Vintage Books, 1987), 78.
8. Office of Educational Research and Improvement, *Youth Indicators*, 94–95.
9. Ibid., 14–15.
10. Ibid., 116.
11. Ibid., 104.
12. Ibid., 102.
13. Ibid.
14. Ibid., 56.
15. Ibid.
16. John Hood, "Funding Focus Should Shift to Content of Education," *Gazette Telegraph* (Colorado Springs, Col.), 4 March 1990.
17. Office of Educational Research and Improvement, *Youth Indicators*, 64–65.
18. Associated Press, "Barometer Shows Drop in U.S. Pupils Science Knowledge: Americans Subpar in All Categories," *Gazette Telegraph* (Colorado Springs, Col.), 11 September 1987.
19. Associated Press, "Test Shows Lack of Economic Knowledge: Students Stumped by 'Profit,'" *Gazette Telegraph* (Colorado Springs, Col.), 29 December 1988.
20. The National Commission on Excellence in Education, *A Nation At Risk: The Imperative for Educational Reform* (Washington, D. C.: 1983).
21. Ibid.
22. Ibid.
23. Ibid.
24. *New York Times*, "Undereducated Employees a Hindrance to Companies," *Gazette Telegraph* (Colorado Springs, Col.), 9 May 1988.

25. Kenneth L. Woodward, "Young Beyond Their Years," *Newsweek* (Winter/ Spring 1990, special issue: The 21st Century Family): 54.
26. Office of Educational Research and Improvement, *Youth Indicators*, 22.
27. Larry V. Stockman and Cynthia S. Graves, *Adult Children Who Won't Grow Up* (New York: Contemporary Books, 1989), 23–24.
28. Richard Lamm, "Young Americans Don't Measure Up," *Rocky Mountain News* (Denver, Col.), 24 September 1989.
29. James Coleman quoted in Landon Jones, *Great Expectations* (New York: Ballantine Books, 1980), 250.
30. B. Eugene Griessman, *The Achievement Factors* (New York: Dodd, Mead, & Company, 1987), 39.
31. Robert J. Sternberg, *The Triarchic Mind: A New Theory of Human Intelligence* (New York: Penguin Books, 1988), 16–17.
32. Howard Gardner, *Frames of Mind: The Theory of Multiple Intelligences* (New York: Basic Books, 1988), x.
33. Napoleon Hill, *The Law of Success* (Evanston, Ill.: Success Unlimited, 1979), 91.
34. Ibid., 163–164.

Chapter 1

1. Lamm, "Young Americans Don't Measure Up."
2. Woodward, "Young Beyond Their Years," 55.
3. Ibid.
4. Office of Educational Research and Improvement, *Youth Indicators*, 122.
5. Ibid., 86–89.
6. Jill Lawrence, "Educators Warn Against Mixing Work and School," *Gazette Telegraph* (Colorado Springs, Col.), 21 July 1989.
7. Mary Bicouvaris quoted in Lawrence, "Educators Warn Against Mixing Work and School."
8. Patrick Welsh quoted in ibid.
9. Lawrence Steinberg quoted in ibid.
10. Woodward, "Young Beyond Their Years," 57.
11. Office of Educational Research and Improvement, *Youth Indicators*, 108.
12. Ibid., 70–71.
13. Ibid., 108.
14. David Klimik quoted in Woodward, "Young Beyond Their Years," 60.
15. Harris, *Inside America*, 78.
16. Associated Press, "Children Form Make-Believe Drug Ring," *Gazette Telegraph* (Colorado Springs, Col.), 10 August 1989.
17. Associated Press, "Survey: White Students More Apt to Abuse Drugs," *Gazette Telegraph* (Colorado Springs, Col.), 19 December 1989.
18. As reported by Woodward, "Young Beyond Their Years," 57.
19. Office of Educational Research and Improvement, *Youth Indicators*, 94.

20. Glen Gabbard quoted in Woodward, "Young Beyond Their Years," 57.
21. Office of Educational Research and Improvement, *Youth Indicators*, 114–116.
22. Ibid., 104.
23. Ibid., 102.
24. Ibid., 66.
25. Ibid., 65.
26. Associated Press, "Barometer Shows Drop in Knowledge."
27. Associated Press, "Test Shows Lack of Economic Knowledge."
28. Knight-Ridder Newspapers, "Americans Lost On Geography Quiz," *Gazette Telegraph* (Colorado Springs, Col.), 9 November 1989.
29. The National Commission on Excellence in Education, *A Nation at Risk*.
30. Al Shanker quoted in Dru Wilson, "Expert: Reform Earns 'F'," *Gazette Telegraph* (Colorado Springs, Col.), 13 December 1989.
31. Dru Wilson, "Expert: Reform Earns 'F'," *Gazette Telegraph* (Colorado Springs, Col.), 13 December 1989.
32. Al Shanker quoted in ibid.
33. Mike Royko, "Responses from Young People Prove Survey Was Right," *Gazette Telegraph* (Colorado Springs, Col.), 17 December 1989.
34. *New York Times*, "Undereducated Employees a Hindrance."
35. Charles E. La Pier quoted in ibid.
36. Ibid.
37. Ibid.
38. Ibid.
39. Joseph Kellman quoted in ibid.
40. New York Times News Service, "U.S. Factories Struggling to Fill Jobs." *Gazette Telegraph* (Colorado Springs, Col.), 25 December 1989.
41. Associated Press, "College Professors Blast Bosses, Students," *Gazette Telegraph* (Colorado Springs, Col.), 6 November 1989.
42. Woodward, "Young Beyond Their Years," 57.
43. Gordon G. Gee, "Communique" (University of Colorado, Boulder, Col.), 1989.
44. Stockman and Graves, *Adult Children Who Won't Grow Up*, 23–24.
45. Susan Littwin, *The Postponed Generation: Why American Youth Are Growing up Later* (New York: William Morrow and Company, 1986), 133.
46. Adrienne Miller and Andrew Goldblatt, *The Hamlet Syndrome: Overthinkers Who Underachieve* (New York: William Morrow and Company, 1989), 19–21.
47. Woodward, "Young Beyond Their Years," 54.
48. Ibid.
49. Hal Dresner, "Those Beverly Hills Kids," *Newsweek* (December 1990): 10.
50. Joan France, "Caretaker Generation," *Newsweek* (January 1990): 16.
51. Woodward, "Young Beyond Their Years," 55.
52. Lamm, "Young Americans Don't Measure Up."
53. "U.S. Living Standard Lagging Behind," *The Spokesman-Review* (Spokane, Wash.), 30 June 1989.

54. Associated Press, "Deficit Threatens U.S. Economic Role, Study Says," *Gazette Telegraph* (Colorado Springs, Col.), 29 December 1989.

55. Associated Press, "Consumer Debt, Weather Troubling Nation's Retailers," *Gazette Telegraph* (Colorado Springs, Col.), 24 December 1989.

56. Associated Press, "Japan's Income Jump Eclipses U.S.," *Gazette Telegraph* (Colorado Springs, Col.), 16 December 1989.

57. Steven Schlossstein, *The End of the American Century* (New York: Congdon and Weed, 1989), 40.

58. Schlossstein, *End of the American Century*, 40.

59. *Information Please: Almanac Atlas & Yearbook 1990, 43rd Edition* (New York: Houghton Mifflin, 1989), 57.

Chapter 2

1. Gordon Grekko quoted in Otto Friedrick, "Freed from Greed," *Time* (1990): 77.

2. Otto Friedrick, "Freed from Greed," *Time* (1990): 78.

3. Ibid., 77–78.

4. Ross Perot quoted in Friedrick, "Freed from Greed."

5. The statistics and events described in the section are based upon information from Bernard Grun, *The Timetables of History: A Horizontal Linkage of People and Events* (New York: Simon and Schuster), 1982.

6. The trends, analyses, and statistics in this section are based upon information from Landon Y. Jones's excellent and comprehensive book *Great Expectations: America and the Baby Boom Generation* (New York: Ballantine Books, 1980).

7. Jones, *Great Expectations*, 21.

8. Ibid.

9. Ibid., 24.

10. Ibid., 39.

11. Clifford Kirkpatrick, *The Family: As Process and Institution* (New York: The Ronald Press Company, 1963), 137.

12. Jones, *Great Expectations*, 43–44.

13. *Fortune* (1953) quoted in Jones, *Great Expectations*, 44.

14. Jones, *Great Expectations*, 44–45.

15. Ibid., 47.

16. Ibid., 48.

17. Christopher Larsch, *The Culture of Narcissism* (New York: Warner Books, 1979), 106.

18. Jones, *Great Expectations*, 55.

19. Ibid., 62–64.

20. Ibid., 58–59.

21. Ibid., 73–74.

22. Ibid., 85.

23. Ibid., 88.
24. Ibid., 300.

Chapter 3

1. As reported by Jones, *Great Expectations*, 139–140.
2. Jones, *Great Expectations*, 140.
3. Ibid., 142–143.
4. Ibid., 94.
5. Ibid., 99.
6. Ibid., 102.
7. Ibid., 102.
8. The events and statistics described in the section are based upon information from Grun, *Timetables of History*, 1982.
9. Jeff Greenfield quoted in Jones, *Great Expectations*, 59.
10. Jones, *Great Expectations*, 117.
11. Ibid., 119.
12. Grun, *Timetables of History*, 1982.
13. Jones, *Great Expectations*, 199.
14. *Information Please*, 807–811.
15. Daniel Yankelovich quoted in Jones, *Great Expectations*, 334.
16. *Boston Globe* quoted in Jones, *Great Expectations*, 302–303.
17. Jones, *Great Expectations*, 251.
18. Ibid., 253.
19. Ibid.
20. Harris, *Inside America*, 113.
21. Ibid., 114.
22. Jones, *Great Expectations*, 250.
23. Ibid., 254.
24. John Barbour, "Shouldering The Blame," *Gazette Telegraph* (Colorado Springs, Col.), 6 August 1989.
25. Ibid.
26. Kent Hayes, *Why Good Parents Have Bad Kids* (New York: Doubleday, 1989), 2–3.
27. Lawrence Kutner, "Latchkey Kids More Likely to Use Alcohol and Drugs," *Gazette Telegraph* (Colorado Springs, Col.), 23 October 1989.
28. Jean L. Richardson quoted in ibid.

Chapter 4

1. Sara Davidson, *Loose Change* quoted in Jones, *Great Expectations*, 293.
2. From *Easy Rider* quoted in Jones, *Great Expectations*, 293.
3. Jones, *Great Expectations*, 298.
4. Ibid., 299.

5. Marsha Sinetar, *Do What You Love, the Money Will Follow* (New York: Dell Publishing, 1987).
6. Harris, *Inside America*, 255–261.
7. John Naisbitt, *Megatrends: Ten New Directions Transforming Our Lives* (New York: Warner Books, 1982), 131–32.
8. Ibid., 150.
9. Ibid.
10. Ibid.
11. Ibid., 151–152.
12. Ibid., 134–135.
13. Tom Ferguson quoted in Naisbitt, *Megatrends*, 136.
14. Naisbitt, *Megatrends*, 37–38.
15. John E. Sarno, *Mind over Back Pain* (New York: Berkley Books, 1986), 9.
16. Bernie S. Siegel, *Love, Medicine & Miracles* (New York: Harper & Row, Publishers, 1986), 2.
17. Ibid., 3.
18. Robert E. Kowalski, *The Eight-Week Cholesterol Cure* (New York: Harper & Row, Publishers, 1989).
19. Redford Williams quoted in Bonnie Jacob, "Are You a Type H?" *USA Weekend* (7–9 July 1989).
20. Rick Ansorge, "Exercise Gridlock," *Gazette Telegraph* (Colorado Springs, Col.), 11 August 1989.
21. Dale Dauten, *Taking Chances* (New York: Pocket Books, 1986), 18–19.
22. Naisbitt, *Megatrends*, 148–49.
23. Paul Hawken, *Growing a Business* (New York: Fireside, 1987), 13.
24. Ibid.
25. Dauten, *Taking Chances*, 27–28.
26. Jones, *Great Expectations*, 299.
27. Ibid., 335.
28. Harris, *Inside America*, 54.
29. Jones, *Great Expectations*, 261.
30. Daniel Yankelovich, *New Rules* quoted in Jan Halper, *Quiet Desperation: The Truth about Successful Men* (New York, Warner Books, 1988), 16.
31. Ibid.
32. Halper, *Quiet Desperation*, 17.
33. Elaine Kurtenbach, "Deaths from Overwork Skyrocket in Japan," *The Spokesman-Review* (Spokane, Washington), 30 June 1989.
34. Halper, *Quiet Desperation*, 21.
35. Arnold Mitchell, "Changing Values and Lifestyles," reported in Dauten, *Taking Chances*, 20–21.

Chapter 5

1. Abraham H. Maslow, *Motivation and Personality* (New York: Harper, 1954).
2. Jim Hasberger quoted in Don Wallace, "It's a Wonderful Life If You Know How to Live It to the Fullest," *Success* (May 1990): 51.

3. Littwin, *The Postponed Generation*, 17.

4. Miller and Goldblatt, *The Hamlet Syndrome*, 41.

5. Jean D. Okimoto and Phyllis J. Stegall, *Boomerang Kids* (New York: Pocket Books, 1987), 56–57.

6. As reported in Littwin, *The Postponed Generation*, 14.

7. Dennis Wholey, *Are You Happy?* (Boston: Houghton Mifflin Company, 1986), 6.

8. Beth Brophy, "Dr. Spock Had It Right," *U.S. News & World Report* (7 August 1989): 49–50.

9. H. S. Glenn and J. Nelsen, *Raising Self-Reliant Children in a Self-Indulgent World* (Rocklin, Calif.: Prima Publishing and Communications, 1989), 46–47.

10. Beverly N. Feldman, *Kids Who Succeed* (New York: Ballantine Books, 1987), 6.

11. The quotations in the section come from Dennis Wholey's excellent and enlightening book *Are You Happy?*

12. Wholey, *Are You Happy?*, 5–6.

13. Norman Cousins quoted in ibid., x.

14. Pat Carroll quoted in ibid., 173.

15. Burt Bacharach quoted in ibid., 175.

16. Theodore I. Rubin quoted in ibid., 52.

17. Ashely Montagu quoted in ibid., 40.

18. Theodore I. Rubin quoted in ibid., 55.

19. Benjamin Spock quoted in ibid., 45.

20. Malcolm Forbes quoted in ibid., 295.

21. Burt Bacharach quoted in ibid., 175.

22. Ruby Dee quoted in ibid., 78.

23. Burt Bacharach quoted in ibid., 175.

24. Ruby Dee quoted in ibid., 78.

25. Theodore Rubin quoted in ibid., 57.

26. Tom Peters quoted in ibid., 121.

27. Helen Thomas quoted in ibid., 102.

28. Burt Bacharach quoted in ibid., 175.

29. May Sarton quoted in ibid., 109.

30. John Naisbitt quoted in ibid., 66.

31. President Kennedy quoted in ibid., 104.

Chapter 6

1. Lawrence D. Maloney, "SUCCESS! The Chase Is Back in Style Again," *U.S. News & World Report* (3 October 1983): 60.

2. Napoleon H. Hill and W. Clement Stone, *Success Through a Positive Mental Attitude* (New York: Prentice-Hall, 1987), xv.

3. Napoleon Hill, *Think and Grow Rich* (New York: Fawcett Crest, 1960), 157.

4. George Gallup and Alec M. Gallup, *The Great American Success Story: Factors That Affect Achievement* (Homewood, Ill.: Dow Jones-Irwin, 1986), 67.

5. Griessman, *Achievement Factors*, 25.
6. Hill, *Think and Grow Rich*, 75.
7. Griessman, *Achievement Factors*, 103.
8. Gallup and Gallup, *Great American Success Story*, 67.
9. Sternberg, *Triarchic Mind*, 211.
10. Ibid., 11.
11. Ibid., 16–17.
12. Ibid., 79.
13. Hill, *Think and Grow Rich*, 38.
14. W. Clement Stone, *The Success System that Never Fails* (New York: Pocket Books, 1962), 255.
15. Sternberg, *Triarchic Mind*, 212–213.
16. Charles A. Garfield, *Peak Performers: The New Heroes of American Business* (New York: Avon, 1986), 141.
17. Ibid., 274.
18. Ibid., 161.
19. Gallup and Gallup, *Great American Success Story*, 67.
20. Garfield, *Peak Performers*, 211–12.
21. Ibid., 26.
22. Ibid., 245.
23. Ibid., 247.
24. Alvin Toffler quoted in "Bleed, Sweat, and Persevere," *Success* (May 1990): 6.
25. Herbert A. Simon quoted in Griessman, *Achievement Factors*, 37–38.
26. Ibid., 38.
27. Ibid.
28. Herbert A. Simon quoted in ibid.
29. Ibid., 38–39.
30. Gardner, *Frames of Mind*, x.
31. Ibid., xi.
32. Ibid., 10.
33. Ibid., 78.
34. Ibid., 80.
35. Ibid., 81.
36. Ibid., 138.
37. Albert Einstein quoted in ibid., 151.
38. Ibid., 152.
39. Sternberg, *Triarchic Mind*, 101–2.
40. Gardner, *Frames of Mind*, 177.
41. Rudolf Arnheim quoted in ibid., 177.
42. Ibid., 190.
43. Steven Hawking quoted in *Minneapolis-St. Paul Star Tribune*, "Physicist Looks to Black Holes for Answers," *Gazette Telegraph* (Colorado Springs, Col.), 25 May 1989.
44. Gardner, *Frames of Mind*, 108–9.
45. Associated Press, "Five-Year-Old 'Virtuoso' Called Genius," *Gazette Telegraph* (Colorado Springs, Col.), 25 March 1989.

46. John Lennon quoted in Gardner, *Frames of Mind*, 115.
47. Ibid., 254.
48. Ibid., 273.
49. Hill, *Think and Grow Rich*, 163–64.
50. Anthony Robbins, *Unlimited Power* (New York: Ballantine Books, 1987), 12.
51. Hill, *Think and Grow Rich*, 152.
52. Helen Gurley Brown quoted in Griessman, *The Achievement Factors*, 81.
53. Erskine Cladwell quoted in ibid., 79.
54. Charles Schulz quoted in ibid., 79.
55. Jacques Cousteau quoted in ibid., 86.
56. Edith W. Martin quoted in ibid., 86.
57. Albert C. Wedemeyer quoted in ibid., 89.

Chapter 7

1. Harris, *Inside America*, 49.
2. Ibid., 40.
3. Woodward, "Young Beyond Their Years," 60.
4. George Sheehan, *Personal Best* (Emmaus, Penn.: Rodale Press, 1989), 7–9.
5. Ibid., 11.
6. Ibid., 134.
7. Holt, *How Children Fail*, 67–68.
8. Karen M. Thomas, "Emphasis Turns to Thinking Skills," *Gazette Telegraph* (Colorado Springs, Col.), 25 June 1989.
9. Jack Snowman, "Critical Thinking Also Means Strategic Thinking," *Educators' Forum* (Boston, Mass.: Houghton Mifflin, 1989).
10. Shirley Gould, *How To Raise a Responsible Child* (New York: St. Martin's Press, 1981), 33.
11. Harris, *Inside America*, 50.
12. The first printing of John Holt's *How Children Fail* was in 1964.
13. Holt, *How Children Fail*, 234.
14. Jerry Conrath quoted in Brad Johnson, "Slow Students Can Make the Grade with Teachers' Help, Educator Says," *Gazette Telegraph* (Colorado Springs, Col.), 16 November 1989.
15. Ibid.
16. Edwin S. Ellis, "The Role of Motivation and Pedagogy on the Generalization of Cognitive Strategy Training," *Journal of Learning Disabilities*, 19 (1986): 67.
17. Barbara Z. Presseisen, *At-Risk Students and Thinking* (Philadelphia, Penn.: National Education Association/Research for Better Schools, 1988), 8.

Chapter 8

1. "Today's Horatio Algers," *USA Today* (19 May 1989): 2b.
2. James Michener quoted in Milton Nieuwsma, "Michener, Like His Novels,

Goes On and On," *Gazette Telegraph* (Colorado Springs, Col.), 27 December 1988.

3. Doris L. McCoy, *Megatraits: 12 Traits of Successful People* (Plano, Tex.: Wordware Publishing, 1988), 37.

4. Robert Dedman quoted in ibid., 83.

5. Karl Eller quoted in ibid., 87.

6. Griessman, *Achievement Factors*, 7.

7. Jack Nicklaus quoted in ibid., 29–30.

8. Stone, *Success System that Never Fails*, 52.

9. Ibid., 53.

10. Jack Nicklaus quoted in Griessman, *Achievement Factors*, 30.

11. Mary Kay Ash quoted in ibid., 35.

12. Charles Schulz quoted in ibid., 35–36.

13. Andy Rooney quoted in ibid., 35.

14. James Michener quoted in Nieuwsma, "Michener, Like His Novels."

15. Charles Schulz quoted in Griessman, *Achievement Factors*, 57.

16. Ibid., 60.

17. Stone, *Success System that Never Fails*, 3.

18. Louis L'Amour quoted in Denver Post Wire Services, "Old West Writer L'Amour Dies," *The Denver Post* (Denver, Col.), 13 June 1988.

19. Ray Charles quoted in Griessman, *Achievement Factors*, 55.

20. Ibid., 53.

21. Lee Trevino quoted in McCoy, *Megatraits*, 208.

22. Nadja Salerno-Sonnenberg, *Nadja on My Way* (New York: Crown Publishers, 1989), 5–6.

23. Ibid., 37.

24. Ibid., 38.

25. Marian Christy, "A Hush Is Holy," *The Evening Bulletin* (Providence, R. I.), 13 January 1989.

26. Bart Scott quoted in Tim Mimick, "8-Year-Old Still Growing Strong, Takes Boys State Juniors Crown," *Gazette Telegraph* (Colorado Springs, Col.), 14 June 1989.

27. Steven Spielberg quoted in Dan Olmsted, "Ex-Boy Scout Makes Movies," *USA Weekend* (28–30 July 1989):4.

28. Ibid.

29. Ibid.

30. Ibid., 5.

31. Warren Penn quoted in Carol Byrne, "Writer Caught Poetry Bug as a Child," *Gazette Telegraph* (Colorado Springs, Col.), 16 September 1989.

32. Maloney, "SUCCESS!", 60.

33. Susan Reed quoted in Lynne H. Williams, Henry S. Berman, and Louise Rose, *The Too Precious Child: Letting Go of the Super-Parent Syndrome* (New York: Warner Books, 1989), 18.

34. Ibid., 17.

35. Ibid., 22.

36. Neil Kurshan, *Raising Your Child to be a Mensch* (New York: Ballantine Books, 1987), 8.
37. Frank Halloran quoted in Susan Dichter, *Teachers: Straight Talk from the Trenches* (Los Angeles, Calif.: Lowell House, 1989), 237–38.
38. Ibid., 172–73.
39. Beth Brophy and Erica E. Goode, "Amazing Families," *U.S. News & World Report* (12 December 1988):78.
40. Beth Brophy, "Amazing Families," *U.S. News & World Report* (12 December 1988):81.
41. Miriam Horn, "Amazing Families," *U.S. News & World Report* (12 December 1988):83.
42. Alvin P. Sanoff, "Amazing Families," *U.S. News & World Report* (12 December 1988):85.
43. Kathryn D. Sloane, "Home Influences on Talent Development," in *Developing Talent in Young People*, ed. Benjamin S. Bloom (New York: Ballantine Books, 1985), 440–41.
44. Marlene F. Shyer, "Vivian Ayers-Allen: On Raising Creative Kids," *McCall* (February 1990):72.
45. Sloane, "Home Influences on Talent," 454.
46. Ibid.
47. Lauren A. Sosniak, "A Long-Term Commitment to Learning," in *Developing Talent in Young People*, ed. Benjamin S. Bloom (New York: Ballantine Books, 1985), 487.
48. Ibid., 481–82.
49. Kathryn D. Sloane and Lauren A. Sosniak, "The Development of Accomplished Sculptors," in *Developing Talent in Young People*, ed. Benjamin S. Bloom (New York: Ballantine Books, 1985), 110.
50. Ibid.
51. Sosniak, "Long-Term Commitment to Learning," 489.

Chapter 9

1. Sternberg, *The Triarchic Mind*, 11, 65.
2. Gardner, *Frames of Mind*, x.
3. Hill, *Law of Success*, Lesson One, 91.
4. Salerno-Sonnenberg, *Nadja On My Way*, 70–71.
5. Sloane, "Home Influences on Talent," 473.
6. Stone, *Success System that Never Fails*, 14.
7. Edwin Diamond, "How to be More Successful," *Organize Yourself*, ed. by the editors of *Reader's Digest* (New York: Berkley Books, 1982), 136.
8. Stone, *Success System that Never Fails*, 44.
9. Griessman, *Achievement Factors*, 106.
10. Edward G. Bulwer-Lytton quoted in Ari Kiev, "A Strategy for Daily Living,"

Organize Yourself, ed. by the editors of *Reader's Digest* (New York: Berkley Books, 1982), 190.

11. John Foster quoted in Kiev, "Strategy for Daily Living," 190.
12. Griessman, *Achievement Factors,* 19–20.
13. Helen Gurley Brown quoted in ibid., 18.
14. Vincent Van Gogh quoted in ibid., 12.
15. Isaac Asimov quoted in ibid., 10.
16. Claude M. Bristol, *The Magic of Believing* (New York: Pocket Books, 1969), 111.
17. Stone, *Success System that Never Fails,* 118.
18. Norman V. Peale, "Eight Steps to a New Life," *Organize Yourself,* ed. by the editors of *Reader's Digest* (New York: Berkley Books, 1982), 235.
19. Hill, *Law of Success,* Lesson Two, 32–33.
20. Griessman, *Achievement Factors,* 152.
21. Ibid., 155.
22. Michael LeBoeuf, *Working Smart* (New York: Warner Books, 1979), 53.
23. Griessman, *Achievement Factors,* 83.
24. Mike Hernacki, *The Ultimate Secret to Getting Absolutely Everything You Want* (New York: Berkley Books, 1988), 20.
25. Robert Anthony, *The Ultimate Secrets of Total Self-Confidence* (New York: Berkley Books, 1984), 54.
26. John R. Noe, *Peak Performance Principles for High Achievers* (New York: Berkley Books, 1986), 53.
27. Ibid., 72.
28. Sternberg, *Triarchic Mind,* 66, 71.
29. Dennis E. Mithaug, James E. Martin, Martin Agran, and Frank R. Rusch, *Why Special Education Graduates Fail* (Colorado Springs, Col.: Ascent Publications, 1988).
30. Sternberg, *Triarchic Mind,* 298.
31. Jim Abbott quoted in "One-Handed Pitcher No. Eight Overall Pick by Angels in Draft," *The Denver Post* (Denver, Col.), 2 June 1988.
32. Ibid.
33. Ibid.
34. LaShawn Brown quoted in Mike Spence, "Ohio Girl Overcomes Childhood Accident to Help Capture Gold Medal," *Gazette Telegraph* (Colorado Springs, Col.), 29 July 1989.
35. Julie Wallace quoted in Mike Spence, "Wallace Focuses on Future, Not Past," *Gazette Telegraph* (Colorado Springs, Col.), 23 July 1989.
36. Associated Press, "Computer Becomes Lifeline to Mute, Paralyzed Man: Ex-journalist Stricken by Lou Gehrig's Disease," *Gazette Telegraph* (Colorado Springs, Col.), 13 August 1989.
37. *Minneapolis-St Paul Star Tribune,* "Physicist Looks to Black Holes."
38. Griessman, *Achievement Factors,* 30.
39. Ibid., 31.

40. Herbert Benson, *Your Maximum Mind* (New York: Avon Books, 1987), 59–60.
41. Stone, *Success System that Never Fails,* 17.
42. Noe, *Peak Performance Principles,* 86.
43. Ralf Waldo Emerson quoted in Fredelle Maynard, "Turning Failure into Success," *Organize Yourself,* ed. by the editors of *Reader's Digest* (New York: Berkley Books, 1982), 246.
44. Fredelle Maynard, "Turning Failure into Success," *Organize Yourself,* ed. by the editors of *Reader's Digest* (New York: Berkley Books, 1982), 244–45.
45. Benjamin S. Bloom, "Generalizations about Talent Development," in *Developing Talent in Young People,* ed. Benjamin S. Bloom (New York: Ballantine Books, 1985), 510.
46. Salerno-Sonnenberg, *Nadja On My Way,* 5.
47. Ibid.
48. Sosniak, "Long-Term Commitment to Learning," 478–79.
49. Ibid., 496–97.
50. Ibid.
51. Sloane, "Home Influences on Talent Development," 440.
52. Dichter, *Teachers,* 172–73.
53. Lauren A. Sosniak, "One Concert Pianist," in *Developing Talent in Young People,* ed. Benjamin S. Bloom (New York: Ballantine Books, 1985), 62–63.
54. Howard Gardner, "The Academic Community Must Not Shun the Debate Over How to Set National Educational Goals," *The Chronical of Higher Education,* 8 November 1989, A52.
55. Salerno-Sonnenberg, *Nadja On My Way,* 37–38.
56. Judith A. Monsaas, "Learning to be a World-Class Tennis Player," in *Developing Talent in Young People,* ed. Benjamin S. Bloom (New York: Ballantine Books, 1985), 247.
57. Sloane, "Home Influences on Talent Development," 440.
58. Thomas Gordon, *P.E.T. Parent Effectiveness Training* (New York: New American Library, 1975), 195.

Chapter 10

1. Hill, *Think and Grow Rich,* 152.
2. John Sculley, *Odyssey: Pepsi to Apple . . . A Journey of Adventure, Ideas and the Future* (New York: Harper & Row, 1987), 90.
3. Ibid.
4. Michael Meyer, *The Alexander Complex: The Dreams That Drive Great Businessmen* (New York: Times Books, 1989), 24.
5. Steve Jobs quoted in Phil Patton, "Jobs' Comeback Fueled by Power of New Machine," *Gazette Telegraph* (Colorado Springs, Col.), 6 August 1989.
6. Meyer, *Alexander Complex,* 169.

7. Ted Turner quoted in ibid., 225.
8. Ibid., 219.
9. Andy Rooney quoted in Griessman, *Achievement Factors*, 35.
10. Anthony G. Kalinowski, "The Development of Olympic Swimmers," in *Developing Talent in Young People*, ed. Benjamin S. Bloom (New York: Ballantine Books, 1985), 187.
11. Derek Mithaug, "True Grit," *The Juilliard Journal* (October 1989):4.

Chapter 11

1. Cox News Service, "Report Paints a 'Bleak Portrait' of American Student Achievement," *Gazette Telegraph* (Colorado Springs, Col.), 27 September 1990.
2. Ibid.
3. Schlossstein, *End of the American Century*, 468.
4. Ibid.
5. A. L. Williams, *All You Can Do Is All You Can Do But All You Can Do Is Enough* (New York: Ive Books, 1989).
6. McCoy, *Megatraits*, 194.
7. Staffan Burenstam Linder quoted in ibid., 90.

Index

About the
Author

Dennis E. Mithaug, professor of education and director of the Center for Educational Research at the University of Colorado–Colorado Springs, is a former dean of education and author of numerous research articles, instructional materials, monographs, and books in special education. He has a bachelor's degree in psychology from Dartmouth College, and master's degrees in sociology and special education and a doctorate in sociology from the University of Washington.